M000281493

Hope Dancing

Finding purpose and a place to serve among the Maya

Leslie Baer Dinkel

Founder of Local Hope, Guatemala's "Xela AID"

Edited by Barbara Smythe

Cover and Title Page Design by Betsey Binét

G_T

**GlimmerTwin
Publishing**
London • Los Angeles

HOPE DANCING: FINDING PURPOSE
AND A PLACE TO SERVE AMONG THE MAYA

GlimmerTwin Publishing 2019
Copyright © 2019 by Leslie Baer Dinkel. All rights reserved.

100% Profits to Charity

Benefitting
Local Hope / Xela AID Partnerships for Self Reliance
111 W. Ocean Blvd. 4th Floor
Long Beach, California 90802
www.xelaaid.org • info@xelaaid.org • www.facebook.com/xelaaid

Mailing address:
65 Pine Ave. #404
Long Beach, California 90802

The author invites comments, suggestions, dialogue at
leslie@xelaaid.org

FIRST EDITION: August 9, 2019
Library of Congress Cataloguing-in-Publication Data
Baer Dinkel, Leslie 1958-
ISBN: 978-1-7328856-0-8

Edited by Barbara Smythe
Cover and Title Page Design by Betsey Binét

Praise for *Hope Dancing*

"This is a wonderful book filled with adventure, compassion, and with powerful insights that resonate long after you have put it down—if you can put it down."

— Denise Danks, Chandler/Fulbright-winning Author of *Phreak, Baby Love,* other titles, and upcoming with co-author Brendan O'Neill, *Meet Mr. Sticks: Keeping the Beat for Rory Gallagher*

"A candid, hopeful, and fun read about one person's quest to make the world better, and the extraordinary challenges along the way…"

—Jeremy P. Tarcher, Publisher, *Personal Mythology: The Psychology of Your Evolving Self* and other titles

"Leslie's life is what happened when someone crossed Indiana Jones with the Singing Nun. It comes through in this story which is both entertaining and insightful. A delight!"

— Abdi Sami, Former CEO, Dream Quest Pictures

"A testament to the immense goodness that can be manifested when one dares to 'know thyself,' follow their heart, and take the not-always-popular-with-others path for their one, precious life."

—Dorothy Baldwin Satten, Author, *Real is Better than Perfect*

"Whether you believe in Divine Intervention or not (the author herself is not convinced), this book is an inspiring must-read for any of us who are pursuing our own life's highest purpose."

—Joy Parker, Co-Author, *Maya Cosmos* and other titles

Dedication

To my husband Mel and my son Oscar who share a pair of rose-colored glasses when it comes to me, and I love them for it.

Preface

When I was compelled by a series of extraordinary events to breach my comfort zone and head to Guatemala, my intent had been to visit only briefly to begin to learn Spanish. But what I found during my time with the Maya, who for decades had been plagued by poverty and oppression, turned my plans (and my life) upside down.

Somewhere between a child's death and a firefight, the Guatemalan people's plight became my own. I promised my heart to them, and never looked back.

That said, I am happy to tell you that this book is not about atrocities. It's about hope, and finding purpose. It's about people who care, coming together to help one another in times of chaos and suffering. Post-war, it's a story about the art of community development across cultures—listening, sharing ideas, hashing through misunderstandings, becoming humble, and in all ways working together to collaborate toward solutions to make lasting, positive change. It's about hope, *dancing*.

I believe wholeheartedly that every person has the power to change the world for the better, and that we do so, as Mother Teresa advised, not by seeking to do great things but by doing small things with great love. I share this book in the hope that it will encourage others to seek their passion and purpose, and to work for positive change day to day with all the love they can muster.

Imagine it. All the goodness created in the world by human beings began with *a single positive action* taken on a single day by someone.

Someone just like you.

Leslie - Atitlán, 2019

Gratitude

For Hope Dancing

Joy Parker was a gifted writer who told me, "every person has a book inside them." She worked with me for more than a year to identify the essential stories that would become the bones of this book. Joy passed away before its publication, but the spirit of hope and loving kindness she embodied during her lifetime lives on in these pages. She was an inspiration to all who knew her.

My long-time friend and accomplished storyteller Denise Danks helped get me unstuck. She urged me to begin this book with the defining moment that at age 33 set my life on an entirely new course. I followed her advice, and as she said it would, the story flowed logically from there. Such has been the fruit of her insight and encouragement over our decades of friendship.

Barbara Smythe, who I met when she was editing for the *Chicken Soup for the Soul* franchise, is an inspired writer. She had lots to teach this journalist who'd spent a career sticking to facts, not feelings. When she completed her delightful memoir, *Confessions of a Misfit Pastor's Wife*, my autographed copy contained a challenge to finish this book. She knew I couldn't resist. She wrangled my drafts into shape for which I am deeply appreciative.

Betsey Binét is a talented artist and editor I've been fortunate to work with for decades. She created stunning designs for my music albums, for the book *Real is Better than Perfect* which I collaborated on, and for numerous other projects over the years. The elegant cover and title page for this book are her creations, and I once again offer her my heartfelt thanks.

I am exceedingly grateful to my loving and patient husband, Mel, for those years of road trips where he drove in silence as I typed away on my laptop. While we traveled together to far-flung, exotic and oft-times romantic destinations, he generously shared me with my other passion — *this book*. It was his unfaltering support that finally made *Hope Dancing* possible. As a bonus, he turned out to be a talented proofreader, too. I am deeply grateful to him for his support for this book, and so much more.

Thank you, too, to my friend and preeminent copy editor Linda Williams, and to beta-readers Mel, Barbara Smythe, Denise Danks, Oscar and April de León, and Wolfram Alderson, and the twenty other readers on our Launch Team. Your eagle eyes and memories helped me get it right.

In addition to others mentioned in this book, Michael Stuart Ani was an early influence. He found his passion and purpose living among indigenous people and advocating for their rights. His insight and humor encouraged me as I found my way.

For Local Hope, Xela AID

This book is the essence of the story of how Local Hope — known first, and in Guatemala as "Xela AID" — came to be. The organization's success has been the result of the efforts of hundreds of people who, over the years, have served on its Board, donated their precious time and resources, volunteered, sponsored programs, helped build buildings and otherwise lent their heartfelt support.

I am deeply grateful to Xela AID's dedicated staff, to its Boards past, and present (below), and to every single person and organization that has collaborated to bring health, education, jobs and a greatly enhanced quality of life to the hardworking, shockingly resilient people of the San Martín Sacatepéquez region we are privileged to call home. At the risk of sounding cliché, I'll echo Margaret Mead's sentiments about the power of "a small group of thoughtful, committed citizens" to change the world. In the Guatemalan highlands, they have, and continue to. It's exciting to see this legacy of hope-in-action continue.

The Author

CONTENTS ✚

"He who sincerely seeks his real purpose in life is himself sought by that purpose."

— Hazrat Inayat Khan

Introduction

For nearly three decades the stories in this book lived on the pages of my personal journals, in file folders, and in the memories of the group of us who'd macheteed our way through bureaucratic red tape and tip-toed through the mine fields of cultural misunderstanding to launch the human development organization *Xela AID* (the first word pronounced SHAY-luh). It was named this because we based our efforts near Xela, the name given by the local Maya to the Guatemalan city Quetzaltenango. "AID" is an acronym for "Agency for Integrated Development."

Xela AID (also known in the U.S. as Local Hope) was initially an emergency relief project inspired by great need in a time of war. But we soon evolved diverse programs spanning health, education, business development, clean water and more to simultaneously address the insidious effects of poverty while staying true to the "integrated development" moniker. We wanted to be more than a Band-Aid® project, and to empower people and communities for the long run.

Guatemala's Civil War (roughly 1960-1996) was raging during many of the years the stories in this book took place, and telling them too soon would have endangered people involved, especially those in Guatemala. In 1999 after a Truth Commission assembled in Guatemala had announced its findings and the nation was in the painful process of officially recognizing the atrocities committed against the population during the war, I reached out to Guatemalan friends regarding completing this book. Many were afraid that those who had been in power still might be able to hurt them or their families. So I set the project aside, and waited.

In the years after the Truth Commission report, the military was largely disbanded. The patrols of armed-and-dangerous 15-year-olds who had been trained to terrorize, torture and kill and had been dispatched to largely rural, indigenous communities, returned to their homes in other regions of Guatemala. One by one, war criminals were convicted, put under house arrest or died off. After the death of a particular Guatemalan politician nearly

25 years after Xela AID had come with its first volunteer group, there was consensus among those who'd been involved that it was safe for the story of Xela AID's founding to be told. This book's time had finally come.

Fear. The terror perpetrated by the Guatemalan military and its allies on the civilian population during that country's Civil War was so complete that even today, many people are still afraid to acknowledge the horrors—truly, the *genocide*—that occurred. Mass graves have been unearthed, witnesses have come forward, books written and the conversation is not going away. Reconciliation has been a slow, contentious process with many still in denial—but there is progress.

That said, at the suggestion of an advisor familiar with ongoing corruption investigations in Guatemala, Guatemalan politics, and the contents of this book, I have removed the names of select politicians and blurred dates to stay above the fray. For private citizens who had any misgivings or weren't sure about being included, I've changed their names and omitted just enough detail to safeguard their identities, or left them out altogether.

Style. From the years I spent as a writer and reporter, as a matter of habit, I carried a pocket-sized journal and used it often. I've used quotation marks where I made notes of what people said at the time of the event, or very close to it, and felt I had reliably recorded their words. Where I ended up with too many gaps, I've instead summarized from the best of my recollection and the recollection of others who were there. Where chapters contain multiple stories, I've used subheads.

Parts. Part I of this book, "Terror on the Mountain," recalls the surreal event in Guatemala and the days leading up to it that set my life on a decidedly different course. "The Company We Keep," Part II, jumps back several years to make sense of how a young woman with a demanding professional career in communications, a love of singing and songwriting, and *zero experience* with human development, ended up in Guatemala founding an organization focused on the latter. It does this by introducing several of the truly extraordinary people who inspired me to find and pursue the cause I felt most passionate about, wherever that might lead.

4

"Spiritual Things," Part III, returns quickly to Guatemala and continues in a roughly chronological telling of the story through Part IV, "Forging Local Hope." In Parts V and VI, "Insights," and "Finding Our Wings," I share some of the moments that most impacted me along the journey to establish a meaningful help organization. The last chapter, "Wings," for example, recalls a young woman whose spirit and ultimate triumph over adversity touched me deeply. A single sentence she whispered to me convinced me that all our efforts over the years had been worth it.

The Epilogue wraps up some loose ends, while the Addendum includes an update on where people are decades later at this writing. In the Addendum there is a Key Dates section for readers who are especially interested in how our development project evolved, or would like to consider this story against the backdrop of other key events taking place simultaneously in Guatemala. I've included a hefty End Notes section with original articles clickable as PDFs on my Author website (lesliebaerdinkel.net).

Politics. With some hesitation, I've included information that some readers might find political. There is a lesson in history as it relates to U.S. foreign policy. There are two accounts of encounters I had with members of the diplomatic corps that were relevant to our work in Guatemala. While I would have preferred to skirt politics all together, I realized that if I didn't share the events that shaped my thinking as I decided to work in a war zone, my motives wouldn't make sense to you, the reader, nor would my evolution in thinking. Whether you agree or disagree with my conclusions and the course I charted because of them, at least you'll know what I was thinking and feeling.

Hope Dancing is a snapshot of my path to discovering purpose. It includes my first-hand recollections of key moments in the founding of a human development organization, including early challenges, adventures we had getting launched, and stories about the people I met along the way who inspired me and gave me the courage to keep on going. Since much of the book is focused on the early years and founding of Xela AID, it is not by any means an all-inclusive account of the amazing growth and development of the organization. Its success has involved the love, devotion and significant efforts of *hundreds of volunteers* over the years.

Of particular note was the year 2013, a watershed moment for the organization. A passionate Board of Directors and Advisors fueled its transformation and catapulted the organization from the broad field of non-profits that fade away with their founder, and set it on a sustainable course. This is further detailed in "Milestones and Key Historic Dates." I am deeply grateful to each of the individuals mentioned, and the balance of the Board.

Hand-Up Model. The delay in writing this book may have been fortuitous in that it allowed Xela AID to mature. While in early years we focused on emergency relief, we quickly learned that there was an infinite sea of human need and that a "give away" model was both unsustainable and ineffective for long-term, positive change. Xela AID's hand *up* rather than hand *out* model was guided by plenty of mistakes we made on our own, the mistakes of non-profits that came before us, and on the smarts of experienced and energetic volunteers who joined our leadership team over the years. The sincere desire to serve that we always had remains, but we now know a great deal more about the terrain and the pitfalls. Over the decades, we've come of age.

To all of you who guided me in my personal journey, and who poured your heart and soul into the development of Xela AID over the decades, I will be forever grateful. I thank you, also, on behalf of those we serve.

The Author

PART I ✚ TERROR ON THE MOUNTAIN

December, 1992

1 - Just After Midnight

MACHINE GUN FIRE echoed in the night. It cut a line in the dirt just a few inches from my feet! I bolted up, half asleep, and drew my legs to my chest. A strange wind beat down, and blew up a cloud of dust that engulfed the lean-to the dozen of us had been sleeping under. I leaned forward and peered up, squinting to see. The night sky was flickering with lights, like fireworks. Then, a bright light flooded down. A helicopter hung in the sky, roaring.

I froze and shivered, not able to grasp what was happening. When I tried to move, my arms and legs would not obey. I felt like I was stuck in a nightmare I couldn't wake up from. But I was awake...

The strafing continued as the structure flattened against the press of the wind. I wondered if anyone had been injured, killed, or would be. No one dared move.

In the darkness I could hear screaming—women, children, everyone. How *had* I ended up here?

2 - Forty-Eight Hours Earlier

"**N**O POLITICS" had been part of the bargain to keep everyone safe, and those were the rules I'd agreed to when I entered the country and started my Spanish lessons at *Escuela Juan Sisay*. The school was located on a windy side street in the highland town of Quetzaltenango, called "Xela" (SHAY-luh) for short. I'd been studying for almost two weeks, and now, it was just a few days before I was to leave Guatemala. Before I did, I wanted to learn more about what was really happening here, and why I had an uncomfortable feeling...

Walking along the cobblestone streets I marveled at the beauty of *trajes*—the bright, woven blouses and full, pleated blue skirts worn by local women. Most wore their hair in two braids with a colorful ribbon running down each. I learned that this *Quetzalteca* outfit was specific to Xela, and the Quiché people. They speak a language of the same name, and are one of approximately 21 surviving Mayan cultural groups in Guatemala. The graceful, skirted women carried baskets on their heads and strolled with their goats and pigs along the streets. The Christmas season was in full swing. A six-foot-wide nativity scene filled a bakery window. It seemed a picture-book scene, but had an ominous undertone.

Every day on the way to Spanish school I passed soldiers. Their tent cities filled green spaces like *Parque Central* at the center of town, and a triangular park in front of the town's cemetery near where I was staying in an area known as *Calvario*. Young soldiers dressed in khakis and carrying guns moved among the beautifully dressed women who looked down at the ground and walked quickly. The facade of the 16th century Catholic Church flanking Central Park with its seven saintly figures, arms outstretched in gestures of peace and hope, looked down on this scene. The stark contrasts made the setting surreal, eerie.

I'd read the basics about Guatemala's 30-year Civil War. The poor wanted better living conditions, land, education, and a voice—in short, hope for the future. Those in power wanted to maintain the status quo whereby 70 percent of all productive farmlands and large businesses were owned by roughly 2 percent of the population, and the government assigned very few resources to poor rural areas. Most of the people who lived outside major cities were people of Mayan descent, indigenous people, and in rural Guatemala they commonly lacked adequate access to basics like clean water, medical care and schooling for their children. According to one study I read, eight in 10 Guatemalans, 8 million people, were without clean water, medical care and enough food.[1] It was these subhuman conditions that had fueled the Civil War.

And now I found myself in the middle of it and wanted to understand from the people who were living it. So during one of my last Spanish tutoring sessions, I asked my Spanish teacher, Gaby, some pointed questions:

"Why are there soldiers in the streets and camped out in the parks?"

"Why do the women walking along the streets avert theirs eyes, quicken their pace and duck behind doorways as the soldiers approach?"

"Why are there almost no men on the streets, or children in the schoolyards?"

Gaby was a small-framed woman who most often kept her long, black hair pulled back tightly in a ponytail. With a decisively serious look on her face, she glanced over each shoulder then drew near me over the desk. She spoke in a hushed tone.

"The soldiers are here to watch us, and to listen to what we are saying," she told me. "And the women are afraid, because many people have 'disappeared.' Anyone who disagrees with the government disappears...

"Men disappear more than women, and even young boys are often taken and forced into the Army."

She stared at me with her deep brown eyes, watching for my reaction. These revelations were shocking and sent a chill down my spine. No wonder the fear was palpable. She had my attention.

Gaby leaned in and whispered, "Leslie, do you want to see what's *really* happening in Guatemala?"

"Yes," I agreed immediately, perhaps foolishly. It's always best to know the truth I thought, even if it is painful, or scary. I sensed from Gaby it would be both. Maybe that drew me to it even more.

"I will arrange it then. We will take you to see some things in the evenings after our lessons."

Our first outing had been to a factory. But our second outing shrouded in secrecy and under the cover of darkness, *that* was the bombshell.

Gaby and her husband Marcos drove me along the Pan American Highway in their aging Datsun pickup truck. I'd gotten to know Gaby well during our many days of practice conversations. She was of Quiché decent, 23 years old, a student at local San Carlos University and had been married to Marcos for several years. Marcos was nearly 30 and also a student at the University. He was perhaps 5 feet, 8 inches tall, of medium build and well muscled, as if he did lots of heavy lifting. Like Gaby, he had dark hair and expressive brown eyes. Both were Catholic, and they lived in her family home and took care of her parents. They wanted to have a baby, but hadn't had any luck—"maybe because of all the stress of the war," she'd confided.

I'd shared my story with Gaby, too. I was 33, married, spiritual but not religious, wrote for a living, played the guitar and composed music. As an avocation I coordinated volunteers for the Missionaries of Charity Brothers and Sisters, Mother Teresa's order. I shared details about experiences I had on Skid Row in Los Angeles, in part, with people who spoke only Spanish. I was in Guatemala to improve my dismal Spanish skills, I'd told her. We quickly became friends. I trusted her, and liked her husband, Marcos, too. He seemed like a good-hearted person, if a little intense.

13

We continued our drive and soon reached a small home, a shack, really, in the middle of nowhere. Marcos got out, walked to the house and disappeared inside. I noticed that behind the house was a garage or storage space of some sort fashioned out of tarps.

"This is the house of a friend," Gaby explained. "We will get out here."

Marcos exited the house with a man who looked to be in his forties, not only older but quite a bit stockier than Marcos. Marcos then came back to us and jumped in the car, while Gaby got out and told me to follow. I grabbed my small pack containing my water bottle and a little money, exactly what Gaby had told me to bring. The man walked to the tarp structure and pulled back the front tarp revealing a truck that was larger than Marcos and Gaby's, and even more beaten up.

The man got into the truck and managed to turn the engine over after a few foiled tries. He backed it out of the space as the truck belched out smoke, and Marcos pulled his vehicle in. The man left the truck running while he and Marcos secured the large front tarp back in place, obscuring Marcos and Gaby's truck. He then got back into the driver's seat and I followed Marcos and Gaby as they piled in.

"He will take us the next part of the way," Gaby explained.

I figured that the road conditions up ahead must have precluded using Marcos and Gaby's little truck, and I was right. Not too far down the road we turned onto a dirt path rife with potholes, and headed up into the mountains. As the sun set, Gaby told me that we wouldn't be with this man for long, as we'd soon need to get out and hike.

All the driving, the car swapping, and the secrecy about where we were going had piqued my interest. I became more persistent in my questions about where we were headed.

"It's a CPR village," Gaby explained. "This means, 'Civilian Population in Resistance.'

"This village and many others were created as families fled Xela and other cities fearing violence, and that the Army would take

14

their young sons and force them to be soldiers," she explained, adding, "It's not too far…"

I imagined a short hike to a village of huts, perhaps well stocked as the families waited out the war.

We drove up the dirt road for nearly an hour before coming to a place where the road further degraded and looked impassable for anything but a four-wheel-drive vehicle. The man stopped the truck, making it clear that this was where we would get out. Marcos thanked the man, and as darkness firmly set in, we began our hike.

It was at first misting, but soon turned to rain. I'd worn a thin raincoat but the rain was seeping in. I got chilled as we climbed, and it was *not* a short climb, at least by my standards. The "not-too-far" hike Gaby had described ended up being close to two hours, almost straight up in places, and in the pouring rain!

I was grateful when, finally, Marcos announced we were nearing our destination. I could smell something burning. "Fires in the village," Gaby explained. By this time, we were all sopping wet and muddy, and I imagined getting to warm up by a fire and have something hot to drink. This was a pipe dream.

We entered the village with no fanfare. There were no huts, but leaky, lean-to structures. As we walked by, people peered out wearily. Most wore tattered clothes, and those moving about did so slowly. The people were gaunt and listless.

We walked by a small fire with a young woman and four children crouched close to stay warm. A flat piece of tin sat on rocks to hold it over the fire, and the woman was cooking on top of it. She was scrambling what looked to be a single egg. I watched her pull apart a plant and mix it in with the egg. I recognized the plant as goosefoot—a weed back home. The cupful of food on her makeshift grill would mean no more than a mouthful for her and each of the children. I began to understand the gravity of what was happening in this camp.

As we walked further along the muddy path I caught a whiff of a sewer-like smell. It grew stronger and soon became overpowering, finally, making me gag. It dawned on me that there must be at least a hundred people encamped here, if not more, and there were no outhouses that I had seen. I wondered where they went...

Things got worse. We came upon a group of women huddled in a circle. As we got closer, I could hear the women crying. One woman began *wailing*, and instinctively, I wanted to run to help. I sped up my pace.

When we reached the women I could see that they were gathered around something. I was shocked to see it was a young boy. He was lying face-up on the ground, arms at his side, eyes closed, on what looked like wet pieces of cardboard. His thin little body lay motionless, and I began to realize, slowly, the state of the child. I felt panicked and my heart pounded. I hoped I was wrong, but soon understood. He had died. He was lying on a makeshift coffin.

Gaby translated to me as the wailing woman spoke between sobs.

"This is his mother," she told me. "She says he died from a sore throat..."

A sore throat! My mind raced.

I was horrified. How could it be that just a five-hour plane ride from my comfortable home in Southern California this mother had no access to simple antibiotics that would cure such things?

My thoughts flashed to a moment a few weeks earlier when I'd cleaned out a medicine cabinet at my home and had thrown away antibiotics that were about to expire. *Those antibiotics might have saved this little boy's life,* I thought. Tears welled in my eyes, and I tried not to let the women see that I, too, was crying.

We continued our walk through the camp and when we'd finished, it was late—nearing midnight. Gaby, Marcos and I, along with several people Marcos called *testigos,* "witnesses," from the United Nations, were given pieces of plastic and shown to a lean-to much larger than all the others. This was where we would bunk down. Men were directed to one side and women to the other. Gaby and I lay alongside one another looking out at the night sky. When I asked her why "witnesses" were needed here, she told me that our presence helped to stave off attacks on the civilian village, but didn't ensure the villagers' safety.

Attacks from whom? I wondered, but was emotionally too spent to ask.

I laid down and covered myself with the plastic, using my backpack as a pillow. The image of the boy lying there on the ground played over and over in my mind. I squirmed and continued tearing up. After the hours of driving and hiking in the rain and all I'd just seen, I felt physically and mentally exhausted, shaken to my core, and desperate for sleep. It came, but I was tormented by the image of the boy. Then, I began to dream. In my dream, a whir in the distance grew louder and became a storm. I drew my feet up, out of the dreamt storm. But then, it had not been a dream at all…

The strafing had continued for just a few minutes, but it seemed like an hour and as if it were happening in maddening slow motion. It was like one of those dreams where you're trying to run with all your strength but your legs don't move and the monster is gaining on you. And just when you think the monster can't get any scarier, it did.

The helicopter hovered over us, shining a light down. When the light moved away and was no longer in my eyes, I could see the helicopter body illuminated. At the back end of the fuselage just below the back rotor I saw four letters clearly visible above numbers. The letters read, "U.S.A.F."

I gasped. Was this a United States Air Force helicopter? If so, what was it doing raining down bullets on women and children —*civilians?* I was bewildered, confused, in shock.

After the barrage stopped and the helicopter flew off, the village fell deathly quiet except for the sobs of children. We had been lucky that night. There were a number of injuries, but no one was killed. But this kind of violence and the fear and uncertainty it brought, I realized, was *daily life* for the people who'd fled to these mountains. They'd done nothing wrong, committed no crimes. They were here only to protect their families, and especially, to keep their children from being taken into the Guatemalan military. This was routinely done with boys as young as 13 (and even younger, by some accounts). Although the families in this camp were there trying to avoid being drawn into the Civil War, the war kept coming to them. They were living a nightmare.

I went to Guatemala expecting to be nothing more than a Spanish student, and ended up being a witness to terror. And now I, too, had been drawn in.

3 - Soldiers at Dawn

AFTER THE ATTACK, Gaby said we should stay put until morning, and told me to try and get some rest. So much was running through my mind. Why were we strafed? Thank goodness no one was killed. And 'U.S.A.F.,' my God! What was my country doing involved in Guatemala's Civil War, and terrorizing civilians?

I was frozen in a sitting-up position under that leaky lean-to, exhausted, in a daze. The letters on the fuselage rolled eerily through my thoughts. I wrestled with what this meant. It's like the moment you hear that someone you love has died, and you hope it's not true—a kind of panic. I felt sick to my stomach. I forced myself to lie down.

Many hours passed, and perhaps an hour before dawn, I finally fell into a sleep. But I didn't get long to rest as soon, the sun peeked up from the horizon. Within moments of sunrise, we were abruptly awakened. A man rushed up to the lean-to and in a loud whisper called, "Marcos!" I couldn't understand the barrage of whispered words that followed in Spanish, but Gaby sat up and began translating to me in a croaky voice as both of us tried to fully wake up.

"There are troops, many soldiers, not far away," she translated.

Gaby then leapt up and she said to me, "You are from *Los Estados* Leslie, you will be safe!"

Marcos was up, too, and whispered, *"¡Vamanos!"* Before I could get a question out, they had disappeared. I had no idea what was happening, so I sat there, thinking, trying to get my bearings and decide what to do next.

But just minutes later, Gaby and Marcos returned to the lean-to, breathless.

"There is one Jeep in the village, but Marcos and I can't drive it out," Gaby told me. "The soldiers are filling the road!"

My mind raced. "What if I drive?" I blurted out.

The two of them looked at each other and quickly discussed the possibility. "That could work. They may not stop you," Gaby said.

The terror in their eyes told me that Gaby and Marcos were facing something horrific if the plan didn't work. The naiveté that had been both my blessing and bane on this trip to Guatemala fueled my sense that nothing bad could possibly happen to me, and to them by extension, if I was driving.

I told them again that I would drive, and insisted we go "Now!" They didn't hesitate.

The Jeep was painted white and bore the stylized deep-blue world-cupped-by-wheat logo that was synonymous with the United Nations. I had no idea of the whereabouts of the person who'd driven it there. But the keys were in the ignition and we climbed in either borrowing, or stealing it—the former, I preferred to believe.

As if skilled in this drill, Gaby and Marcos jumped in the back and squeezed down onto the floorboard as the man from the village who'd awakened us came running up with a precious wool blanket and hurled it over them. Without making a sound, the man motioned frantically to me with his arms to go, and quickly.

I turned the keys in the ignition and the vehicle jerked to a start. It took me a minute to get the hang of the clutch, and we bolted several times. Soon I'd backed out and was winding my way around obstacles on a path that looked like it would lead to the road we'd hiked in on.

When I found the road, I made a sharp turn to hightail down the mountain. But almost immediately, I had to slam on the breaks. About 250 yards in front of us, the road was completely *filled* with soldiers coming our way.

I felt my stomach somersault and the blood drain from my face. My hands and forehead began to sweat. *What should I do?* I didn't dare say anything out loud that might elicit a response from Gaby or Marcos that could give them away to the oncoming soldiers.

Keep driving down the road. If anyone tries to stop you, just smile, wave, and keep going, I thought.

Then, shots were fired! I shuddered. I was relieved to see soldiers stopped along the shoulder of the road shooting into the air recklessly, and laughing. I continued driving slowly toward them. To my surprise, when I reached those in the front rows, they began to part for our vehicle to pass through—surreal, like the parable of the Red Sea.

As we entered into the press of soldiers my heart raced and I hoped no one would speak to me, or try to make eye contact. There were soldiers in front, behind and on either side of the Jeep. I could have reached out and touched one of them. I kept steady on the gas and on the wheel, tried to look relaxed and confident, and kept my gaze straight ahead and a slight smile on my face.

The soldiers thinned out. My heart was still racing, but I was beginning to believe we would pass through without incident. Then, to my dismay, I heard someone call out something unintelligible, and saw a soldier ahead and to the left waving his hand and motioning me toward him. Nervously, I smiled. It occurred to me to act as if I was in a hurry. I looked directly at the soldier, smiled broadly, raised my eyebrows and pointed to the watch on my left wrist as if to say, "Hey, I gotta be somewhere, O.K?"

I kept the vehicle rolling slowly. The soldier hesitated. One, two, three seconds passed and my heart pounded in my chest as I thought about what could happen next. Then, amazingly, the soldier waved me on and continued walking straight ahead with the rest of his unit. I felt a surge of relief.

When it appeared that the last of the soldiers had disappeared from around us, I was wet with sweat and hoping this reprieve from calamity was not too good to be true. I wanted to tell Gaby and Marcos that the danger had passed, but wanted first to make sure we were far from the soldiers.

I didn't speak a single word until we came to a main road about 30 minutes later. In all the commotion, I couldn't remember the direction we'd come from, but assumed I should go back toward the man's house who'd driven us up the road.

"*¿A la derecha, o la izquierda?*" (Right or left?) I croaked out without looking back. "Left," Marco whispered. I turned left and stepped on the gas.

I drove down that road for a good 15 minutes before I pulled to the side. I looked in the side mirrors and around nervously to make sure we hadn't been followed, then told Gaby and Marcos I thought it was safe. I thanked my lucky stars. As the two of them came out from beneath the blanket, I opened the driver's door and jumped out. I was shaking. Marcos crossed from the back seat and into the driver's seat without exiting the vehicle. Gaby got into the front, and I climbed into the back where I sat down and breathed a sigh of relief. We were silent for some time.

Gaby was first to speak. She warned me that I mustn't tell anyone where we'd been or what had happened. There could be *problemas* for her and Marcos, and for me.

"The Army believes that refugees and the *guerrilla* are one and the same," she explained. "We could be accused of conspiring against the government, and you could too!" (I took Gaby's warning seriously, by the way, and did not tell a soul what had happened *for nearly a decade.)*

We drove along silently for a number of hours. My mind was like a tangled yarn-ball of emotions, and I couldn't find an end to follow one thread. I had a lot to think about.

I was staying in Guatemala with a family that hosted students who were there to learn Spanish. That night in my tiny room, I didn't sleep much, and morning came too quickly.

Playing in my head like a jingle you can't quell was a loop of images of the horrific conditions at the refugee camp. The boy who had died. The hovering helicopter barraging us with bullets. The lingering smells. I felt afraid, sad, and angry all at once. And "U.S.A.F."...that *hurt*. My government was involved in terrorizing unarmed civilians in the night. I'd seen it with my own eyes. I couldn't come up with any explanation, other than the country I loved was on the wrong side of history. I felt devastated. I knew that what I'd experienced in Guatemala was something I would never forget, even if I wanted to—and it would change my life. How, I didn't know.

I lay awake that night and replayed all that had happened. Then, I thought about the twists and turns that had landed me here. It all began with the casual suggestion of a friend who'd found his purpose.

PART II ✛ THE COMPANY WE KEEP

4 - The Rebel Peter Hickman

WHEN MY JOURNALIST BUDDY Bob Rhein introduced me to Peter Hickman in 1984, he told me he thought we were kindred spirits. The longer I knew Peter, the more flattered I felt that Bob thought so. Peter had found his passion and purpose, and with these, a courage of conviction unlike any I had seen firsthand. He was utterly *fearless,* and wise beyond his 30-some years. I wanted more of what he had, and I had a sense he would help me grow. I couldn't have known then that Peter's intuition would lead me to Guatemala.

Peter amazed and inspired me.

On December 5, 2001, he stood on the stage of the Eastman Theatre in Rochester, New York, where more than 3,000 people had gathered. Filling the theatre were reporters and curiosity seekers, but largely, the faithful from Catholic traditions around the world. Peter shared the stage with Mary Ramerman, a long-time leader in her Rochester Catholic community. She was devoted to serving the poor and ministering to the sick. But Mary's large, active community had gotten the attention of the Vatican when she regularly broke the rules—like wearing vestments and sharing the altar with a priest during masses (only men were allowed to be priests). Their church also allowed non-Catholic believers to receive Holy Communion, and welcomed openly gay and lesbian people to take communion and even *marry* in the church. These were all major no-nos.

This gathering would become an historic event.[2] [3] Those Roman Catholics who dared to attend were threatened with excommunication by the local diocese. Peter was one Catholic who wasn't afraid. And truth be told, he wasn't just any old chum of mine, either. He was actually *Bishop* Peter Hickman, widely recognized as founder of the ecumenical, "Old" Catholic movement that because of its progressive practices is a thorn in the side of Rome.

On this day in an act forbidden by the Roman Catholic Church (although progressives had confidentially expressed support), Bishop Peter ordained Mary Ramerman as *the first female Catholic priest*. It was not an act of defiance, but one of conscience. He is a staunch advocate for a Catholic Community that is inclusive, which by current definition would have to be independent from Rome. Over a couple of decades, he formed, then expanded an international Ecumenical Catholic Communion[4] that welcomes married priests, people whose gender identity or role is non-traditional, and encourages parishioners to follow their conscience on matters such as birth control and divorce.

The booming movement has singlehandedly changed the face of the Catholic Community in the United States, making Bishop Peter Hickman an inspired Holy Man to some, and a heretic to others. For me, he is the wise and inspired friend whose invitation to serve changed the course of my life.

The 14th century poet Hafiz wrote, "First, the fish has to say, 'Something ain't right about this camel ride—and I'm feeling *so damn thirsty.*'" One day that same year Bishop Peter ordained Mary Ramerman, I figured out I was thirsty. I felt well rooted spiritually. I loved writing and editing for a living, and wrote and played music as a delightful avocation. I was happily married, had a loving extended family, and had collected a nurturing circle of friends. I felt strong and empowered. But something was missing.

The longing I felt was captured in an Edmond Everett Hale poem I had read in my teens, "I Am Only One." It acknowledges that no one can do everything for the world, but that we each can do something—and should. I was trying to figure out what that "something I *can* do" to make a positive difference might be. I went to Peter for guidance.

Red-haired and with piercing green eyes, Peter is unassuming and soft-spoken. Over the years I'd seen him add a unique perspective to conversations and quell conflict. Why was it, I asked him, that despite the embarrassment of riches I enjoyed on so many fronts, I still felt restless and unfulfilled in my life?

"I've got an emptiness I can't figure out how to fill," I told Peter.

My husband Sam, on the other hand, always seemed cheerful and content—happy with things just the way they were. I shared with Peter that I felt foolish and self-absorbed for not being as content as Sam was.

I'd met Sam at a conference of high-tech journalists in the mid-1980s when I was the editor of a computer magazine. The realm I worked in belonged overwhelmingly to men—writers, editors, sales people, and publishers. There may have been one woman for every 50 men in that industry. I often attended conferences, and since I wasn't looking to meet someone, at evening events I'd occupy myself listening to the band. Sam played keyboards, guitar, and sang with a group I was watching one night. He talked to me during a break. I learned that besides his other talents, he also composed music. I played guitar, sang, and composed music, too. He was especially kind and a great listener—something of a natural counselor. We kept in touch, and eventually, started dating. We married in 1989. My discontent these few years later had nothing to do with Sam, but everything to do with a hole in my life that had preceded him.

Peter let me do most of the talking. Having worked myself into a desperate state, I sat there with him feeling lost and defeated. When he was sure I'd said everything I needed to, Peter spoke slowly and thoughtfully. He told me he had no doubt I would discover what seemed to be missing in my life. "Just keep on searching and moving forward," he encouraged.

Then, in what seemed to be a non sequitur, Peter asked if Sam and I would be willing to help him out by playing music at Mass at his church the next Sunday. As a devotee to Eastern spiritual traditions for most of my life (I attended Catholic church only as a young child), my repertoire of Catholic hymns was all but non-existent. Sam had grown up a Southern Baptist. But Peter said the music didn't have to be Catholic, *per se*, and that we were free to reach deep into our spiritual wells and pull out some inspirational music to share, however eclectic its origins.

Peter was clever, but it occurred to me what he was doing. While our participation might offer some ancillary benefit to his congregation, I was sure his request was largely for my benefit. He was coaxing me out of the realm of worrying about the void in my life and offering me the opportunity to fill it with something meaningful *that very week*. I was grateful for the gesture, and decided to go with it. I had nothing to lose.

I ran the idea by Sam who was amused at imagining a Catholic-Jewish-Buddhist girl like me (it's a long story) and a lifelong Baptist such as himself playing music for a Catholic mass. We both agreed to accept Peter's gracious invitation.

The next Sunday we were welcomed with open arms into the St. Matthews Ecumenical Community of good-hearted people, and we were made to feel at home. Soon we were playing at masses weekly and rocking the congregation with titles spanning classic Baptist hymns to secular songs that had messages of hope and love. For me, it was an exciting step in the right direction. Something felt right about my involvement at St. Matthews under the watchful eye of my friend and mentor, who we came to know in the St. Matthews Church context as *Father Peter*.

Within months, Fr. Peter encouraged me to become involved with the Church's program to provide food to families in need, and I jumped in with both feet. We asked parishioners to bring canned food to service on Sundays, and then afterwards, a group of us sorted the donations, bagged them up, and delivered them to an organization that specialized in distributing food to those with great need. When we dropped the donations off, we'd sometimes see families waiting in line. One day I watched a young boy whose eyes lit up as he and his mother drew close to the bags. The boy, who was about four years old, actually licked his lips in anticipation. I'd never known what it meant to be hungry. Seeing this young boy react in this way gave me the tiniest inkling of what hunger might feel like.

Collecting food for people with real need was incredibly satisfying. The world's problems are big, but knowing I could do something small to help a few people was inspiring and empowering. I wanted to do more.

One day at St. Matthews I was passing through the lobby when I noticed a shelf containing a small assortment of inspirational books. I was attracted to one with a picture of Mother Teresa on the cover. I opened it at random, and the page contained one of her quotes. It read, "In this life we cannot do great things. But we can do small things with great love." I felt as though I'd been personally challenged.

I decided I would make a conscious effort to add more love to the things I did for others, and to do more for others. I was curious to see where that would take me. I wrote down that quote and put a copy on the mirror in my bathroom where I knew I would see it each morning.

As it turned out, working at this had an almost magical effect. Day by day, I felt more positive and energized. The tough days got noticeably fewer. I began to really see and appreciate how fortunate I'd been in my own life, and because of that, how much I had to give. I had never felt so grateful, and it was changing me from the inside out.

That change led to a place I never imagined finding myself— smack dab in the middle of Skid Row.

5 - Christine Washington

SKID ROW IN LOS ANGELES is a sprawling tent city. Across a ten-block area,[5] thousands of people are relegated to sleeping in the cold, washing in drinking fountains, foraging for food in trash bins and defecating behind buildings. I couldn't have imagined worse conditions if I tried.

I'd been so inspired by my experiences at St. Matthew's, that I wanted to work on a larger scale. When an opportunity to volunteer with a similar program focused on that ten-block area came along, I jumped at it. This small thing I could do to help turned out to be a *big step* out of my comfort zone.

San Pedro at 7th Street was the heart of Skid Row, and where I met Christine. Each Saturday morning she filed into line to pick up her bag lunch. She was about 35 years old and thin framed. Her dark skin had been weathered by the sun in the brutal way reserved almost exclusively for people who are homeless. Her lips were cracked, and cheeks darkly scarred from sunburns. The sandwich, apple, chips and water we gave her weren't much in the scheme of things, but she was grateful...she was *hungry*.

When Sam didn't have a wedding to play, he'd come along to Skid Row to help. Fr. Peter, although neck-deep in growing his church, also made time for this service work. We all knew that handing out food wasn't going to end poverty, but agreed it was a satisfying activity, and a step. After all, there's *no hope* for a better life for someone who starves to death.

The first time I volunteered on Skid Row, we met other volunteers at 9 a.m. on the outskirts of Chinatown, about a mile-and-a-half from downtown, and parked to carpool. The idea was to take as few vehicles as possible. The streets where the group set up food lines were frequented by people with drug addictions. Getting money for the next fix ruled their lives, our handlers explained, so any vehicle was at a high risk of being broken into.

About a dozen of us piled into two old vans we'd stacked to the roof with flats of water and boxes containing filled lunch sacks.

We were told that these had been prepared by the early shift of volunteers who'd met around 6 a.m. I had no idea what to expect, and around every corner wondered if we were there yet.

When we did get to the homeless encampment lining San Pedro Street, there was no mistaking that we had arrived. There were tents, shelters made of cardboard, plastic bags, umbrellas and other reclaimed items stretched as far as I could see down both sides of the street. I learned that upwards of 7,000 people called Skid Row home.[6] It was a sea of human suffering—a vast collection of downtrodden people, the likes of which I'd never seen before. Their stories shook me to my core.

I met people who'd been given drugs and alcohol before they could walk. People who'd grown up on the streets with no parents to guide them. Veterans who'd seen hell in combat and lost their ability to cope, and in some cases, lost their will to live. People who'd been beaten, or sexually abused by their own parents. The very first day, I saw a heroin user cook his dope with a cigarette lighter under a bottle cap and shoot up right in front of me, as casual as if he were eating a sandwich.

I felt like I'd gone to a parallel universe where the rules and norms were completely different than those I knew—a dark, Gotham-like place. Yet many people I met had not given up hope of one day getting off the streets and having a normal life. Seeing the ramshackle physical and mental state of many of the people I met, I was astounded that they had any hope left at all.

I soon realized that we were not just a meal ticket for these human beings living at the dark, forgotten edges of humanity. Truly, we were their lifelines. We were "normal" people they could talk to—people who affirmed their very existence.

"We are invisible. *Invisible!*" one man told me. I thought about it. I'd often give out a dollar or two to someone on a freeway exit, but that was from the safety of my car. Before I started working on Skid Row, I'd never spoken to a homeless person walking near me. Their collective plight was too great a problem to solve, and that made me uncomfortable. So I'd cross the street to avoid them. I never made eye contact.

It must be painful to be invisible, I thought.

Christine was someone I'd seen on that very first day on Skid Row. She caught my eye because despite her tattered, dirty clothes and ruddy cheeks, she was smiling. She was full of thanks when we handed her a food bag and some water—so grateful for so little. It amazed me that she could muster so much gratitude in her situation and mean it—no small feat. I admired her attitude.

After a few weeks of handing out food bags, my curiosity won out. I overcame my trepidation enough to sit down on a curb next to Christine and just chat. That day, she told me her story.

She'd split up with her perennially drunken husband and father of her two children. She worked the night shift at a convenience store, but on minimum wage, couldn't support the children and wasn't collecting anything from their father who had disappeared. She relocated her children to their grandmother's house for their own good. Then, overcome by loneliness and despair, Christine, too, started to drink. Soon, she began to use drugs.

"I *hurt*—but not as much when I was drinkin' or lit," she told me. "I knew I was makin' it worse, but I couldn't stop."

It was a downward spiral. First despair, then drinking and drugs to kill the pain. Soon she was not able to get up in the morning. Finally, she lost her job. She couldn't bear to face her children, or her mother, so she stopped seeing them. More despair, drinking and drugs...

In desperation, Christine began to prostitute to pay for her drug fix and the rent on the single-room, run-down apartment she'd moved to. She was eventually evicted after being late with the rent "more than a few times," she crowed, chuckling. Then, she got pregnant from one of her johns.

"I ain't got no idea which one," she told me, shaking her head. "Hell was I *all alone!*"

Christine was living on a city backstreet in a tent when the baby was born. She'd screamed during the birth, and no one came to

35

help. Conversely, she "thanked God" that no one came. "Who knows what kind 'a bad dude it might 'a been…"

She got through the birth on instinct and "What I saw on TV," she told me. I thought about how lonely she must have been then, and how afraid…

She named the baby boy Jeremiah, "After the prophet that God promised to rescue." *A wish for him, and for herself,* I thought.

Each part of Christine's story was more heartbreaking than the last. When Jeremiah was about three weeks old, she was sitting on a street curb like the one we were sitting on. She was cradling him in her arms and about to go into her tent to feed him when a woman in a tailored suit and two police officers showed up. The woman told Christine she was from Social Services, and that she was there to make sure Jeremiah was safe.

When Christine told the woman she was living in a tent, the woman replied that she'd need to accompany them to the police station. The woman talked to her in a calming voice, Christine recalled, and one of the policemen asked her to pass Jeremiah into his arms.

"Hell no!" she told him.

When she refused…when she couldn't bear to give up her child, one officer restrained her. The other policeman took the baby from her arms, she recalled, her eyes now welling up. But she didn't blame any of the three.

"I knew it was the right thing to do, but I didn't want to do it. I did not want to lose that little boy."

They took Christine to the police station. She answered questions. Without an address, she couldn't keep the baby, for his own good, she was told. She repeated this to me, agreeing. She walked out of the police station without the baby, alone again.

"God's promise of rescue for Jeremiah was fulfilled," she said matter-of-factly, drying her eyes. She had not been as lucky.

That event three years prior was the last time she'd seen her son. And although she knew it was best for him, it hadn't made losing him any easier.

"My stomach is empty, and so is my heart," Christine told me, poetically, as we sat there on that curb. She was still smiling through the pain.

Her final comment on the matter: "I never recovered from that, and it ain't likely I will."

I saw Christine each Saturday for the better part of a year and cheered her on while she found a drug rehabilitation program to attend, a job on an assembly line, and a place to rent, in that order. It was progress.

Her story touched me so much that I wrote a song about her. She cried when I brought my guitar with me one Saturday and played it for her, the refrain:

Someday we'll get out of here, 'till then I wish you these...

Enough to eat, a place to sleep—and peace to you Christine.

If only.

Christine was the first person living on Skid Row I got to know, but not the last. Of course there were the drug dealers, the violent offenders just out of prison, and others whose extreme behavior placed them on the fringes of civilized society. But I also met and got to know some surprising people living on Skid Row who at one time had been in the mainstream.

Frank, an artist who sold bracelets made of reclaimed telephone wire, had gone to the prestigious Claremont Graduate School and earned a Masters Degree in Fine Arts. He'd gone through a divorce, taken to drinking, and had descended into the seamy world where meals come from trash bins, bathing happens in 7-11 restrooms, and there is no such thing as being safe at night.

A man who called himself 'Sky' was from a middle-class family in Washington State. He'd seen the front lines in Vietnam. Suffering from PTSD and unable to reboot, his wife left him and he began drinking and using drugs. He'd been a successful construction worker. But post divorce, he couldn't hold down a job and ended up on the streets. His story hit home. I had a cousin with a similar history.

A family—a husband, wife and two daughters—had lost their Iowa farm during hard times. It was difficult at first for me to believe that a "normal" family could be reduced to sleeping in a refrigerator-shipping box, but they had. Worse, they were not the last family I met that had ended up homeless. It was mind-boggling to believe this was happening in America.

Getting to know these people challenged and changed my perception of the homeless. Many of the people I met on Skid Row shared a common story: They'd been living along the spectrum of "normal." They'd experienced a major crisis. They had little or no support from family or friends, no safety net, and fell. I understood that this perfect storm was all that separated me from the Christines, Franks and Skys of Skid Row.

A few years later I left Skid Row thinking differently about the homeless, and poverty in general. I was more grateful than ever before for my family and friends who stuck with me during my own dark times.

Truly, we are saved by those who love us.

Enjoy this related song:

• Christine

www.lesliebaerdinkel.net/HopeDancing/Songs/

6 - Brother Simon, Mother Teresa

"**T**HERE'S SOMEONE I think it would be beneficial for you to meet," Fr. Peter mentioned, nonchalantly, one day. He couldn't have been more right.

Brother Simon was a tall, fit fellow with a short, dark beard, wide smile, and eyes like Fr. Peter's that sparkled with a hint of mischief. He was a monk in the Order of Mother Teresa's Missionaries of Charity, and was not at all what I had expected. He was down-to-earth, outgoing, athletic and a real jokester—not like the staid, pondering and portly pontiffs of film or the imagination. The work of the Missionaries of Charity in Los Angeles ran the gamut, spanning food for the poor to halfway houses for boys and girls with a range of challenges. As soon as I began working with the Brothers, I had a profound sense that I was right where I should be. Fr. Peter had great intuition.

At first I worked helping a group of about a dozen Brothers and numerous "Co-Workers," lay volunteers who assist the Brothers, Sisters and Fathers of Mother Teresa's Missionaries of Charity Order. We collected foodstuffs appropriate for the homeless, that is, food that didn't need to be cooked. We'd bag it up and deliver the bags to the homeless where they lived in alleys, beneath bridges, and in every unsavory nook and cranny you could imagine—places where angels should fear to tread. In many cases, people were grateful to the point of tears. Some said they were living off the groceries we delivered each week. One day while we were packing I calculated the cost of each bag. Fifteen bucks seemed a bargain to perhaps save a life.

There wasn't a Brother among the lot who wasn't a character in his own right. Brother John, like Brother Simon, packed and delivered groceries each week. Expressive, excitable, and with a flare for drama and dance, he was another Brother who didn't fit the mold. Brother Joseph was also a constant in the food outreach effort. Originally from Scotland, he ran a halfway house for young boys to help them get off and stay off drugs and out of gangs. He kept the young men on the straight and narrow with a mixture of Scottish wit and tough love. His 24-7 devotion to his mission was impressive. Brother Stephen was medium height, thin, well read, soft spoken, and witty. He sought out opinions and gathered up new ideas like an investigative reporter. He was a thoughtful, kind man. The Brothers were an enthusiastic and dedicated group, and I counted myself extremely fortunate to work among them.

One day, Brother Simon extended an invitation to Sam and me to join a group of Brothers and Co-Workers on an excursion to a special event in Mexico the next weekend. Sam had a wedding to play, but he encouraged me to go. It was an outing I couldn't even imagine missing. An opportunity to see and hear the humble, small-framed woman from Calcutta who not only was awarded the Nobel Peace Prize in 1979, but who many were characterizing as "The Living Saint."

I accepted enthusiastically, and began counting the days.

It was a crisp, cloudless, winter day as I walked with Brother Simon and a group of Brothers and Co-Workers along a Tijuana dirt road toward a large auditorium in the distance. As we got closer I could see the structure was in desperate need of repairs and paint. It was the best location this border town had to offer, I reckoned.

We walked amidst *thousands* of people who streamed toward the ailing structure to be in the presence of Mother Teresa of Calcutta. The Catholic nun was nothing short of a legend among the faithful and the unchurched alike for her selfless work with the poor of Calcutta, most of whom were Hindu. I had asked the Brothers for the inside scoop on Mother T. when Brother Simon had invited us, and they hadn't disappointed. They shared the official stories they'd been told as Brothers, but also, others they'd heard on the inside—and in some cases, first hand. Some were pretty juicy.

Like when young "Sister Teresa" had rebelled against her Order. She'd found a man lying in the gutter being chewed on by rats, still alive. She hoisted him up, and with some help, got him to the convent. The Mother Superior refused to admit the man because he was of an "untouchable" class in the caste system of India. (Castes have since been outlawed, but persist.) It was that incident that compelled Sister Teresa in 1948 to slough off her traditional black-and-white habit, don her now widely recognized white sari with blue piping, and start her own Order—The Missionaries of Charity. (White is the color of purity, and the blue piping was her tip-of-the-hat to Krishna, sacred to Hindus as a messenger of God and often depicted as a blue baby or blue man playing a flute.)

The Missionaries of Charity, or "M.C.'s" as they are known, were officially recognized by the Roman Catholic Church in 1950. They vow to "give wholehearted free service to the poorest of the poor."

In another story, then-Sister Teresa had walked out on a Pope. He'd asked her to come to Rome to meet with him, but when she arrived, she got a less-than-warm welcome from his handlers. Her blue-piped sari would not suffice for an audience with His Holiness, they told Sister Teresa as they handed her a black-and-white "formal" habit to change into.

According to the Brothers, she replied, "If my sari is good enough for Jesus, it's good enough for everyone," and then took her leave to the dismay of stunned Vatican officials. (At the telling of this story, the Brothers were fairly certain that Sister Teresa was the only Catholic in modern history to blow off an audience with The Most Holy Father.)

Some years after she'd shunned a Pope, her Missionaries of Charity Order had grown from a handful of like-minded young nuns to *thousands* of nuns. In 1964, Pope Paul VI went to Calcutta to visit *her*. At the end of his trip, the Brothers told me (and it has been documented), the Pope left Mother Teresa his limousine as a gift. She thanked him kindly. As soon as he left, she had it sold to help finance a leper colony she was building.

My head was filled with these and other stories that circulated among the Order's inner circle as I shuffled along excitedly with our group. I was ecstatic that I would have the opportunity to see and hear this amazing woman for myself, someone who had surely found and was fulfilling her purpose.

When we arrived at the stadium, we were not afforded special seating, but took our places within the crowd in the stands. Below, at the level of the stage, a sea of nuns and priests in formal wear flowed in and among each other creating a moving patchwork of black and white. The sounds of the crowd echoed, and at times, were deafening.

We sat for about 30 minutes, when suddenly, the blare of not one, but two bands began, drowning out the crowd. Positioned on either side of the auditorium were two bands, both featuring trumpets and drums. In *oompah* style, they began to play a song I didn't recognize. It seemed they were trying to coordinate, but had no such luck. The result of the two bands being slightly out of sync was an assault on the ears that was so crazy sounding as to be comical. It made all of us smile, and chuckle a bit.

Minutes later, I could see the crowd begin to move below, then part. I soon saw that this was for someone who was entering the auditorium. Studying the edge at which the crowd was parting, I could make out a small, frail-looking form. Draped in her renowned sari, and moving slowly forward, it was indeed Mother Teresa. This tiny figure was followed by an entourage of Sisters dressed in the same garb. The group of perhaps ten made their way through the crowd and took their seats in front of the stage.

A man then stepped upon the stage and took to the podium, introducing someone in Spanish.

"He just introduced the Mayor of Tijuana," Brother Simon explained to me, taking the opportunity to tease me a bit about the need for me to improve my Spanish for occasions such as these.

"Noted," I replied, adding that to my mental list of self-improvement goals.

The Mayor then took the stage, and the applause quickly died down. He began an introduction that went on for more than several minutes, that "in essence," Br. Simon told me, emphasized how thankful he and his constituents are that God had brought "The Living Saint" to Tijuana. When the Mayor called for a round of applause, the bands started up once again. They meant to play a moving version of "Ave Maria" in unison.

"It sounds like something from the Mayberry band," Brother Simon quipped, referring to the Andy Griffith Show we'd both grown up with. We had a good laugh.

The excitement grew. The figure, now much more defined apart from the crowd, stood up and climbed the stairs onto the stage. She made her way to a too-high microphone, which she grasped, pulling its gooseneck down by half its height. A hush fell over the auditorium as she began to speak in her thick accent. (She was born in Skopje, Macedonia, to Albanian parents.) I readied my journal and took notes.

"Brothers and Sisters, friends of Jesus, I am so pleased to be with you on this beautiful day that God has made..."

I listened intently, as if in a dream. I was transfixed. I felt at that moment like I was living in a book I couldn't put down. I wrote down everything I could capture. She spoke for about ten minutes.

In closing, Mother Teresa said this:

"All my young life, I was troubled by the suffering of the poor. But now that I have spent many years searching for an answer, I can share with you what I discovered to heal my own troubled heart. It is this:

"Meditate, for in silence you will find prayer—a humble voice in which to speak with God. With God you will find a boundless love, and the desire born of this love will lead you to serve the Almighty by serving His people. In this selfless giving to others, finally, you will find peace.

"God bless you."

Time stood still. I sat stunned at how these words had touched me. I felt somewhere between a dream and being hit by a lightening bolt. *Meditate. Love. Serve. Find Peace.* It was spiritual advice that sounds so simple to do, but I knew would take years to consistently put into practice. Like, "Love thy neighbor..." It's easy until they call the police because your music is too loud, fail to pick up their dog's calling card on your lawn or refuse to go in halves on a new fence, right? This mental discipline would be a life-long practice. If such things were easy, we'd all be saints.

I thought about how the sequence Mother Teresa described had applied in my own life, and the great peace I felt when I was serving others. I had a sense that these words would become even more meaningful to me over time, as I practiced.

Momentarily, the crowd was silent. But soon the silence gave way to applause, the applause gave way to cheering, and both the bands began blaring once again.

I didn't want to move from that spot. I wanted to contemplate Mother Teresa's advice for a good long while. I read her words again, savoring them, until Brother Simon nudged me, urging that I follow. Our group was moving, I thought, to a place where people who had carpooled would meet and head back to Los Angeles.

I was wrong.

I followed Brother Simon and several others from our group through corridors and back toward what looked like an office area rather than the public space of the auditorium. We came to a room where I could hear voices inside, and we entered. There, surrounded by nuns, priests, monks, and others, sat *The Living Saint.* She looked up momentarily when we walked in, then continued speaking. I felt humbled to be among this group— many of whom no doubt had given many decades of their lives to serving the poorest of the poor in conditions I couldn't even imagine. I quietly took an empty chair, listened and wrote.

"Never give up," she advised the group. "I started by picking up one person, and now together we have shared God's love and mercy with many thousands.

"When you feel sad and unworthy, remember that the world is not your responsibility—only the one person in front of you at that moment…"

We listened for more than a half an hour as Mother Teresa shared her wisdom—simple, yet profound. At a natural breaking point, the group began to stir and many began saying their goodbyes, bowing to Mother Teresa before leaving the room. It was then that Brother Simon approached her. He took my arm, and before I knew what was happening had me standing in front of her. I flushed. For maybe the first time in my life, I felt *shy*.

"Mother," he said, cupping her hand, "This is Leslie. She has been helping us in Los Angeles. We think she would be a great coordinator for our Co-Workers [of Charity]."

Since Brother Simon and I hadn't discussed this idea, I was *entirely* taken aback. The conversation that followed, went like this:

"Dear girl you are Catholic?" Mother asked.

Since I was officially unchurched, I began to confess, "Well, I…"

"She is modest Mother," Brother Simon interrupted. "She demonstrates her love for God through her service to the poor."

"And you are willing to make sacrifices in your life to serve the needs of the poor?" she continued.

"Well, yes, Mother, I'm willing, but I'm afraid that I'm not…" Again, Brother Simon broke in.

"Not worthy? Mother, I've explained to her that we're all unworthy servants of God…"

I was now not only feeling shy, but on this rare occasion, I was also *speechless*.

Mother Teresa concluded, "Jesus thanks you for your service to his poor and forgotten and I will pray for you as you work hand in hand with the Missionaries and Co-Workers of Charity."

She put her hands together and bowed in my direction. A pleased Simon whisked me from the room, thanking Mother Teresa as we backed out.

When we were well out of earshot of the group I protested to the good Brother, "But I'm not Catholic!"

"Shhh," he said, grinning mischievously. "You'll do a lot of good work—Catholic or not."

I knew I would do my best and smiled in the face of Brother Simon's shenanigans. I also trusted his intuition. He had a sense of content and knowing about him, and his enthusiasm was infectious. He was hard to disagree with. Fighting back tears, I nodded my head in agreement.

Later that evening I reread my notes from the event, and feeling the power in these words, reviewed them many times.

"In this selfless giving to others, finally, you will find peace."

7 - Sister Thomas Moore's Turkeys

S HE LED THE SISTERS of Charity in Los Angeles, appointed by Mother Teresa herself. A woman in her late thirties, I guessed, I was immediately impressed with how lively and talkative Sister Thomas Moore was. I'd always thought nuns would be more demure and soft spoken. But "T.M." (as the Co-Workers called her for short, but not in front of her) *had* to be a firecracker to get the job done. She'd taken on the challenge of presiding over a home for pregnant, under-aged girls who lived temporarily at the M.C. Sisters' Home for Unwed Mothers until giving birth.

The first time I visited, I could see that they were a rambunctious group. I could hear fighting over who was next in the restroom and when T.M. intervened, she got some lip—but she didn't tolerate much of it. She quickly laid down the law and the girls respected her.

These were girls who, in most cases, had little parental supervision in the first place. Then, after getting pregnant, they'd run away. The ones I observed on my first visit to the Home were cocky, strong-willed survivors. With the help of just one other Sister, T.M. oversaw up to *18 girls at a time* under the single roof of a repurposed old mansion in a low-income neighborhood in Lynwood. T.M.'s rules required the girls to take turns cleaning and cooking. There was a 7 p.m. curfew, and of course "no monkey-business is allowed," she told me. (Translation: No boys in the house.) I looked forward to getting to know Sister Thomas Moore!

Riding high after meeting Mother Teresa and having a job assigned (although awkwardly acquired), I'd stepped up my visits to work with the Missionaries of Charity Brothers and Sisters. I took the Volunteer Coordinator post seriously. Brother Simon gave me a calendar of events and a list of donations the Brothers needed including clothing for adults and children, simple medical supplies; canned foods like corn, peas, Spam, and cooked hams and cranberry sauce (for the holidays). It was he who introduced me to T.M., who also had a long list of needed items.

Between the two lists and the growing number of people who needed food each week, there was a *warehouse* of items we needed to collect. At first I thought it would be a piece of cake given the many Co-Workers there must be. But when Brother Simon showed me the Co-Worker list that included about 200 addresses, he added, "Only the thirty or so with stars next to their names are active Co-Workers." Given the vast need, *thirty* was a scary number. I figured we'd need at least *three times that*, or that I'd need to quit my day job to do nothing but collect donations!

I began recruiting more Co-Workers by visiting Catholic churches where I was afforded a few words before Mass. A complication of recruiting was the M.C. rule that nothing could be requested using Mother Teresa's name. I could talk about the work of the Co-Workers in support of the Missionary Brothers and Sisters, with no mention of Mother Teresa, and ask that interested volunteers join up. This rule was to help ensure that "volunteers understand they are serving God, not Mother Teresa," Brother Simon had instructed me. Although it made recruiting tougher, I was impressed by the preventative measures Mother Teresa took to avoid becoming a demigod.

Over a few months, we added several dozen volunteers to the corps. This was on the promise of doing good work alone, and that you didn't have to be a Catholic to join. This appealed to some of my good-hearted, giving and religiously uninclined musician friends and other friends who signed up. Since most people worked during the day, I scheduled our help activities for evenings and weekends. In recognition of the growth of the Co-Workers, and because they were fun-loving guys, the Brothers surprised me one day with something that couldn't have been more unexpected. I arrived at the main house to find that one of the small bedrooms had been designated for me, complete with a sign above the door sporting my new, honorary title, "Brother Leslie." This was all in good fun, but it choked me up.

While there had been success getting new recruits and we were getting lots of good work done for the Order, my new role wasn't without bumps in the road. The first and biggest bump occurred during my very first major assignment from none other than Sister Thomas Moore.

It was T.M.'s desire to hold a great Thanksgiving feast. She and the other Sister who worked with her at the Home for Unwed Mothers, along with several M.C. Sisters from other locations, would serve a dinner. They'd serve this dinner not only to the girls living at the home, but also to their relatives, the local poor, and the homeless. To do this, T.M. predicted that based on past years' attendance, 48 turkeys would be needed—no more, no less.

That will be a cinch, I thought to myself. That's because at my place of employment at the time, each November, all employees were given with their first paycheck of the month a certificate good for one turkey at a local grocery store.

As soon as I left our meeting, I began telling fellow employees about the upcoming Thanksgiving shindig and asking if they could spare their turkey certificates. I was surprised at how willing people were to help, and quite proud of myself when I'd collected enough certificates to claim 45 of the 48 turkeys needed. We were close to success, and *it must be in record time* I thought of my first major assignment. I couldn't wait to tell Sister Thomas Moore that just *days* after her request, we were nearly done corralling turkeys for the cause.

But there was a problem. When I went to share the news, I discovered that besides never using Mother's Teresa's name to recruit help, "M.C.'s and Co-Workers never directly *ask* for donations." T.M. explained this to me, patiently, even as I displayed to her the pile of acquired turkey certificates.

"I appreciate your (pause) *energy*," she continued. "But our way is to pray.

"Our prayers are answered *without* us having to ask," she gently admonished, further instructing, "Have faith!"

At first I couldn't believe how badly I'd screwed up *already*. I was in Rome, and when in Rome I guess I should have known what

49

to do and what not to do. I *wanted* to acquire those turkeys in the Missionary-of-Charity-approved way. And I guess more than anything, I wanted to experience faith delivering real-world results in the way that Sister Thomas Moore seemed to feel so confident that it would. So, I took her advice to heart, and packed away the certificates. Off I went…to pray.

I prayed. And not only did *I* pray, but I assembled a cadre of Co-Workers and we prayed together. I waited and watched for a sign from the end of the first week of November, and into the second. I thought I might receive a phone call offering turkeys. Or perhaps one of us would hear about, enter, and win some kind of turkey lottery. I quietly imagined turkeys falling from the sky—all 48 of them.

Nothing yet.

Then, something incredible happened.

My brother Justin—who knew almost nothing about my work with the Missionaries of Charity, and *nothing at all* about my turkey search—called me out of the blue. He said that through his work he had come into something he wondered if I might have a use for: Three frozen turkeys.

What were the chances?

With the certificates I'd already collected, Justin's three turkeys made exactly the 48 we needed. I was floored.

I told him the story. He confirmed that he had known nothing about my search, but had been offered the big birds by a client, and for some reason, had immediately thought I might have a use for them. *Amazing!*

So midweek the second week of November, we had three turkeys on ice. I shared the news with several of the Co-Workers who were elated. And we kept on praying…and praying.

On Monday November 25th, with just three days 'til show time, I made phone calls and arranged for Co-Workers to cook turkeys on Thanksgiving eve at their own homes. I arranged for all 48 to be cooked. This included the three birds from my brother, and the 45 birds that, as of yet, had not materialized and for which I continued to have faith would, without asking, show up through Divine Intervention.

But on the Tuesday before Thanksgiving, I finally buckled.

I shuddered at the thought of all those people the Sisters had invited going without a hot meal on Thanksgiving Thursday—or, a more likely scenario, us Co-Workers scrambling around in utter panic on Wednesday. I made a logical, but perhaps cowardly decision. I still had in my possession exactly 45 turkey certificates. I called 11 Co-Workers to meet me on short notice at a Ralph's grocery store near the mission home in Lynwood. There, the dirty dozen of us went about our blasphemy picking out frozen turkeys and redeeming them at checkout. It was a faithless, but necessary business, I'd decided.

After checkout, we carpooled to the Lynwood home. I advised the Co-Workers that they would stay in their vehicles until after I had confessed to Sister Thomas Moore—this botched turkey round-up was my doing, and I'd take the blame.

On the drive to the Home I thought about how I'd tell her. I'd let her know about my brother's call and donation—which I had *not* asked for. Then I'd take the fall for the turkeys acquired by the certificates I'd *asked for* and would ask for T.M.'s forgiveness.

That all sounded lame, even in my head. It was a long drive.

The grand old Lynwood house had a dozen bedrooms on two floors and in the attic. But when I pulled up this time, the house looked even bigger—*gargantuan*. Given the task at hand it loomed like a haunted mansion on a Freddie Kruger film set.

I parked directly in front of the walkway to the front door. The other Co-Workers parked on the same side of street in front and behind my car, and dutifully stayed in their vehicles while I got out and closed the driver's side door. I circled to the passenger side, which I opened to take out one of several, bagged, frozen turkeys on the seat. With a turkey cradled in my arms I walked slowly up the walkway to face T.M. It felt like the scene from

Jaws where the shark is coming. (I could practically hear the music.)

Standing in front of the door I felt it shake, telegraphing the mayhem inside. Several teenage girls pounded down the stairs like a herd of buffalo yelling four-letter expletives. I rang the bell. In a few moments, who opened the door but Sister Thomas Moore in the flesh. My stomach turned a somersault.

"Sister Thomas Moore!" I said, excitedly, trying to put a positive spin on what I was about to confess. "This past Monday morning, my brother contacted *me* and had turkeys to donate..."

Upon seeing the frozen turkey squarely in my arms and hearing what was meant to be just Part One of my story, a broad smile spread across the Sister's face. Before I could get another word out she declared with delight, "Now you see what happens with prayer!"

"Well...uhm," I stumbled, but upon seeing the various cars outside, she interrupted.

"Bring in the rest," she said, motioning excitedly with her hands.

As she took the frigid bird from my arms, T.M. gave me a shoulder-to-shoulder squeeze and continued. "Everything is possible with faith!" It was another rare occasion where I was speechless.

She headed toward the kitchen while I stood there momentarily as frozen as the turkeys, then made another split-second cowardly decision. I would shut up now, while I was in her good graces. I'd tried it the M.C. way, done my best, after all.

"O.K. I'll get the other Co-Workers," I called with just as much enthusiasm as the Sister.

I headed back to my car, relieved, but feeling guilty. I motioned to the others to come on ahead with the rest of the turkeys. The dirty deed was done.

As far as I know, none of my Co-Worker co-conspirators ever spilled the beans about our turkey caper. Still, I wondered if somewhere in the back of her mind Sister Thomas Moore questioned what had become of the certificates I'd collected. Had she wondered if that year's feast was by virtue of birds of that forbidden feather? If she had, she never asked—and I never told.

My conclusion about prayer—a powerful mental construct to be sure—and my own responsibility as a carnate, able-bodied being in this decidedly physical reality, is summed up by this story that's been told in many versions, origin, unknown:

A man's boat had been wrecked in a storm and he was thrown into the sea. Upon realizing the gravity of his situation, he began praying to God to save him. Soon, a boat appeared, and the captain yelled, "Friend, I have a rope here. Let me throw it to you now!"

"No thank you," the drowning man replied matter-of-factly. "God will save me." The boatman shrugged and moved on.

The drowning man continued to pray, and as fate had it another boat came by. The captain of this boat, too, offered to recover the drowning man, but he refused. "God will save me," he said. Away the second boat sailed.

A third boat came by, but once again, the drowning man sent it away.

Unfortunately, before long, the man drowned.

Upon entering heaven, the drowned man had a chance to speak with God and asked, "Why didn't you save me?"

God's reply was brief, and to the point: "I sent you three boats!"

Enjoy this related song:

• Let Me Be Your Hands

www.lesliebaerdinkel.net/HopeDancing/Songs/

8 – A Family's Simple Joys

December, 1991

THE DROOPY LITTLE Christmas tree propped up in a corner and adorned with toilet paper would have looked pitiful to me a year earlier. But today it looked like a minor miracle. Christmas was Brother Simon's favorite time of year. He explained to Sam and me that it was the time he got to play Santa, in a sense, making rounds to share small gifts, groceries and hot cider with families in need. He'd asked Sam and me to join him this Christmas Eve as he made his rounds.

The three of us set out to visit half a dozen families living in low-rent apartment complexes near downtown Los Angeles. With most of the families, we delivered groceries and gifts to the door. Sam carried a guitar, and on some stops, we'd sing a few Christmas songs. But at this, our last stop, lived a family Brother Simon took a particular interest in. They'd fled Guatemala's civil war that had already claimed the life of the husband-father of the family. Brother Simon's arms were twice as full as at the other stops as he carried a five-foot pine tree someone had donated, along with a bag full of used ornaments and gifts he'd wrapped for every member of this family. Sam and I followed with the guitar and two standard-issue bags of groceries.

Brother Simon set the tree down to the side of the door, just out of sight, and knocked. A short woman with long, dark hair opened it, and a wide smile spread across her face. The two exchanged hugs and warm greetings in Spanish. The woman's name was Lourdes. She hugged Sam and me, too. Lourdes was quickly joined by her three young daughters, Susana, Alicia and Robin, each of whom greeted Brother Simon and the two of us with loving hugs. I guessed that Susana, the oldest girl, was about 10 years old; Robin, the youngest, was maybe 5, and Alicia was somewhere in between. I was touched by how warm and welcoming the family was to Sam and me, even though we were total strangers.

Lourdes motioned us toward the kitchen where we put the groceries on the sink. I made myself useful by taking them out of the bag and on to the counter. I noticed that Lourdes was moving about with some difficulty on wooden crutches. I then saw that her left leg hung motionless, swinging slightly as she moved.

"¡No funciona!" she said, sweetly, having seen my eyes linger.

"I'm sorry," I replied with a smile, not having meant to stare.

In the small dining area opposite the kitchen, four plastic chairs sat around a small folding table. It was neatly set with four place settings, the dishes and silverware mismatched. I looked around and realized there was no furniture in the living room. *Nothing.*

No sooner had we put the groceries down than the girls took Brother Simon's hands and excitedly led him, Sam and me, into the single bedroom of the apartment. There, we found a queen-sized mattress on the floor with a blanket over it, and clothes stacked neatly around the walls. There was no dresser or any other item of furniture in the room.

In one corner of the bedroom propped up stood the small, sagging tree—one of the saddest, but most touching Christmas trees I'd ever seen. It wasn't really a tree at all, but a single pine branch with two smaller branches on it. The family had stuck the branch into a large, sturdy milk bottle with rocks in the bottom, added water, then propped it in the corner to hold it upright. They'd twisted long strands of toilet paper then sprinkled them with glitter to make gold garlands, which they'd carefully draped across the few branches. I inspected angel ornaments they'd made. They had cotton-ball bodies and wings of toilet paper cut to shape and stiffened somehow, maybe with white glue. Each angel had a halo made from a pipe cleaner rolled in gold glitter. On the angel's backs they'd glued a soda can pull-top and used it as a hanger.

The makeshift Christmas tree oozed holiday spirit, and Lourdes' love. I thought about all her effort to acquire it, and to decorate it with the very little she had. Lourdes worked as a baby sitter, Brother Simon told us. Sometimes she'd earn as little as $4 an hour, and some months, make just enough to pay the rent. In those months, the food Brother Simon brought wasn't just a help, but a lifesaver. Brother Simon told us that the canned ham, jellied cranberry, Christmas cake and other holiday fare we'd brought along with beans, rice, salt and cooking oil would be a special treat. These gifts would probably be the only ones the family would get.

Brother Simon returned to the front door, opened it, and brought in the donated Christmas tree. He expertly offered it to Lourdes and the girls without implying any deficit.

"Here's an extra one for the living room," he told the family in Spanish.

The girls looked excitedly at the full-sized tree, took it to the living room and set it up in a corner on the attached, crossed-wood stand. Brother Simon then handed them the bag of used ornaments. The girls' faces lit up as they unpacked each ornament and placed it on the floor in a neat row. They looked to their mother, who told them to go ahead and place them on the tree. They did it with watchmaker concentration and precision. I'd never seen children take a task so seriously or decorate a tree so methodically.

At the bottom of the bag were their gifts—one each, with their name printed on it. The last one was for Lourdes. All the gifts were tagged, "From Santa." The girls placed them under their living-room tree, then passed out hugs again, all around.

"*You* are Santa!" Robin, cried out, pointing at Brother Simon who vehemently denied it as Sam unpacked the guitar.

I played Jingle Bells and a few other simple Christmas songs that the six of us sang while Lourdes, who didn't know much English, listened intently. We shared songs and stories for about an hour before we packed up to go. With tears in her eyes, Lourdes thanked Brother Simon for helping to make the girls' Christmas a happy one, and for bringing them something special to eat for Christmas dinner. More hugs were shared. Turning to Sam and me, Lourdes said, "*Que Dios les bendiga,*" (may God bless you).

I was deep in thought as we walked from the apartment. I remembered my idyllic young life—always having enough to eat, having both parents, a furnished house with the cupboards stocked with food and having my own room no less—and *lots* of Christmas gifts. I never wanted for anything. I fought back tears thinking about this family's tenacity, their grace in the face of hardship, and their ability to find joy in small things—like an adorned, withering pine branch in the corner of a bedroom.

I felt humbled.

"Thank you for bringing us with you," I told Brother Simon, still teared up. And then, unable to hold out any longer, tears slid down my cheeks and I blurted out, "It seems so unfair that some people have to struggle so much!"

Brother Simon smiled a knowing smile. He'd worked with lots of newbie volunteers over the years who, like me, were not yet accustomed to seeing the every-day challenges faced by those living in poverty.

"They are struggling. But here they have running water, electricity, and a warm place to sleep. They were in a much worse situation in Guatemala," he shared with me.

Brother Simon had served as an M.C. Brother in Guatemala for some years. He talked about those times fondly, and it was obvious he had a deep love for the country and its people. I asked him why he'd left. As the Guatemalan civil war raged on, the M.C.s had decided for safety reasons to minimize their presence there, keeping just an orphanage run by Sisters open in the capital city.

He went on to describe the primordial beauty of Guatemala—the lush, green landscapes and the volcanoes, some active, at every turn. He recalled the 16th Century architecture and ancient ruins of the Maya. But it was the kindness and gentle spirit of the people that had impressed him the most.

"You'll have to visit Guatemala some time," Brother Simon told me. "Your Spanish could use some improvement—*major* improvement!" he teased, once again, maybe for the tenth time.

"You never know," I quipped back, even though given the wartime conditions he'd mentioned, the idea seemed far-fetched.

We reached Brother Simon's car and he opened the door and retrieved three items from the front passenger seat. He smiled and handed me a copy of *501 Spanish Verbs*, a rather thick book he had once called "the bible" for anyone serious about learning Spanish.

"It's an extra copy I had laying around," he said, chiding, "I hope you'll use it."

His persistence about my dismal Spanish and need to improve made me smile. Learning a language was a long-term commitment, but given the vast number of Spanish-speaking people I was now working with, he was right to push me to do it. And it was something I intended to do.

"Yes I will," I said, and thanked him.

He then handed Sam and me two other gifts, both in beautifully woven bags.

"It's a small gift for each of you, for your Christmas tree," he said. "Thank you both for coming tonight."

I knew that the Brothers had only a small allowance to use each month—about $35 for the barest of necessities. Gifts for others meant he'd given something up. I was a little embarrassed to accept, but thanked him.

Sam took the wheel, and just after he drove off, asked me to open his little bag. I found a note, which I left for him to read, and a lovely little Christmas tree handcrafted of beads with a beaded hanging loop. Sam commented on how thoughtful the gift was.

I then loosened the drawstring on my bag, and inside, found another beaded item. It was a green bird with a red breast, a yellow beak, and long, green tail. Like Sam's little Christmas tree, it had a beaded loop that could be used to hang it. My note read:

Dear Leslie,

Thanks for your work with the Brothers. I got this quetzal as a gift the first time I went to Guatemala. It's a special symbol to Guatemalans. Maybe some day you'll visit and see one.

Your Friend,

Brother Simon

When I read this, I had the oddest of feelings that one day I *would* visit Guatemala. Maybe it would be when the war ended, I thought.

That Christmas Eve, I could never have imagined what happened next to propel me to Guatemala, and how soon my visit would actually come to pass.

9 - Death at Dragon's Back Ridge

MY FATHER STOOD in the doorway of my dark bedroom silhouetted against the light in the hall. He walked in and sat down beside me. I sat up, still half asleep. "Mom died," he croaked out, and then began to sob. I hadn't understood how sick she'd been.

I went through the confusion and depression expected of a 14-year-old girl who loses a parent. I was lost for a time. Then, when most teenage girls are fixated on boys, I began a spiritual quest. I had a new respect for time, and committed to not wasting it. Trying to beat the grief, I amassed an arsenal of wisdom books from the gamut of religions and philosophies. My mother's death and my resulting journey landed me, just having turned 15, in a spiritual community where I'd stay until I was 27. The silver lining to being utterly lost was learning that there are many paths to being found. I also learned that grief takes its own sweet time.

Over the years I gained some self-awareness and eventually, made peace with my mother's death. I thought I would be better prepared the next time someone close to me died. But when it happened again in my early 30s, I didn't feel prepared at all.

June 1992. I received the dreadful phone call not long after arriving at work. Brother John was direct.

"Simon is dead," he told me through tears, barely able to speak. "It was an accident during our spiritual retreat near Mammoth Mountain."

I gasped, and covered my mouth.

"The police are still investigating..." he continued, his voice trailing off until he couldn't speak another word.

"I'll be right there!" I reassured him in a full-on panic.

In shock and disbelief at the news I grabbed my purse and leapt for the office door and as I ran out, told my boss that a friend had been involved in an accident. I was filled with urgency, as if by getting to the Brothers' house in a flash I could change things, and Brother Simon wouldn't really have died.

I drove silently through the traffic, my heart pounding. I could hardly believe what I'd heard, and didn't want it to be true. Had I misunderstood? I hoped against hope…

I arrived at the Brothers' main house and first talked to Brother John. I was relieved to see him so I could hear from his lips that I'd misheard. I wanted so desperately to have misunderstood. I asked him if the news was true. He nodded in the affirmative.

I went into the kitchen where the balance of the Brothers had gathered, and they told the story of how Brother Simon had disappeared. He'd never come back from an early morning trek into the woods to meditate on his own, as he often did. When he'd been missing about eight hours, the Brothers called the local authorities. After a few hours search they'd found him. His body lay at the bottom of a gorge about 75 feet below a cliff. Nothing more was known, but there should be more information forthcoming, they said.

I spent the day with the Brothers and the Co-Workers who arrived after they were called with the terrible news. At first, I was immobilized. I felt so ill that I actually vomited. We were all so very sad and sick. One by one we found the strength to plow through, and soon, I joined in notifying people about the tragedy. They were heart-breaking phone calls to make.

Sam arrived at the Brothers' house to help. He consoled me, but I was numb inside—inconsolable. I was horrified that a man of just 38 had died, but moreover, that one so utterly caring about others and who had positively influenced *so many lives* had died *so young*. The massive amount of good he could have done in coming decades was a bitter loss. And all those who, like me, he would have inspired in the future—that was a tragic loss as well. It seemed outrageously unfair.

I was assigned the awful task of calling Lourdes (we'd brought the tree and gifts to her family at Christmas), and I dreaded it. When I managed to croak out that Brother Simon had died, there was dead silence. But rather than the upset I had expected, she told me the strangest story. She'd had a dream the previous night about Brother Simon. He had come to visit the family. He had walked them to a river. At the river, he presented Lourdes with a small refrigerator. He then told her that she shouldn't worry, because going forward, she would be able to take care of herself and her family. He then stepped across the river. The dream seemed an amazing coincidence full of metaphors predicting Brother Simon's death.

After telling me the dream, Lourdes began to cry, softly. We cried together over the phone. I imagined what it was going to be like for her to have to tell her girls, and the pain they would feel at the loss of the man who had been like a father to them—their own personal Santa Claus. Lourdes told me the dream would keep her strong, and that she was sure it was a communication from Brother Simon—a reassurance that she would share with her family.

Who knows what is possible? As Brother Simon once told me, "Some things are just a mystery."

The police investigation took about a week. The Brothers called me and a few other Co-Workers together to share the findings. They said Brother Simon had hiked into an area known as Dragon's Back Ridge. The breathtaking, lesser-known hiking trail in that area was especially dangerous because of its sheer cliffs. Brother Simon had found that trail and began to walk it, when, the authorities said, it looked like he'd come upon a bear and been chased by it. *What were the chances?*

Along a thin, unstable part of the trail with a water jug strapped to his belt, he had apparently lost his balance, slipped, and had plunged to his death.

An early morning walk in the woods, an unlikely encounter with a bear, one misplaced step and an untimely death. It was hard to imagine the place and how Brother Simon had fallen. It all seemed so surreal.

Days after the tragedy, I couldn't kick the "surreal" feeling, and a depression that had set in. I felt compelled to go to Dragon's Back Ridge where Brother Simon had died and see it for myself. I called Brother John who felt similarly compelled. He said he would see if any of the other Brothers wanted to go.

We set a date.

Two weeks had passed when Brothers John, Stephen and I started our journey to Mammoth Mountain in the dim light of the very early morning. When we arrived hours later, we made our way up the rocky footpath. It was a steep and somber climb.

At the top, we were confronted by a giant crater. It was the upper mouth of Hole in the Wall, known as a dangerous winter ski run. Dragon's Back Ridge is a half-circle outcropping less than six inches wide which makes up the front wall of the foreboding crater, a place where few dare to walk. The investigation had concluded that this was probably where Brother Simon had fallen. The bear explanation seemed more plausible now. Surely he would have treaded that six-inch-wide, dangerous path only if he'd been forced to. But we would never know for sure.

The three of us sat down and flanked by one another, stared incredulously at that ridge.

"I hate you," I uttered under my breath to that thin outcropping, my vision blurring and tears beginning to roll down my cheeks.

Brother John hooked his arm through mine and soon, Brother Stephen did too—the three of us now a human chain in solidarity.

"I know it hurts. We all loved him. He was our rock," Brother John consoled.

The wind passing through the crater howled like a wounded animal. Soon, we were all sobbing in grief, and at one point,

Brother Stephen picked up a hand full of stones and peppered the outcropping with them. For what seemed like an eternity, we sat there, arm's linked on that lonely, windswept ridge hoping for an answer, a sign. I scanned the scene and caught a glimpse of small birds flitting through the landscape, but nothing more. The silence was deafening. Then, I remembered I had once asked Brother Simon if through his vocation as a Brother he'd found his purpose. *What a heavy conversation to have had in the Brothers' kitchen putting cans of beans and rice and napkins into grocery bags,* I thought. I smiled slightly as I remembered.

"I don't think about it like that," Brother Simon had told me, nonchalantly. "I don't worry about if it's my purpose—you really can't know. I just try to make sure I'm always taking the next right step in my life."

"How do you know what that is?" I'd asked him.

"It's usually obvious—right in front of you."

That had been profound.

Remembering it was my sign.

Over the following months, I contemplated Brother Simon's kitchen wisdom and made a conscious effort to watch for my own next right step. It was a tough time. I was still grieving the loss of my friend and mentor. I'd fall into the trap of wondering *why* this had happened to Brother Simon, and how senseless it was that a young man who'd devoted his life to helping others had plunged over a cliff. This kind of thinking only piled needless suffering on top of normal, predictable grief. And while I knew that such thoughts would only take me to a dark place, I couldn't seem to break free from them, for a time.

One day about four months after the accident, I caught myself diving back into the black hole of *why*, and in a moment of clarity, decided I'd suffered enough. I was done. In that moment, I gleaned some insight and resolve from Brother Simon's comments in the kitchen. I realized that what had earned him that daily content he exuded wasn't contemplating the *whys* of the past, or worrying about the future. His content had come in his full presence in the here and now, and in taking his "next right steps" when the time came. It was time for me to rise above the sadness of loss, and to do the same.

I didn't know what my next right step would be, but finally, I was ready to find out. Oddly, it turned out to be another trip to Tijuana.

10 - The Home for Abandoned Grandmothers

BROTHER SIMON ONCE TOLD me and a group of Co-Workers, "It's a process." We'd asked him for some words of wisdom about how to become more humble and compassionate. At the same time, we'd asked for guidance on how to keep our emotions and judgments under control in the face of shocking expressions of poverty. How *did* the Brothers and Sisters of Charity keep from gagging from foul smells coming from clothes and hair that hadn't been washed in weeks or months? Or grimacing or crying in the face of oozing, open sores? Or shying away in the face of off-putting (and sometimes scary) behaviors associated with mental illness? It was important that we worked on this, because with all the indignities a poor person suffers, the last thing they need is pity, tears, or judgment.

For reasons none of us understood at the time, Brother Simon recommended we take a trip to the Home for Abandoned Grandmothers. Ten months after his death, a group of us did just that. It's there I learned that there's nothing like scrubbing a floor, cleaning a wound, or emptying a bedpan to find out where you are on the continuum of humility and compassion.

"The Missionary of Charity Sisters in Tijuana Need Our Help!" was the headline of the phone call I received from Brother John. It had been pouring rain for several weeks in that town just south of the border between the U.S. and Mexico. And with its unpaved and already deeply rutted and eroded back roads, Tijuana had become even less navigable than normal.

For several weeks, the weather conditions had precluded the normal stream of Missionary of Charity Co-Workers with mere automobiles from making the journey to help. Thus the two Sisters and one "Novice" (a young woman in training to become a full-blown nun) had been left at the waterlogged Tijuana compound to manage on their own. Volunteers were now needed to bring in food and medical supplies, clean, help wash clothes and help with so much more at the home that sheltered up to 33 elderly women at any given time. I put out the call that we needed volunteers with four-wheel-drive vehicles where possible, and soon, a small fleet of us was headed to Tijuana.

Our group was accompanied by Laura Saari, a reporter for the Southern California newspaper the *Orange County Register*. I don't think the scene could have been better set than it was in Laura's article about the trip, which started this way:

Up a steep, pocked road in the southeast most reaches of Tijuana, past the deceased cars and shriveled dogs that distinguish so many border towns, only a block of bright blue paint serves to set apart the gate through which dozens of women go to die. There is no sign on the house, although it has a name: The Home for Abandoned Grandmothers...

When we arrived at the complex, we knocked on the door and the Sisters welcomed the dozen of us in and offered us some hot tea. After passing it out, they sent us on a short tour of the facility with the young Novice who was quite shy and smiled sweetly. She was very attentive to our group and seemed glad to have some company.

She walked us through the cement-block complex which had a dozen rooms for the residents, one of which she showed us. The room had three cots, each with a simple wooden dresser along side. The beds were neatly made, and the room looked impeccably clean. Since there was no closet space, one had to assume that all the worldly possessions of each person staying in the room were contained within the small dresser. When I asked the Novice, she told me that was so.

There were three bathrooms to serve the residents. The Novice showed us one of them, which had a toilet, sink and shower. I made a mental note that with three bathrooms and up to 33 residents—that meant 11 women per bathroom. I thought about the traffic jams that would mean.

The Novice then took us to see the Sisters' room. In keeping with Mother Teresa's intention that the Brothers and Sisters of Charity live like the people they serve, the Sisters' room was as simple as the rest, except that they had small beds instead of cots and each bed had a wooden cross over it. Their room, too, had a small wooden dresser for each bed just like the residents' dressers we'd seen. Although the bathroom looked just like the others, the Sisters had the "luxury," the Novice told us, of an ensuite bathroom for just the three of them. *That's a very small luxury,* I thought.

The kitchen was large, as one might expect to serve that many people, and with lots of cupboard space to allow for enough food storage to feed all the residents at any given time. It had a large but very old refrigerator. The complex had none of the other conveniences of home—no heating or air conditioning—and the dishes were hand-washed as a service activity the residents took turns doing each day, the Novice explained. The dishes that had been washed that morning were meticulously sorted by size and drying in metal racks.

The walls throughout the complex were bare except for wooden crosses at various locations including in the living room, some of which were adorned with palm leaves (likely from the previous Palm Sunday). And there were also several framed posters featuring Mother Teresa that included some of her most memorable quotes. These included the "Do small things with great love" quote that had challenged me, and "If you judge people, you have no time to love them." There was also the more controversial, "We are not social workers." (The latter had raised the ire of some who felt the Missionaries of Charity should do more to *cure* rather than just *care for* the sick and dying.)

Although the word had been put out that the Sisters were in urgent need of assistance, the place *looked* amazingly clean and tidy, like you could eat off the floors that, though cement, had a sheen. There was a noticeable sense of order to the place, by design. "Order is comforting to the residents because they have suffered from so much chaos in their lives," the Novice said.

The Novice then led us to a large living room area with couches all around the walls. Some were back-to-back, and others were perpendicular to the walls to create more space. There sat dozens of women, some talking softly together and some sitting alone. The women looked to be age 50 and up. Most had long, black-

and-gray or gray hair, and some had braids. They were clad in clean, modest shifts or pant outfits. Many had wooden canes next to where they sat.

The Novice introduced us to the women in Spanish, and most looked up to greet us and smiled or uttered a few words. Some waved, and we waved back. I thought about the stories that each of them must have to tell—stories of their lives, their families, and the heartbreaking tales of how they ended up here, alone, without their families. We were there to help and to brighten the women's day, I reminded myself as I began to get a little misty-eyed.

This Home exists, first, because of perennially sagging economies in Mexico and Central America and the resulting poverty and suffering. For decades, lack of jobs and low wages—and more recently, gang violence—have incentivized people trying to improve their lives to look beyond their borders. It exists, secondly, due to rivers, deserts, barbed wire fences and drug cartels—just some of the dangers migrants face when trying to enter the United States illegally.

Families fleeing poverty with hopes of finding a better life are willing to face just about anything to reach the United States, which is largely viewed as *the promised land*. But when hopefuls near the border, they learn more about the dangers of crossing to the States from others who've tried and failed. Hiding overnight in drainage pipes and on rickety barn roofs. Being packed for 24 hours or more in the false bottoms of swiftly moving trucks. Walking sometimes for days across blazing deserts with limited food and a gallon or less of water. These are just some of the risks that are taken to pursue the better life they believe they'll find in *El Norte*. But these were conditions that, most likely, *Abuelita* (Grandmother) would not survive.

It was the man of the family, most often the eldest son, who had to make the terrible decision: For her own safety, *Abuelita* must be left behind. I can't even imagine the pain of such a decision for the one making it, and for the entire family.

The Home for Abandoned Grandmothers is the Missionaries of Charity-run sanctuary for some of those grandmothers who were left behind. It's a safe place to take shelter, to find comfort and fellowship, and sometimes—as Laura pointed out in her story—to lament the predicament they find themselves in as they await the return of their families, "stuck in limbo between abandonment and hope."

Flor Padilla and Dolores Alvarez were two of those grandmothers.

After our short greeting, the Novice asked us to gather to hear the list of chores that needed doing: mop floors, dust, clean walls, clean windows, change bed sheets, clean and bandage a wound, help prepare lunch, visit with residents, and more. ("Clean and bandage a wound," I noted. That sounds a bit unsettling....)

The Novice had been excited to see I'd brought a guitar. As one of my assignments for later in the afternoon, she designated me to provide a soundtrack for our activities. But first, I'd be mopping floors, then (as fate would have it) helping one of the sisters "clean and bandage a wound." That figured. Like my mom had told me on more than one occasion (later stolen and made famous by the Rolling Stones, or was it the other way around?), "You get what you need."

The mopping was mindless work and I did it effortlessly and in good cheer. The long-suffering women who lived there would at least have shiny-clean, good-smelling floors to walk on. It was a small thing I could do and feel good about. The wound cleaning and bandaging was another matter, and something that had a profound impact on me.

Flor Padilla had been bedridden for nearly a year the Sister told me as she handed me a basket of supplies we'd need to clean and re-bandage Flor's wound. These included gloves, a soft washcloth, a bottle of Johnson's Baby Shampoo, a roll of gauze, several absorbent pads, a roll of white surgical tape, and a commercial-sized tube of antibacterial ointment. She then picked up a medium-sized round metal basin filled with warm water and led me towards Flor's room.

When we walked into the room, I was shocked to see that the wound we would dress was not something manageable like a small patch on Flor's arm, leg, or shoulder. Flor's *entire head* was wrapped like a mummy with only her nose and mouth showing. I couldn't imagine what kind of a wound we were talking about.

"She has face cancer," the Sister whispered to me, kindly, yet matter-of-factly. "We must clean the wound each day."

I felt my heart speed up and a slightly sick feeling come over me. Then, I heard my Dad's voice. *You can do anything you set your mind to do.*

I can do this, I told myself.

"Flor dear, I am here with a friend," the Sister said softly, taking her hand. Flor squeezed it.

"*Hola* Flor," I offered, my voice cracking unexpectedly.

"*Hola*," she offered, in a whisper muffled by the bandages partially covering her mouth.

I smiled and tried to stay in good cheer, remembering again that we were there to serve. *Don't you dare cry.* I told myself. *Hold it together and do what you can do to help!* I kept a few feet away and focused all my attention on helping the Sister.

The Sister told me I'd be handing her what she needed. She put on the gloves, then leaned over Flor. Gently lifting her head, she began to unwrap the gauze.

As the wound became visible, my heart raced even more than it had been, and a great knot grew in my throat. This was not just a patch of cancer on poor Flor's face, but the opposite. The skin of her face appeared in patches amidst the cancer. This cruel, malicious disease had virtually devoured what had once been Flor's face!

What I saw was something unimaginable, suffering that no human being should have to endure. It made me feel sick and sad and furious all at the same time.

Completely against my will, my eyes welled with tears that flowed onto my cheeks. Then all the feelings morphed into a sort of panic, a flight response that caused my legs to feel rubbery. *This,* I thought, *is what it feels like to begin to faint.*

Before the Sister noticed my legs shaking, I planted myself firmly on a stool next to the bed, determined to regain control over my body and to complete my assignment. I felt selfish and ridiculous, and shook my head to snap myself out of it.

"Could you please hand me the shampoo?" the Sister asked. Her request did me good. It broke the spell I'd been under momentarily, refocusing me away from the horror of it all and back to the task at hand—a simple, caring act with certain concrete steps to complete.

I handed her the shampoo which she squirted on the cloth she'd dipped in warm water, and the Sister began her loving service to this poor woman. I took deep, steady breaths, and after several minutes, my eyes dried. The knot eased, and the shaking stopped. I needed to look away to stay focused on the Sister's words, and to keep from falling back into the riptide of emotions. But I felt I'd taken an important step in the right direction.

This experience had given me an idea of where I was along the continuum of humility and compassion the Brothers and Sisters of Charity had spoken about to the Co-Workers.

I realized how far I had to go.

At lunchtime, tray tables were set up throughout the living room and we were invited to sit on the couches and eat cheese sandwiches with the residents. The other volunteers' assignments had focused entirely on cleaning and maintaining the property, rearranging foodstuffs in the kitchen and preparing lunch. They were in high spirits and chatted with the ladies. I wondered how long Flor would still be able to eat. And then what?

I was still thinking through it all and had gone inward. I shifted my thoughts to being grateful—grateful that I was healthy, that the people I loved were healthy at the moment, and that we were all able to see a doctor when we needed one. I had so many supportive friends in my life, and I wanted to thank every one of them the next time I saw them. I don't think I'd ever felt so grateful as I did at that moment. It was yet another reminder to count my blessings, and to do it often. I was grateful, too, to the Sisters who had dedicated themselves to helping Flor, and all the other women living here. If there are angels among us, I'd met them.

When we'd finished eating, several volunteers began taking our plates when the Novice called to me.

"The women love music!" she encouraged, and emerged into the living room carrying a folding chair in one hand and my guitar case in the other. She placed the chair strategically so that everyone would be able hear, and set the case next to it. I was relieved to change gears. I moved to the seat and took the guitar out of its case and into my arms, then begin to play my favorite songs of comfort, like John Denver's *This Old Guitar,* and *Annie's Song...* I sang the sweetest, most soothing songs I knew. They were the one gift I could give at that moment. I melted into the music, and soon felt more myself again.

Some of the women closed their eyes as they listened. I knew a few songs in Spanish, like *"De Colores"* which immediately brought smiles to their faces. *I'm going to learn more songs in Spanish,* I thought.

After about 30 minutes, I put down my guitar to take a break. A woman ambled over and sat down beside me.

"Dolores," she told me, holding a hand to her heart.

"Leslie," I said in reply.

Her frame was small and bent slightly at the hip, and her hands were aged with hard work and arthritis. I thought of the children she'd held and bathed and raised with those weathered hands— how long had it been since she'd seen them? Her hair was long, graying and braided, her smile tentative, and her eyes hopeful. She spoke to me in such simple Spanish and so slowly, that I could understand.

"My son's name is Juan Carlos Alvarez," she told me. "He was going with his wife and my little grandson to *el pueblo de Los*

Angeles, and when he found a place to live, he was going to send for me. I have not heard from him. Do you know him? It has been *six years...*"

My heart sank.

Of course there was little chance I'd have run into her son in a city of some 3.5 million people (at that time). But Dolores couldn't imagine the size and expanse of "The Village of Angels" Juan Carlos had gone to. And with my limited Spanish, I couldn't explain it to her. I told her sincerely that I would look for her son.

Upon my return, I did.

There were not two, nor twenty, but *hundreds* of telephone book listings with the combination of Juan or Carlos Alvarez. I found none with the combination of all three. (This was before the Internet, and Facebook. I quickly ran out of places to look for him.)

I dreaded making the call, but about a week later, I did call the Home to let Dolores know I'd been unable to find her son and his family.

As a Sister translated, I heard Dolores begin to cry, her hopes of being reunited with her son, daughter-in-law and grandson, dashed. I hung up demoralized, for the moment. But the experience of the Home for Abandoned Grandmothers was not lost on me. It made me ponder the question of what it would take so that one day, people of few means, like Flor, could have access to medical care. And, why couldn't families like that of Juan Carlos Alvarez stay at home in their own country and prosper and never have to leave an *abuelita* like Dolores behind? The experience made me even more committed to the work with the Brothers. It also planted a seed—the idea that, maybe someday, I could do even more to help.

PART III ✚ SPIRITUAL THINGS

11 - 501 Spanish Verbs

"SPIRITUAL THINGS DON'T HAPPEN TO ME, but they do happen to Leslie," my long-time friend and fellow journalist, Denise Danks once commented to a newspaper reporter. The series of unlikely events that happened next probably qualify under Denise's "spiritual things" designation, though they could also have been nothing but coincidences.

It all started with the copy of *501 Spanish Verbs* book Brother Simon had given me on Christmas Eve, six months before his death. I'd barely cracked it open. It was thick and daunting. Its 640 pages were overflowing with grammar lessons, tips, the 501 most-used Spanish verbs and their 18 possible tenses, each—that's 9,018 chances to be verb-tortured. Also, it reminded me of Brother Simon, the accident, all the good he would have done had he lived… No wonder I'd avoided diving in.

It was Day of the Dead, a popular holiday in Southern California. The celebration spans October 31st to November 2nd. I'd joined in years earlier by creating a section on the mantle of our fireplace where I kept a picture of my mother and me together during my childhood, snaps of a few friends and other relatives who had died, and a collection of photos of loyal dogs and cats who'd also passed. After Brother Simon's passing, I added his photo to the friend's section. While perusing the photos, it occurred to me that I should get serious about improving my Spanish, as Brother Simon had suggested. Sam and I didn't have anything planned that night, and this would be as good a time for me to start as any.

I walked to the bookshelf in our office and pulled down *501 Spanish Verbs*. I opened it at random, figuring I would begin memorizing whichever verbs I opened to. But I happened to open the book to the back, first. There on the inside back cover I found something quite unexpected. Reading it gave me a chill:

Leslie,

Did you learn Spanish yet?! Take your time using this, but use it!

—Blessings,

Brother Simon

He'd used clear packing tape to hold together the spine and other parts of the book (which had seen better days), and had also laminated that message. Then, on a sticky-note over the tape like an afterthought, he'd written:

P.S. Go to Guatemala. There's something there for you!

When I read this, the hair on the back of my neck stood up. I took a long, deep breath and let it out.

Maybe it was because it was Day of the Dead. Maybe it was because I was now actively watching for my "next right steps" as Brother Simon had called them. In either case, I read his sticky note as a sign. Maybe there *was* something for me in Guatemala? But it was a war zone! It conjured up images of Vietnam, the first televised war. A gun to a man's head. Gaunt women and children crouching wide-eyed behind reeds in a swamp. Families clutching each other in terror. These were my only reference images for a war zone. Why would I go *there?*

I read the P.S. sticky note a few more times, and slept on the idea. In keeping with my fears about Guatemala, in the morning I conveniently decided that Brother Simon's emphasis had been on *learning Spanish*, and not on *where* I learned it. I would get serious about learning and would immerse, somewhere. But Guatemala was not on that list. I decided to look in Mexico. It was close, and would probably be about as inexpensive as Guatemala.

That's where I began.

To find a Spanish school in Mexico, I headed to the International Center at my alma mater, Cal State University, Fullerton. The Center was inside a large building, and was itself a sprawling area of bookshelves around tables where materials could be read. I walked through the glass doors and to a long reception desk where a woman sat reading a book. When I asked about Spanish schools abroad, she barely lifted her head from her book, but pointed me toward a large wall of book shelves perhaps 30 feet away. They were *packed*.

I walked over to the bookshelves and upon closer examination saw that they contained *thousands* of books and brochures about Spanish study in various countries. The area dedicated to Mexico was not obvious.

The shelves were so overwhelming that I returned to the receptionist for help, asking if she could recommend a Spanish school in Mexico, specifically. She declined, since she had not studied in Mexico. She did tell me that I'd find Spanish language schools in Mexico on a bookshelf at the far left of the rest, then turned her attention back to her book. (So much for customer service!)

I made my way back to the "Spanish Study: Mexico" area and stood staring at the bookshelf she'd indicated. It was about four feet wide, and was filled with materials mingled and stacked every which way on a half dozen shelves. Even this single bookshelf was a blur of choices. But among the mess, I noticed a simple, tri-fold brochure sticking out on the upper shelf. I squinted to read it, and could make out a word that took my breath away: *Simon*.

I did a double take. I stretched up to reach the brochure and pulled it down. The mention of "Simon" was in reference to "Saint Simon." The paragraph explained that this particular Saint was honored with daily ceremonies in a village nearby this language school. It venerated the "unorthodox Saint" who the Church had worked to synchronize with a widely worshipped deity the Maya called "Maximón." In this reading, he looked after marriages, and also represented the earth, fertility and the harvest.[7]

"The Catholic Church then added Saint Simon to its rolls to make itself more welcoming and familiar to indigenous converts," it read.

Then came the kicker. *Escuela Juan Sisay*, the school whose brochure I held, was not located in Mexico at all. It was located in a town called Quetzaltenango, in *Guatemala*.

This brochure had obviously been misfiled, and why it was sticking out was anyone's guess. But of course the brochure had me at "Simon"—at least for a good look.

Somewhat reluctantly, I took the brochure to the receptionist and asked if I could take it with me. She said I could not remove it, but directed me to a photocopier and grunted, her nose still in her book. She told me that I could copy up to five pages each day for free.

"Just put your name, phone number and number of copies on this list," she said, handing it to me.

I needed just two pages copied—the front and back of the school's brochure. I copied it, thanked the receptionist, tucked it into my purse and left. I was a bit annoyed at myself for coming away with no information about Spanish schools in Mexico, but finding that brochure had been such a strange coincidence that it rattled me a bit when I thought about it. I decided to sleep on the whole language immersion idea, and think about it again in the morning when I was refreshed.

The next day, something *else* strange occurred—or really, a couple of odd things in sequence.

First, the receptionist at the International Center called me. I wondered how she'd gotten my phone number, but remembered I'd left it when I'd signed for the copies. She was calling to see if I needed help booking time at the language school I'd found in Guatemala. *How had she known about that?*

It turned out I'd left the original brochure on the photocopier, and she'd found it. She may have felt guilty about how she'd ignored me, or was feeling especially (and uncharacteristically) helpful that day. Whatever the reason, she *had* called me.

I told her I wasn't ready to enroll yet, but thanked her for the call.

"And by the way," I asked just before hanging up, "You seemed really absorbed in the book you were reading yesterday. What was it?"

"It's a great book. You should pick it up," she advised. "It's called *I, Rigoberta Menchú*—a story about an indigenous woman from *Guatemala.*"

I couldn't believe my ears. This felt less like a coincidence and more like a conspiracy to convince me that all roads lead to Guatemala!

Perhaps for me, they did.

After taking stock of the events of recent days—the newly discovered note from Brother Simon, the Guatemalan Spanish school pamphlet in the Mexico section, the odd call from the university receptionist and the book she was reading about a famous Guatemalan woman—I couldn't help but feel that no matter how much I tried to fight it, my "next right step" was staring me in the face. It was right in front of me as Brother Simon said it would be. *Guatemala.*

I contacted the language school and booked two weeks of study. Once I'd decided, I began to feel excited about going. But not everyone shared my excitement.

When I talked to Sam about my plans, he was understandably concerned. My father, normally supportive but skittish about international travel, was mortified that I'd be heading off to study Spanish in a war zone, but he wasn't surprised. Both he and my mother had told me since I was a little girl, "You can do anything you set your mind to." I believed them. That encouragement had come back to haunt them more than once. Including the time I'd run away to the Hawaiian islands to find myself after my mother's death—while just 15. I met two sisters with a condo to bunk with, sold *puka* shell necklaces by day, and played guitar and sang in a nightclub in the evenings (passing for older than 18, the drinking age in that state). I stayed away three long months. I returned unscathed, with enough money to buy a car and with an inflated sense of invincibility. Now, almost two decades later, my patient, doting, and long-suffering father hoped to temper that sense.

"I don't like the idea of you going to Guatemala and all those other dangerous Mexican countries," he said in a geographic and a cultural *faux pas* (forgivable considering his lack of travel outside the U.S. and his advanced age). I overlooked the gaffe and tried to assuage his fears, and failed, mostly.

But no one was going to change my mind. The idea had taken hold in me, rooted in the signs.

To hell with the civil war.

———

Enjoy this related song:

• Be Here Now

www.lesliebaerdinkel.net/HopeDancing/Songs/

12 – Guatemala

Early December, 1992

SAM DROVE ME DUTIFULLY to the airport. Understandably, he was not a huge fan of this trip of mine. He felt it was risky. I couldn't argue with that. Yet he had helped me read up, prepare and pack.

"Can I ask you one last time not to go?" he said.

But I *needed* to go. It felt as right as breathing. I told him so, and I could tell he understood while at the same time he fought to swallow his objections. I appreciated his effort.

My father had asked me to promise I would *just learn Spanish* in Guatemala, and that I wouldn't get involved in any causes. I had no intention of getting involved in anything, but he'd made the comment several times. My father knew me better than I knew myself.

When we reached the airport, Sam parked and walked me to the gate. He heaved a sigh and gave me a hug that was longer than usual. I understood that he was genuinely concerned for my well-being. But rather than trepidation, I was feeling the exhilaration of beginning what I sensed would be a great adventure...something leading me in the right direction for my life.

"Bring me back some great coffee!" he called to me trying to be cheerful as we waved to one another. I lost sight of him as I disappeared into the secured area for ticketed passengers.

It was a remarkably short flight—not even five hours to Guatemala which, heading south from the United States, is the first country below Mexico and begins Central America. I could see from the plane as we neared Guatemala City, the country's capitol, that the area was surrounded by stretches of greenery, at least one active volcano (there were puffs of smoke rising from it), and large areas of colorful, tightly clustered homes.

After we landed, I trundled through the small airport and quickly reached the one and only conveyor belt for luggage where my single bag soon appeared. A sign on the wall directed me to the *Aduana*, Customs. The plane had only been about half full, and the short line moved quickly.

"Why are you in Guatemala?" the Customs agent asked me rather forcefully in broken English as he perused my passport. A bit nervous at his fervor, I replied that I was there to study Spanish "and get to know the country."

The agent paused to get a good look at me. Had I said something wrong? After sizing me up and apparently deciding that I was just a naive tourist who'd decided to study Spanish in a war zone, he warned me.

"This is a dangerous country right now—especially for a young woman traveling alone. You should not leave the area of your school or attend political events. We cannot be responsible for the safety of persons who leave tourist areas," he said.

I noted the slightly ominous tone of his voice and nodded in the affirmative. Deal. I had no intention of doing either. He stamped my passport and handed it back to me.

As per the instructions from my Spanish school, upon exiting the airport I kept a tight grip on the handle of my luggage and moved quickly through the crowd of people awaiting relatives, selling mementos, and asking for money. But I couldn't help notice a particular young man of perhaps 15 who had no working legs, but folded them to one side and moved around on a skateboard. I dug out a U.S. dollar and gave it to him and he thanked me enthusiastically with a "*Gracias!*" and a broad smile. It was a tiny bit of help, I knew, but little kindnesses add up for people—they had in my life.

I stepped into the next cab in line and said as I'd been instructed by the school, "*Galgos.*" This was all I needed to say before we were off, and it was a good thing because it was one of just the few dozen words in my Spanish vocabulary.

Just about 10 minutes later we arrived at the country's equivalent of a Greyhound Bus station, complete with a line drawing of a greyhound painted on the side of the busses.

"Quetzaltenango," I told the woman behind the counter, who told me *"Cuarenta y ocho,"* for 48 *quetzales*, about six dollars. It was a bargain for what my language school contact had told me would be about a five-hour bus ride. And this was no "chicken bus," she assured me. This referred to the over-crowded, ramshackle but colorfully decorated and somewhat renowned converted school buses from the U.S. that speed along Guatemala's highways. This was a "luxury bus" she said, that would keep a reasonable speed, would not pass on dangerous curves, and would have a bathroom on board, which was good news. I took a seat just a few rows behind the driver on the half-full bus and hunkered down for what would be my first look at Guatemala. I fixed my gaze out the window.

Guatemala City was a jumble of cars traveling at high speeds on freeway-like roads but with no lanes painted on them and lots of horns honking. We wound through architecturally mismatched buildings—old, Spanish style and concrete modern—some crumbling, while trucks and busses that flanked us belched out smoke. The roads were lined with people, many of them in colorful clothing and women mostly in skirts. From time to time groups of people darted into the road in front of us to get across, causing my heart to skip a beat each time. On several occasions, the bus swerved to avoid hitting pedestrians, and based on the driver's outbursts (which I assumed to be cursing), it seemed there were at least one and maybe two near misses. Despite the school's assurances about this being the best bus service available, I could see it was going to be a wild ride.

As we set out I thought about the young man on the skateboard I'd seen at the airport, and how his quality of life would have been different had he been born into my world. His options here had been limited enough to land him on a skateboard begging at an airport. In the United States, even if he'd been born poor, this young man would have had more and better options. Early detection might have made it possible to intervene to correct his disability, or physical therapy may have made him more mobile.

Prosthetics might have been a solution, or even a simple wheel chair. The inequity was stark.

Escuela Juan Sisay was located in the highlands some five hours away from the airport, and I wondered how different that area might be. I was hoping it was substantially different. Based on what I'd seen so far, Guatemala City was on disrepair steroids and seedier than most back-streets in metropolitan areas I'd seen in the U.S.—even when I worked on Skid Row.

I was relieved when we began to wind up a mountainous road and the scenery began to change. Tall buildings and bustling parking lots were replaced by tall trees and fields of corn and other crops. Soon, small homes dotted the countryside. The sense of trepidation that had gathered in my neck and shoulders while we were in the city began to dissipate. I felt myself settling in.

About three hours into the journey, I had additional cause to be tense. I was unpleasantly surprised to learn that the single restroom on the bus was out of service (and probably had been for months by the looks of it when I poked my head in). *"No sirve"* (It doesn't work) a woman seated near by offered, wagging her finger back and forth. *"Gracias"* I acknowledged, half smiling.

I made my way up to the front of the bus and tried to communicate my need to the driver. He indicated, as far as I could tell, that this was a direct bus, no stops. This played out and I was fairly uncomfortable for the next two, final hours of our journey.

I was eager to disembark when the bus finally dropped us all off at a small terminal in Quetzaltenango. I stepped off, retrieved my luggage as the driver unloaded it from the outside compartment in the bus undercarriage, then hurriedly searched for a restroom. Luckily there was a *baño* at the back of the terminal. Here is where I got my first lesson about toilet paper in Guatemala; it's best to *carry your own*. Luckily, I had a few tissues in my purse. Secondly, the paper does *not* go in the toilet. I had wondered why there was a small trash basket next to the toilet full of wadded-up toilet paper. Unfortunately, I didn't understand this rule until noticing a scrawled note on a scrap of paper tacked to the back of the stall door, "No *papel en* tolet (sic). *En* tratch (sic) only," at which time it was too late. I did not fish it out.

I exited the bathroom in time to see the bus I'd been on noisily pull away spouting diesel fumes. I then dug into my purse and retrieved the *Escuela Juan Sisay* brochure. To my surprise, I found no phone number, and what looked to be only a partial address since it contained the street but no street number. *The town must be small enough that everyone knows where it is*, I thought, and I approached the reception window.

"*Escuela Juan Sisay?*" I asked, and got only a blank stare from the older gentleman behind the counter. I showed him the brochure which he looked at intently, then shook his head and waved his finger, as in *No, I have no idea where this school is.*

"Telephone book?" I asked in variations of *Spanglish* hoping I'd be able to look up a phone number and the full address for the school. He looked at me quizzically, then reached behind the counter and pulled out a thin, dog-eared pamphlet about ten pages thick in total. This couldn't possibly be the phone book for all of Quetzaltenango, could it? A quick thumb down the E's found no *Escuela Juan Sisay*, nor did it appear in the J's or S's. The tiniest bit of anxiety shook me as I contemplated my predicament. *A taxi driver will know where the school is* I thought with relief, and thanked the man before approaching the single, waiting cab.

It was an old vehicle, and well used. The paperwork I could see on the wind wing convinced me it was a real cab. But I was reluctant to get in, for two reasons. First, the driver looked to be of an advanced age, which wouldn't have mattered as much on its own. But more importantly and related, his eye glasses were Coke-bottle-bottom-thick. Being that his was the only cab I could see, I got in anyway.

What followed after I threw my bag onto the back seat and got into the front was crazy!

I showed the gentleman the brochure, which he held an inch away from his face to examine. He then took me on a Mr.-

Toad's-Wild-Ride*esque* adventure darting through and around traffic on winding streets. Stop signs were for him only a suggestion, or non-existent. And the only thing that saved us from being T-boned at high speed on several occasions was the horn he applied while speeding through intersections. My heart pounded in my chest and I held on for dear life!

At one point, clearly lost, the old man pulled the car to the side of the road and brought it to an abrupt halt. He then exited the car to stand within *two feet* of a street sign on the side of a building so that he could read it.

"Oh my God," I said under my breath. At that moment, if by luck or fate, I looked out the window and about half-a-block down the street saw painted on a yellow building an image of a man wearing a bandana. The man's image matched the one on the brochure, and sure enough, under it read the words, "*Escuela Juan Sisay.*" No one had to ask me to exit the taxi. I bailed!

I paid the driver the 15 *quetzales* he'd asked for (I would have gladly paid double just to be out of that cab), grabbed my bag, thanked him, and exhaled a deep breath of relief. I collected myself and half-dragged my bag down the street to the school. "I should never have gotten into that car," I said, under my breath making a mental note: *Next time, I will follow my instincts.*

13 - Gaby, Dena, and the Bank

I'D BARELY KNOCKED when a woman flung open the metal door to *Escuela Juan Sisay*. The Spanish school was named for a man who was "a painter and courageous human rights advocate," the brochure read.

"I am Gaby." the woman said warmly, and immediately gave me a hug and welcomed me in. "We are so glad you have arrived!"

Gaby said she worked at the school and would be my teacher. She was short in stature with thick, black hair and bronze skin. Her wide-set eyes and striking cheekbones suggested her Mayan ancestry. She had a gentle firmness about her, and within minutes I knew we'd become fast friends. I was looking forward to getting to know her during our Spanish lessons.

As I entered the building, a woman and two children leapt to their feet. Gaby introduced them to me as Dena and her two children, Hugo, age 6, and Claudia, 11. They were the family I would live with during my stay. Dena introduced herself, telling me that she worked at the government-run phone company. I learned that this was a coveted position, since unemployment in Xela ranged an unimaginable 60 to 80 percent for able-bodied adults.

It was very late in the afternoon and I felt bad that Dena might have been waiting for me at the school for hours. There was no way for me to explain the challenges I'd had in finding the school, nor to apologize effectively. And so I experienced my first bout of many of the frustration of not being able to communicate.

The two children excitedly took my hands and hugged me around the waist. It was an incredibly warm reception. The people I'd met so far were as kind and welcoming as Brother Simon had described. Gaby told me Dena and the children would take me to their house after she gave me a quick tour of the school.

The school building was made of concrete blocks, some of which were painted and some not. The tile floors had been polished so often that the design had worn off of many of them, and in some places, the walls were actually crumbling underneath the paint. Numerous small rooms were divided by simple wooden walls, each with a desk and a chair on either side of it. There was an upstairs, too, which was actually outside. About a dozen desks with two plastic chairs, one on each side, sat in open air far enough apart to provide semi-private places for one-on-one Spanish lessons. If it was sunny at lesson time, upstairs in the outdoors is where I'd be.

As we headed back toward the front door, I noticed several green-and-red-beaded birds hanging on the walls that were nearly identical to the one Brother Simon had given me. I realized that there was one on about every wall. I'd noticed them on the money, too, and wondered about the meaning of this elegant, long-tailed bird.

When the tour was over, Gaby took me to Dena, Hugo and Claudia, said a few words to Dena and at the same time held up seven fingers and said, *"¡Lunes!"* I understood her to mean I'd need to be at the school by 7 AM on Monday. *Thank goodness for body language.*

I said goodbye to Gaby, and we walked out to Dena's waiting car, I thought. But no. That this family had a car was a silly assumption. Off we walked along cobblestone streets, me with my suitcase in one hand and a child holding the other.

About 20 minutes later we arrived at Dena's home, which was cozy. Her small living room was furnished with just three plastic chairs against a wall and a small table containing an old radio about the size of a shoebox. Off the living room was a very small kitchen with a plastic table, three matching chairs, and a very old refrigerator—an off-brand, with bulbous, round corners that looked to be at least 20 years old. There was a short hallway that led to two small bedrooms, one of which would be mine. There was a bathroom off the hall, and in my room, a single bed and a wooden desk. I was surprised to see that I had a private bathroom, which upon closer inspection, was just big enough to turn around in. The bathroom included a flush toilet, and a showerhead poking out from the wall that I learned had been installed just for me. Dena proudly demonstrated it, and though it produced only drizzles (and cold water at that), I was grateful—and humbled.

After I sat my bag on the bed, we retreated to the small kitchen table which was now one-seat short. When I hesitated, Dena insisted I sit down and told me she'd make me some coffee. I love a good cup of coffee, and didn't argue. Dena, Claudia and I sat at the table while Hugo stood. We "talked" as best we could. The children didn't seem to understand how limited my Spanish was, and asked me many questions and at high speed. I could only look at them blankly and shake my head, alternately feeling embarrassed and frustrated, again, that I couldn't understand or reply. But the frustration only deepened my resolve to learn. I soon retreated to my bedroom, unpacked and hung a few things on a nail on the wall so the wrinkles would fall out, then quickly fell asleep.

Dena must have understood how tired I'd been, as neither she nor the kids disturbed me the next morning. But when I awoke at about eight a.m., several hours after my normal time, she was ready with coffee and a series of choices I could make for breakfast, among them, eggs, black beans, tortillas, fruit, and *mosh*—a Malto-Meal-type hot cereal served soupier, she explained. I chose mosh to try something different, and fruit, and knew that I would not starve in this home. Dena served me a huge bowl, enough for two people at least, and a plate of fruit that took me the better part of 30 minutes to eat. Seeing that they had little, I ate every bite. I also stretched my vocabulary to let her know that in the future, she could serve me smaller portions.

It was a fun, if frustrating breakfast trying to make small talk. But I could see the logic of staying with a family. I couldn't cheat my immersion program by speaking English, since they wouldn't understand. And I could already see that my desire to get to know the family would be a powerful motivator to increase my vocabulary.

Knowing that my sleeping accommodations and food needs were going to be met took the edge off, and I began thinking about putting another uncertainty to rest, that being, changing dollars to local currency. Dena said she would accompany me to the bank.

I was grateful that she did.

Dena and her little family lived in a section of town that included the local cemetery, called *El Calvario.* The area was not the safest, Dena managed to communicate, as we began our trek of 20 minutes to *Parque Central* where I'd be able to change dollars at one of the banks there in the town square. What I saw next was something I'd missed the night before, but didn't know how. The only explanation I could come up with was sheer exhaustion.

As we turned the corner from the street Dena lived on to the main street leading back toward *Parque Central*, there was a triangular park in front of the cemetery. There, I saw perhaps twenty pitched tents and dozens of armed soldiers pacing and as watchful as cheetahs.

"Look only at the ground," I understood Dena to say and demonstrate. She took my hand and her pace quickened. She looked straight at the ground and whisked me along. Realizing she was afraid, or more aptly, *petrified*, I followed suit fighting the urge to look at the camp and the soldiers. I had no idea if the soldiers were protecting or antagonizing the populace, but Dena's fear said the latter. As we passed local people, I saw that they, too, were looking at the ground and walking swiftly, to the point of scurrying. It was a fear so thick I could feel it in the air. It left me feeling unsettled, and curious.

As we left the park and soldiers behind, Dena's mood lightened. She looked up long enough to point out women walking along the streets who were dressed in colorful blouses called *huipils* with pleated skirts.

"Clothes *Quetzalteca*," she said, smiling, "*La moda* (the style), Quetzaltenango."

The outfits were stunning, as were the women's long, black hair, most often braided on two sides with a colorful ribbon passing through. Focusing on the women's clothing was a helpful distraction from the soldiers. I wondered why Dena was so afraid…

We soon reached *Parque Central*, Quetzaltenango's large central park flanked by roads on all four sides and lined with numerous banks. Dena brought me to one where she thought I'd be most likely to be able to change dollars. In front of her bank of choice were two armed guards. I looked up and down the street and across the square and saw that there were armed guards at every bank. Dena exchanged a few words with the guard at this bank, and I was allowed to pass inside. She was not allowed in, and communicated that she'd wait outside.

The line was long. Ahead of me were about 15 indigenous people. Many of the men were dressed in formal suits and the women, most often in the *Quetzalteca* outfit Dena had pointed out. It appeared that everyone was in their Sunday best to come to the bank and I admired the formality of it.

I'd been standing in line only about three minutes when something happened at the front of the line. The bank teller seemed to be shouting something, and momentarily, all eyes were upon me. I had no idea what was going on.

I then realized that the bank teller was calling to me, motioning me to come to the window—*perhaps to tell me that I was in the wrong line?*

I made my way up to the front of the line to receive instructions from the teller, but when I arrived, he asked how he could help me. I then realized he had called me to the front of the line to serve me ahead of all the local, indigenous people who were waiting. I immediately became uncomfortable, and told him that I would be happy to wait my turn. I headed to the back of the line, when the bank teller called out to me again. What came out of his mouth took me aback.

";No hay que preocuparse. These *indios* can wait!" he said in Spanglish with a smirk and chuckle. As if we were old buddies, he motioned me back to the front of the line.

I could hardly believe what I'd heard. My heart began to race and my face flush. I did not look back, but continued to the back of the line where I took my place. But the teller did not let up.

";No hay problema!" he shouted after me, continuing to beckon me to come forward. He smiled reassuringly, as if this was common practice, no big deal. And it probably was.

Then, when I thought I couldn't feel any more uncomfortable, it got worse. As I took my place at the back of the line, the people ahead of me refused to move up in line. Some had their eyes fixed to the ground, and several of the men were motioning me forward to take my place in front of them. I felt slightly sick as I began to realize how completely accustomed these people were to this kind of discrimination. I tried quickly to make sense of what was happening, but felt short-circuited—I couldn't think.

I didn't know how to respond, and in my bewilderment, gave in to a flight response. I bolted from the line and fled from the bank and down the steps outside to where Dena was waiting. I couldn't explain to her all that had happened and what I was feeling, but communicated that I had not been able to change money in the bank. I was tearing up, but hid it from her.

Dena shrugged her shoulders and quickly took me to another bank without question. This made me think it was common for people staying with her to have difficulty changing dollars, and it was. I learned some banks wanted perfect bills, and others required a passport, which the person may not have on hand.

I eventually changed money, but couldn't stop thinking about what had happened in the first bank. No person should be treated as if they are less than another. It was disturbing.

On Monday morning and each school day thereafter, Dena made me a breakfast of *mosh*, eggs and black beans, and prepared me a cup of hot coffee. She poured it into what appeared to be a prized plastic carry-cup. The cup sported an image of Bambi, and was kept on a high shelf well away from the children, reserved for houseguests only. We set out for the language school each morning promptly at 6:30 a.m.

Being December, the cold, dry season in the highlands, the air was cool and crisp and the steam coming off my coffee was visible in the air as we walked to school. I'd sip it as we made our way past the soldier camp at the park at *Calvario*, for Dena, a patch of terror. I hated that Dena had to walk back alone, but she insisted on walking me to school each day. Her near-cowering as we passed the soldiers suggested something had transpired with them—something very scary.

I didn't ask, and she didn't tell.

I couldn't get the bank incident out of my mind. That Monday during lunch, I had some time to talk with Gaby about what had happened. I was grateful she spoke some English, and that my Spanish was improving. She listened patiently, then spoke slowly and deliberately.

"Here, indigenous people are seen as inferior. I wear modern clothes, but I am *Quiché* (an indigenous person). I always suffer when my last name is revealed."

Gaby went on to explain that the majority of Mayan people in the rural areas of Guatemala can't read or write, and that many in the Quetzaltenango area speak Quiché and little or no Spanish.

"Because of this, many people are very isolated," she explained. "Most of us live in poverty, without clean water or electricity. Many can't afford to see a doctor, or to send their children to school. There isn't enough work, and the wages are low. Parents sometimes have to put even very young children to work in the fields to help feed the family. When it seemed that there was no hope left for a better life, some of our people went to war…"

Gaby stopped herself, as if on the verge of telling a secret. I wanted to know more, and I told her so.

"*Otro dia*" (another day), she said.

❖

14 - The History Lesson

WEDNESDAYS WERE CONFERENCE DAYS at the Spanish school. Little did I know that during my second conference, I would lose my innocence to a polished political activist and a pierced, brash and well-informed French girl. It was a brutal awakening.

Conferences were an important part of the school's study plan. The school invited in a speaker who would deliver a lecture entirely in Spanish. Afterward, the teachers at the school would call upon students, in Spanish, to answer questions about the lecture. The students had to answer in Spanish.

This was challenging for those of us who were beginners. But I had pushed my way through it the first week when the topic had been "Guatemalan Waste Management." That turned out to be, largely, an oxymoron. Burning trash or throwing it into open pits was the common practice, as was funneling sewage into rivers where downstream, people watered crops, washed clothes, and most horrifying, collected drinking water. It had been a shitty topic made palatable (or almost) by the laughter generated when all us students slaughtered the Spanish language as we tried to discuss a disgusting topic. It is common to understand more than you speak, at first, and I was surprised at how much I learned in just a week. I figured I'd gotten the gist of about half of the lecture.

My second Wednesday conference topic would be "Guatemalan History," I told Dena as she walked me to school. I had no idea of the scope of the history lesson, but I knew the lecture would be entirely in Spanish. Since like the previous week all us students would be required to comment in Spanish, I knew I was in for another challenge.

Moon Jewel Belamy, about 19 years old, was a student at the school. She hailed from a town just outside Paris, had flaming red hair (a shade that only comes from a bottle), and wore a delicate hoop ring in her left nostril balancing the one that adorned the outside corner of her right eyebrow. She joined me and a dozen or so other young people from European countries including Germany, Spain and the Netherlands. A shy young man from Japan named Yoshi (affectionately called by the teachers *Yoshito*, "Little Yoshi") was also in the group. In keeping with the stereotype of Europeans being multilingual, all the European students did in fact speak English as well as their own language, and spoke one or two other languages as well. It was only Yoshito and I who were forced to speak Spanish to one another if we wished to communicate, and we didn't get too far. I appreciated him for trying. The smile on his face when I tried telegraphed that the feeling was mutual.

For our history conference, a man named Marcos was introduced as our speaker. He had striking Mayan features, bronze skin, black hair and piercing brown eyes. He was introduced as a political science graduate from local San Carlos University, and an expert on everything from general statistics about Guatemala's present economic situation to its political history, both of which would be topics of today's lecture. He was also Gaby's husband, I learned. He held himself confidently, and I thought he and Gaby were a fitting match.

I was nervous at first about being able to understand enough to have thoughtful questions to ask, and even more nervous about having to ask them in Spanish. But I realized part way through the lecture that because Marcos spoke slowly and enunciated well—and perhaps also because I'd gained some vocabulary since the beginning of my stay—I could understand much more than I had during the first lecture. I was also learning new words as he spoke, and making notes of them so I could use them in my questions: *población* (population), *alfabetazación* (literacy), *salud* (health). It turned into a useful (if long) list.

I scribbled down the bleak statistics. Most of the rural population are Maya, the country's indigenous people, and at least 80 percent live below the national poverty line. The Quiché language is prevalent in Xela, and Mám is the top language in the closest villages 45 minutes outside of Xela. Nationwide, illiteracy tops 50 percent, which skyrockets to 70 percent in indigenous villages. And while most city-dwelling children finish high school, most rural children attend school only a few years if they attend at all, rarely reaching sixth grade. So grave is the economic situation—there is up to 80 percent unemployment in rural areas—that like their fathers and mothers, even young children most often have to work in the fields to supplement the family income. That's because while many of the Ladino (mixed Spanish-Maya) people in Xela earn salaries the equivalent of $600 per month or more, indigenous families of five-to-ten people in rural villages "most often earn less than $600 in an *entire year*," Marcos explained. Infant mortality (the number of children who die before their first birthday) is reported at 56 in every thousand births[8] as compared to just nine in a thousand in the United States.

This was important information for me to know, but hard to hear. I let the discomfort sink in.

Soon, we came to the question-and-answer section of this part of the lecture. Several of the more advanced Spanish students trotted out very well-put-together questions featuring present, past, future tenses and tenses I didn't even know. I worked to formulate mine. I wanted to know how long these terrible conditions had existed, and to hear from Marcos what he thought were the root causes. I asked my question, if awkwardly, and to my surprise he understood me.

Marcos paused for a moment. Then, kindly, he began to tell a tale the likes of which I'd never heard before and could hardly believe. Gaby sat next to me and translated what I wasn't sure of.

Marcos described a period of economic reforms that were being undertaken in the late 1940s and early 1950s in Guatemala under the democratically elected president Jacobo Arbenz. These included a higher minimum wage, better worker benefits, and investments in infrastructure. The Arbenz reforms had launched the economy of Guatemala into a growth curve.

"It was a bright time in our history, including for people with few resources because they saw wages going up and prices coming down. They had hope for the future," he said.

Then, he dropped a bomb, prefacing it with, "I have to tell you the truth…" He told us that the U.S. State Department and the

CIA had orchestrated a *coup d'état* toppling the progressive president Arbenz, and in his place, installed the military dictator Carlos Castillos Armas.

"He was nothing more than a puppet protecting U.S. business interests," exclaimed Marcos. With a shrug, he added that with no coalition of support, Armas was soon overthrown by another dictator.

"This action was at the root of the current civil war," Marcos affirmed. "This set back Guatemala's economic development and its development as a democracy, and hundreds of thousands of people have already died, and continue to die."

When Marcos finished speaking, you could have heard a pin drop. I might have been imagining it, but it seemed that all eyes were upon me—the only person in the room from the United States.

I was momentarily speechless and in a state of disbelief. I had never heard about U.S. intervention in Guatemala. Obviously, I was not very well read on international politics or foreign policy in general. I only knew the history I'd been taught in school and the coup Marcos recounted hadn't been mentioned, that I remembered. We'd just elected as our new president Bill Clinton. I wasn't politically active or particularly well informed, but had gleaned that the Clinton administration was generally considered less hawkish than the administration that had preceded it (think Gulf War). In my poor Spanish I offered a brief defense.

"I've never heard about that," I started, "and I hope it is not true. But if it is true, I hope those kind of actions are in the past."

I had everyone's attention (because of my naiveté, although I didn't know it at the time), and felt pressed to say more.

"Many of us are hopeful that our new leadership will be more respectful of other countries' (and I had to say this in English) *sovereignty.*" The word was quickly translated into Spanish by Marcos, who, like Gaby, spoke some English. Marcos smiled and nodded his head politely, but my answer unleashed a kind of furor in Moon, who nearly shouted as she responded to my comment with approximately the following:

102

"You are *so* naive. Your country doesn't care about the well being of the rest of the world. It's about the oil, about the money, *¡tonta!*" (Yes she called me "stupid.")

"Haven't you heard the song they sing about the U.S. in Latin America?" She then sang an excerpt of the song, roughly translating in English as, *"My name is Uncle Sam and I travel 'round the world. In the name of peace and progress, got my fingers in your pockets..."*

No, I hadn't heard that one. And I was distressed to hear it.

Some of the other students laughed and seemed to know exactly what song she was talking about. I was clearly at a disadvantage. Politics was not my thing, and I'd never researched these claims. In fact I was still too young to vote when the Vietnam War had come to an end. With U.S. foreign policy almost entirely outside the sphere of my knowledge I had no informed rebuttal, defense, or meaningful apology I could share.

"I'm sorry you feel that way," was all I could muster for Moon, but I meant it.

I felt like the outsider of this student group, and like I needed to bone up on my own country's history. I wanted to be able to confirm what Marcos had claimed, or to dispute it.

Post lecture I returned to my desk for the last few hours of my Spanish class with Gaby, but I was so upset about by what had been said about my country that I couldn't concentrate. I was eager to do some research, hopefully to *disprove* Marcos' story and Moon's allegations. Gaby could see that my mind was not on our lesson, and offered to take me to a local bookstore where she knew the proprietor.

"No one will mind if you look through the history books, even if you don't buy them," she assured me.

We set out walking and arrived in just a few minutes. When we got there, Gaby introduced me to her friend who owned the store, and to my dismay, he knew exactly the alleged *coup* I described, and took me to an area that had not just *one* book on the subject, but at least *a dozen*. I was dumbfounded. Gaby, seeing the disappointment on my face, must have thought I needed some time alone. She showed me a table at the end of an aisle where I could sit down and thumb through selected books. She told me not to rush, and that she'd bring in coffee for me, and visit with her friend.

"Just let me know when you are ready to go," she said, gently, as you would to someone who was recovering from a traffic accident.

An hour later, I was still reading...

In summary, the CIA-orchestrated coup Marcos had described was well documented in Spanish and in English. One place was in a printed paper from the George Washington University National Security Archive titled, "CIA and Assassinations: The Guatemala 1954 Documents"[9.] It told the story of the U.S. effort to unseat democratically elected Guatemalan President Jacobo Arbenz in 1954, just as Marcos had said, and it elaborated.

Besides the economic reforms Marcos had described, when Arbenz became president, he began enforcing taxation. While required, many companies operating in Guatemala had not been paying their taxes. That included the U.S.-based United Fruit Company, which was at that time the largest employer and landowner in all Central America. It had bought up all its competition, and had a virtual banana monopoly in Costa Rica, Honduras and Guatemala. At the same time, it had mainstreamed bananas, transforming them from an insignificant, homegrown crop for local use to the fourth largest fruit export in the world. As such, there were millions of dollars at stake annually.

United Fruit's highly profitable business was hurt by the Arbenz reforms, and in short order, the United Fruit Company's law firm began working to convince the CIA that Arbenz was a communist who should be ousted. The CIA presented the case against Arbenz to Congress which approved the CIA to move forward with "PBSUCCESS," an operation (now declassified) to overthrow Arbenz' so-called "communist" regime.

During the operation, the CIA deployed approximately a thousand mercenaries who posed as "freedom fighters" for propaganda pictures and took over key radio stations to make it appear as if Guatemalan citizens were rising up to overthrow Arbenz. Convinced that should he not surrender there would be severe civilian casualties, Arbenz stepped down.

After the successful coup, then-U.S. Vice President Richard Nixon flew to Guatemala, congratulated the Guatemalan people on having rescued their country from communism, and installed as president military dictator Carlos Castillo Armas. The accounts confirmed that it was as Marcos had said: This coup initiated decades of authoritarian rule whose brutalities included the "disappearance" and killing of 200,000 to 300,000 Mayan indigenous people (accounts differ). According to each and every of these well-documented accounts, these various murderous regimes were all U.S. backed.

The revelations continued. I discovered that John Foster Dulles who was Secretary of State under President Dwight D. Eisenhower was affiliated with United Fruit's law firm; and it was he, himself, who had in past years negotiated land deals for United Fruit in Central America. His brother Allen Dulles, who sat on United Fruit's board of directors, also happened to be head of the CIA. John Foster Dulles' case against Arbenz as a communist was discredited in later years as his obvious conflict of interest was understood, and the operation was revealed as a move on behalf of United Fruit to stop the reforms, regain an army of cheap labor, and avoid taxation.

I was stunned at reading all this.

Gaby walked down the aisle a couple of times to check in on me, and told me again that she was in no hurry. She and her bookstore pal were catching up.

"Take your time, and don't look so sad. You are on vacation!" she quipped, trying to cheer me up.

Unless a dozen or so hardcopy books citing many sources had been doctored—and I thought that was highly unlikely—I had to admit to myself that what Marcos had described was true.

I felt angry, and betrayed.

I gathered up the books and replaced them on the shelf, except one that appeared the best researched, which I bought. It was only fair considering all the books I'd handled, and I wanted to finish reading it anyway—one day, when I could stomach it.

I thanked the proprietor for his patience with me. I must have looked a wreck, because Gaby commented as we exited the book store.

"*¿Estás bien?*" she inquired with a look of concern.

"Yes, I'm O.K." I replied unconvincingly.

Gaby stopped and put her hand on my shoulder. She looked me in the eyes and said, kindly, "You cannot change yesterday. You can only change tomorrow."

Important advice.

15 - Meaning of the Quetzal

HAZRAT INAYAT KHAN perfectly described my mood after that U.S. history lesson in a far-flung corner of rural Guatemala when he wrote, "There can be no rebirth without a dark night of the soul, a total annihilation of all that you believed in and thought that you were." At first I thought I was just depressed, but *annihilated* was much closer to how I was feeling. I was the one who had always teared up with pride at the playing of the Star Spangled Banner. After all I'd just learned, I was not feeling proud.

After the previous day's drama at the lecture and my disheartening discoveries at the bookstore, I felt ashamed to go back to the school and face those who'd been in the know about my own country's nefarious history in the region. In our positive household, shame was not something I'd grown up with. But I was feeling it now, almost as if I'd given the orders that had led to the C.I.A. coup that happened before I was even born.

I had Dena call the school and tell them I wasn't well. She was determined to cook me up some *atól*, a sweet, corn-based hot drink that in this part of Guatemala is a cure-all like chicken soup in the U.S. or tea in England. I accepted it gratefully, but could muster only a weak and unconvincing smile.

Gaby hadn't believed I was sick, and within a half an hour showed up at the front door. Dena let her in and she was in my room a split second after I'd acknowledged the knock at my door. She gave me a warm hug, then told me a few tales about happenings that morning at the school. I feigned interest, but Gaby could see I was distracted and not myself.

I kept my Spanish books on the dresser in my room on the left-hand corner nearest the door. At the center of the dresser, I had placed a totem, of sorts—the brilliant green-and-red-beaded quetzal Brother Simon had given me. Gaby noticed it.

"*Bueno*, a quetzal!" she exclaimed, her face lighting up. "Do you know the meaning?" she asked.

I couldn't say that I did. She was brimming with excitement to tell me, so I gave her my full attention. She said her mother had told her this story, and that it was a story that her grandmother had told her mother. It had been passed down for as long as anyone in her family knew. (After I wrote this story down, I read it back to Gaby who filled in the details I'd missed and corrected a few words.)

"The Spaniard Pedro de Alvarado arrived in 1524 on the shores of what is now Guatemala," Gaby began. She enunciated very distinctly and spoke more slowly and a little louder than normal—like some English speakers do when talking to people they think speak a different language and must be deaf as well.

"The land was then part of the vast Mayan Empire led by the warrior *Tecún Umán*, The Great Ruler. Pedro de Alvarado, a blood-thirsty *conquistador*, engaged Tecún Umán in a battle which took place both on earth and in the heavens," she continued, her eyes wide and expressive.

"On earth, Tecún Umán and his warriors fought with all their might, but they were no match for the furor the Conqueror unleashed upon them in the form of a fleet of heavily armed and armored soldiers on horseback. In *el cielo* (the sky, or spirit world), Alvarado the Conqueror refused to meet Tecún Umán in honorable, hand-to-hand combat. Instead, in full body armor and seated upon his armored horse, the Conqueror released an arrow that struck the honorable Mayan warrior in his chest. With a cry that echoed throughout all our history, Tecún Umán fell from the heavens!"

I was now on the edge of my seat.

"When The Great Ruler's body struck the earth, he did not die, but was transformed," Gaby continued. "He became the first quetzal—a bird cloaked in emerald green signifying the color of our people's forest home. But the blood that ran down the breast of Tecún Umán did not disappear when he fell to Earth. It was the blood of the Mayan people, and it forever stained his breast, the breast of the quetzal, a deep crimson red.

"It is said that in captivity, the quetzal will die of a broken heart. And so it became a symbol of the Mayan people, and our struggle to be free—from oppression, from war, and from poverty. We see it as a symbol not only for us, but for all who suffer these injustices and share our hope of being free."

I picked up the beautifully beaded quetzal, and held it adoringly, as if the beads were jewels. After hearing Gaby's story, what this bird represented felt incredibly meaningful to my life. After all I'd learned in Guatemala, I wanted more than ever to believe that there was hope for a just world, one day. And I wanted to believe that I could help in some small way. I remembered the night I opened the gift from Brother Simon, and wondered if he had known its meaning when he gave it to me. Perhaps he saw where I was headed before I did.

Gaby's story had distracted me from my self-pity for a few minutes. But she had not told me the story just to share an old family fable. She was also making a case to console me.

"Mine are not a bitter people," she continued in earnest. "They are survivors, forgiving, and full of hope. As Tecún Umán is reborn in the story, so are we.

"You did not do the things your government did, and I don't believe you would ever behave as it behaved. You are innocent."

Her words were salve.

16 - A Dollar a Day

THE DALAI LAMA said at a lecture I was fortunate to attend, that "Every time your heart breaks, it gets bigger." After less than two weeks in Guatemala, I felt that my heart must now be the size of a basketball. I'd be leaving in just a few days, and decided to have a heart-to-heart talk with Gaby. I wanted to find out more about the current state of Guatemala, and how an average person like me may be able to help.

"Do you want to see the *real* Guatemala?" she asked me. My answer, not understanding what it would mean, had been an unadulterated, "Yes!"

One evening after class, Gaby loaded me into Marcos' and her old Datsun pickup truck. She said we should stop to eat something and let it get dark, and then we could continue to our destination. We drove to a little family restaurant that served traditional food—chicken with green *jocón* sauce, black-bean loaf and fried plantains. I had no idea where we were going next, and all through dinner, Gaby wouldn't tell me but only made small talk.

"You have to see this for yourself," she said, dodging my questions. "Whatever I say will not describe it accurately."

After dinner, we drove for about 20 minutes into the countryside. When we reached what looked like an old warehouse, Gaby shut the engine down and we glided in silence to a stop in a grassy area. Her next words to me were in a whisper.

"Speak softly," she said, and still, I had no idea why.

"We are not supposed to be here," Gaby confessed, making me wonder what could possibly be inside the warehouse.

"No *extrañeros* (outsiders)," she continued. "This is what they don't want the world to see."

I was intrigued, if not a little scared.

We got out of the truck and closed the doors quietly, then I followed Gaby through the grass half bent over as she was to avoid being seen, I thought. But by whom? The warehouse seemed to be abandoned. I followed Gaby behind the warehouse where sure enough, there was a partially opened door and I could hear noise inside—the first clue I'd had that something was going on in there. Gaby peered in, then motioned for me to follow. She pushed the door open just slightly and the two of us slipped through. Inside was nothing I could have imagined.

The old warehouse was a hive of activity. We stood in the dark along a wall near the back door and looked out into the expansive room where row upon row of bare light bulbs dangled from the ceiling. Below each light bulb was a sewing machine, each attended by a person—a woman. Dust rose from the floor as the women moved about, giving the illusion of smoke as it was illuminated by the dim light. The women were each sewing what looked to be pieces of denim.

"Jeans are made here," Gaby whispered. "They are expensive designer jeans to be sold in the United States…"

Many of the women had infants wrapped tightly against their backs. I watched one of the women shift a crying baby from her back around to her breast to nurse. She adjusted the sling to hold the baby in place, then quickly returned to sewing. As I looked more closely and scanned the women's faces, I realized that some of them were not women at all, but girls—as young as 11 or 12, I guessed.

"They are afraid to stop working for even a moment," Gaby told me. "They have to sign a paper saying they get minimum pay, but they don't. If they don't sign, they will lose their jobs."

Minimum pay, Gaby explained, was the equivalent of about three American dollars each day. But the women really only received eight quetzales for 12 hours work, she said—the equivalent of about *one dollar*.

Gaby took my hand and we walked along the back wall and on to the other side where women were cutting fabric on large tables.

When these women finished cutting, others came and gathered the cut pieces and took them away, distributing them among women and girls who were operating sewing machines. One girl carrying a bundle looked up and I was stunned to see her face; she couldn't have been more than 10 years old.

"There are laws against children working in factories, but no one enforces them," Gaby explained. "Parents are happy to get work for their children—even starting as young as four or five..."

I must have looked sick with shock, because Gaby put her arm around my waist and squeezed gently in a gesture to comfort me.

We slipped out of the warehouse as stealthily as we had gone in. On the ride home, Gaby asked, "Would you like to know *more* about what is happening in Guatemala?"

I paused for just a moment. I felt like I had when I saw the movie *Alien*. I didn't like the anxiety of watching a horror movie, but once I was committed, I couldn't stop watching. I wanted to know what the monster looked like, and feared knowing at the same time—like now.

"Yes, I *do* want to know more," I blurted out to Gaby.

She told me, "If you want to know, we will take you." But she wouldn't tell me where, and again, offered no details.

"It is something you need to see for yourself," she said.

We would go one evening after class, after she arranged it with Marcos...

The "something" Gaby thought I needed to see for myself had been the camp; the mountain village where refugees lived in squalor with little food to eat or clean water to drink. It's where I would see the tiny, lifeless body of the little boy who died for lack of a $10 antibiotic, and we would come under attack from a helicopter...from my very own country.

It is where I would begin to understand poverty, hunger and injustice in a very personal way, where my illusions would be shattered.

113

That's the conversation that led me to that mountaintop, and changed the course of my life.

Not even a full day had elapsed since Gaby, Marcos and I had made the harrowing return from the refugee village when it was time for me to leave Guatemala. I was still in shock from that night's events on the mountain. I dragged myself from bed, finished packing, and put on the best face I could to meet Gaby and Marcos. When they arrived it was time to say my goodbyes to Dena and leave gifts for her and her children. I thanked Dena profusely for her care and kindness, and gave her a to-go cup for coffee made of porcelain and designed for adults.

"You like Bambi?" she asked, managing to smile. She was clearly sad that I was leaving. I presented Hugo with a Hot Wheels set, and Claudia with a Barbie doll, just two of about a half-dozen toys I'd brought from the states to pass along to children. I left the rest in a small bag with Dena to make good use of.

"You've made it a happy Christmas," Dena whispered tearfully. "I will not be able to buy the children gifts this year."

I thought about how much I have, and how—unlike every member of Dena's family—I'd never wanted for a thing in my life. Not food, shelter, or a toy. I reflected upon how much I'd taken for granted.

It was another lesson in perspective, and gratitude.

The ride to the bus station with Gaby and Marcos seemed twice as long as it had been on my arrival. My Spanish was not good enough to explain all I was feeling. I thought I'd begin to cry if I tried to express myself, so I remained silent during much of the ride. I was still trying to wrap my mind around all I had seen and experienced.

It was a tearful parting, not just because I was sad to leave. I was also angry—*enraged*, really. My government was on the wrong side of human decency. I'd seen it with my own eyes, and I was deeply disappointed and disillusioned. Cloak-and-dagger plots dreamt up in Washington to protect a banana empire had translated into *real-life suffering* for a village full of innocent people. I'd seen with my own eyes. And a lifeless child...

When I was hugging Gaby and Marcos goodbye, I blurted out, "I'll be back!" And with that, I strode into the bus station.

They told me later that many other visitors had spoken similar words, and never returned. They thought they'd never see me again.

They were wrong.

17 - Signs Along the Road

MY RE-ENTRY HAD BEEN STRESSFUL. I was at home in my own bed, but tossing and turning half the night. I couldn't seem to stay focused on my professional work. I wanted to return to Guatemala, but I was still trying to figure out what I might be able to offer there that would be of value. I had short bouts of anxiety when I remembered what had happened in the refugee village, and a couple of times, I woke up sweating.

My cousin Jan, who had served in Vietnam, told me about the hell he'd gone through re-entering civilian life. Having survived front-line battles, he suffered from Post Traumatic Stress Disorder (PTSD) and shuddered, even hit the ground sometimes, at loud noises. The "incongruity" of his return also plagued him as he tried to readjust to the comforts and plenty of life back home. On the front lines, he'd lived for months on end in jungle encampments on minimal rations—not too different from what I'd seen the refugees surviving on. Though I'd experienced just a taste of what Jan had suffered, I had a new appreciation for his lifelong struggle with PTSD, and an understanding of the incongruity he'd once described. I was feeling it.

I had always looked forward to Christmas because I knew our little family would be together at my Aunt June's house. As a newborn, I had come home from the hospital on her lap. She'd been an important fixture in my life, and especially after my mother died. Dad and I would gather there with Aunt June, Uncle Ed, a smattering of friends of the family and in my younger years, my cousins Joel and Jan. But this year, even though we were together and the ham was in the oven and the Spode dishes were on the table, my experience was different. Instead of the sense of warmth, security, and family, every part of our gathering stood in stark contrast to my experience in the mountain refugee village.

We gathered in the warmth of a comfortable home while families shivered in the rain and cold. I was clean and comfortable while innocent people were displaced, muddy and miserable. I stared at a full plate of ham, yams, mashed potatoes and gravy with whole cranberry sauce and had enough food to waste while children on that mountaintop ate weeds and shared bits of a single egg.

I put on a cheery face, but ate little. I'd lost my appetite. I was suffering some level of depression. What I had experienced in Guatemala had changed my perspective. I was seeing the world with new eyes, and I wasn't sure what to do next.

I couldn't *un-see* what I'd seen.

The choice of what I would do with this new information weighed heavily on me. I could carry on with my life as it had been and imagine what I'd seen was for someone else to do something about. If I chose instead to do something (and deep down I knew there were no "ifs" about it), what would it be? I needed to think carefully. If there was one thing I knew about myself, it was that I didn't do things in a small way. When I jumped in, it would be with both feet and I wanted the effort to matter.

For the rest of the month, I let Guatemala sink in. The incongruities continued.

Driving to work, I noticed the well-kept streets and manicured neighborhoods in contrast to Guatemala's faltering infrastructure. On the freeway, for the first time, I noticed that most cars were in good condition, and that often there was just a *single person* in each car; in rural Guatemala, most vehicles were small trucks ready to fall apart packed to overflowing with people who sat or stood in the truck bed in the wind and rain.

My colleagues at work and I were well dressed (I won't reveal how many pairs of near-new shoes I owned). And for the first time, I noticed how much food we'd throw away at lunch time without giving it a second thought.

We have so much and we take it for granted.

I was all over the place emotionally and poor Sam had to put up with me even as he tried to understand. But how could he? He had not been there. He hadn't seen the soldiers on the streets, or the women and girls working by dull, bare bulbs in the jeans sweatshop. He hadn't seen the hunger, smelled the human waste or survived the strafing as I had in the refuge village that night. He hadn't heard the wailing, or seen the boy who had died... And I hadn't told him.

I didn't want to tell him the worst of it, so I didn't tell him about it at all. Had the tables been turned and my spouse had told *me* he'd *barely escaped* a firefight alive, I would have been petrified for him to return to that situation. I wanted my decision about whether or not to return to Guatemala to be my own, without input or pressure.

Even though in the past Sam had been supportive, I didn't want to fight with him over my decision, should he not agree. But it was a mistake to underestimate him and leave him out of the discussion. My penance was having to sort through everything in my head, alone.

Limbo is a painful place. Or as the medieval Sephardic Jewish philosopher Maimonides put it, "The risk of a wrong decision is preferable to the terror of indecision." Luckily, it didn't take me long to know for sure that I *would* return to Guatemala.

When I told Sam, he was quiet at first. He chose his words carefully, saying he could see how much it meant to me. Ultimately, he told me that he would support what I felt I needed to do. Of course, I hadn't told him the whole story. And neither of us could have known how my choice to return to Guatemala would impact our relationship in the future.

Before the New Year rolled around, I knew that Brother Simon couldn't have been more right when he predicted that there was something for me in Guatemala. As I imagined what my return might look like, I was completely energized thinking about all the good a group of us could do.

119

The exchange rate was $1 for Q8 (*quetzales*), and Q8 could buy a dozen eggs. That meant that for a single dollar, at least 12 children could get protein for one day.

I learned that in the U.S., overstocks of medicines were destroyed each year by the *ton*, even before they expired. We could get them donated. Lives could be saved.

Schools in Guatemala were operating with no books and few supplies. We could do a book drive for school books that had been overprinted, or were used. Children could learn.

We could build modest, safe places to live, and with a few pennies worth of chlorine could provide safe drinking water for a family for months.

We could turn our spare change and our throw-aways into treasures for people with great need in Guatemala, and work together on solutions for long-term, positive change.

Once I figured out who the "we" was, we began.

PART IV ✚ FORGING LOCAL HOPE

18 – A Motley Crew

M Y FIRST RECRUIT WAS ACCIDENTAL. I'd gone for my yearly eye exam and before I knew it, was talking with my optometrist about my recent trip to Guatemala and the need I'd seen. I told him about the trip I was planning. We would start by bringing life-saving medicines and health care professionals like him to help. Next out of my mouth was that this would happen sometime in the next six months, "June, most likely." I asked if he'd like to come. Taylor Bladh, a devout Latter Day Saint who had made numerous mission trips to help those in need, said "Yes!" I was momentarily astounded. Volunteer *Número Uno*, check.

St. Matthew Church and Fr. Peter Hickman, who'd introduced me to the transformative power of service, was my next stop. When I told him about the suffering I'd seen and shared ideas about what we could do to help, he invited me to speak at the very next meeting of the St. Matthew Ecumenical Catholic Community Council. The Council was immediately supportive. Fr. Peter himself became Volunteer Number 2, followed by Bob Rook, a Council member who was Number 3.

Fr. Peter suggested that the project could operate under St. Matthew's charitable status, and with that, parishioner Kathryn Tuma became Volunteer Number 4. She took on all the bookkeeping—a substantial task considering the complex accounting rules that Federally approved non-profits have to follow. Fr. Peter, Bob and I firmed up the June dates for our first trip and began a focused effort to recruit additional volunteers.

My old writing buddy Bob Rhein became Volunteer Number 5. He was a great organizer and publicist, and would get us some coverage in local papers to help with recruiting. He had a wonderful sense of humor and was an all-around energizing force. Due to prior commitments he determined he would help stateside, then travel on a later trip (we were already thinking there would be later trips).

Missionary of Charity Brother Joseph McLachlan became Volunteer Number 6. His vast experience working with Latin American refugees while running a home for troubled teenage boys in one of the toughest neighborhoods in Los Angeles made him a shoe-in. He had tons of community organizing experience and would be a huge help all the way around, and especially considering my relative dearth of Spanish (he was fluent).

Rudy Vargas had become one of my dearest friends from my day job in communications and marketing. He'd long been a documentary filmmaker and social activist, and he was in the moment I told him about the project, as Volunteer Number 7. My friend Rick Cass who was Rudy's production partner signed on, too, and with Volunteer Number 8, we suddenly had a film crew to document the effort.

From my life as a musician, I knew singer-songwriter Jeff "Joad" Sherman who agreed with me that no humanitarian effort would be complete without a soundtrack. He was immediately in, recruiting fellow musician Paul Black to join us, locking in Volunteers 9 and 10. St. Matthew's Church parishioner and musician Mirella Morra and singer Carla Nagel were soon on board and we were officially a "band" (and a dozen).

While we continued to add people to the group, we began to seek donations. The two Bob's and a few others went to churches, temples, dime stores and outlets asking for clothing for young children and infants. During a single week, we filled a garage (Sam's and my garage, that is) with donations we hand-carried from various sources. But we didn't count on what happened next.

We'd been so successful in our pitches that phone calls came in from the places we'd visited, and additional donations began to arrive...by the truckload. We ended up with *several hundred* large boxes of clothing! What we had not thought through, however, was where we were going to put such an abundance of donations. In the end we had to beg for spare corners in a half-dozen volunteers' garages all over Orange County.

Another surprise came when we went to sort the donations. We'd specifically asked for clothing for infants and children *only*. That's because I'd learned from Gaby on my first trip that the manufacture of woven *huipils* and *traje* (Mayan blouses and suits) for adults in villages in Guatemala was an important cottage industry. We wouldn't want to disrupt or compete with people's livelihoods by giving away free Western clothing. It had not occurred to us that we'd have to *enforce* that donations included only the children's clothing we'd asked for.

As we opened boxes, we were disappointed to find that about thirty five of them contained adult clothing which, besides being a threat to Guatemalan cottage industry, were unfit for anyone to use.

There's nothing like the dank, "vintage" smell of old clothes. After many hours of sorting and smelling that smell, we borrowed a truck, loaded it, and made several trips to Goodwill. We donated hundreds of men's dress shirts and slacks, ladies slacks and dresses, men's and women's shoes (including high, spikey heels), bathing suits and bras which were all inappropriate donations for a rural village. We loaded moth-eaten, torn and badly stained junk-clothes and shoes for the dump—items that for some reason, some people thought would be good enough for the poor.

Didn't people with limited resources deserve better? Yes.

Had I also been guilty of cleaning out my closet and passing my beyond-saving crappy-old clothes along to Goodwill so I wouldn't feel bad about throwing them away? I had.

Never again.

This was just the first time I noticed my wrong thinking (and the general wrong-thinking) when it came to people less fortunate. Real caring and respect would mean that I would no longer give something I would not wear, eat, or otherwise use myself.

This verse came to mind. "I tell you, whatever you did for one of the least of these brothers and sisters of mine, you did for me." – Matthew 25:40."

"Your project sounds exciting!" Dan Smith told me enthusiastically when I called the office of Direct Relief International (DRI), a then-Santa Barbara-based clearinghouse for excess medicines and medical equipment. "But there's a waiting list to receive medicines from DRI, and it's rather long," he cautioned.

We talked for nearly an hour, and he gave me some valuable tips he'd learned from the many groups DRI worked with in Latin America. These included the need in most situations to keep medicines under lock and key, and the wisdom of having a token charge for exams to help ensure that people valued and would use their medicines.

At the end of our conversation regarding my request for medicine, Dan added, "Let me see what I can do…" He was so upbeat and positive that I knew something more would come of our call.

Not even two weeks after our first conversation I was only partially surprised to hear from Dan who said he'd come into some short-dated medicines, meaning, they would expire in less than a year. He asked if we could use them.

"Absolutely!" I told him. I was elated, making DRI our first partner organization.

With lessons learned fresh in mind from the inappropriate clothing we'd inadvertently collected, Bob Rook and I put together a list of exactly what we needed from DRI and others who could provide medicines. We did extensive research. We'd seek out antibiotics, deworming medications, anti-fungal creams and non-prescription pain relievers like aspirin and ibuprofen as top priorities.

In the process of seeking out samples we also learned that we could get brand-new surgical tools that although never used, had been "present" in an operating room during a surgery, and so were discarded. This included scalpels, scissors, clamps, and other instruments we figured we could use, donate, or trade in Guatemala for what we needed most for a medical mission.

Unbelievably, from just a single hospital we were able to secure *half a truck load* of instruments still in their sealed plastic wrappers.

We waste so much.

Over the coming months, we welcomed a heartening *flood* of additional volunteers. Many of them were from St. Matthew's, or contacts through the Missionaries of Charity. The group totaled a whopping 43 volunteers in all[10]—almost twice the size that would fit into a standard bus. Finding two large passenger busses, booking dozens of hotel rooms, maintaining order and attending to everyone's needs with such a large group would be a challenge, I knew. But it would be worth the effort.

Our diverse group included doctors, nurses, teachers, construction workers and miscellaneous others who wanted to help people. We were a motley, motivated crew!

We sought the help of the Guatemalan Consulate in Los Angeles, and met Rafael Salazar, the Consul General. As a precaution against being detained by government authorities (there was a civil war raging, after all), he helped us execute photo-identification cards for each member of the team and wrote us an official letter of invitation to do relief work in Guatemala, which he signed.

Logistically, we would rely on Gaby and Marcos to be our guides in country. Based on the vast talents of our huge group, we made a list of potential projects and sent them to the two of them to assess and refine into a handful of projects that would fill urgent needs. The two of them pulled in some teachers at the Spanish school to help—Enrique, Freddy, Fernando and Nery. We would come to call these teachers, affectionately, our "Fab Four."

After a few rounds of back and forth by FAX, we agreed to focus on holding emergency medical clinics in some extremely impoverished areas. To lead this effort we recruited three doctors who, as it happened, were quite a diverse group. Dr. Jan Singh was from India. Diep Nguyen was originally from Vietnam. Dr. Juan Ruiz hailed from Colombia.

We would also take advantage of the talent of our optometrist and first recruit Taylor Bladh, and hold a vision clinic. We would harness the talents of the builders among us to construct emergency shelters, or perhaps one small home for an exceptionally needy family.

During all the planning, it became obvious that we needed a name. We would be based in Xela. There, we'd be providing humanitarian aid. "Xela Aid" flowed off the tongue as short and to the point. But from what I already knew, we'd want some day to grow past emergency aid and do true development work—solutions that would last. "Agency for Integrated Development" didn't roll off the tongue, but its acronym, "A.I.D.," was perfect. We lost the periods and "Xela AID" was officially launched.

Graphic designer Thea Makow, who I worked with in my professional life, offered to join the group and to create a logo for us. Something that would communicate the idea of "friends helping friends in Guatemala," I suggested. The organization's first logo featured two hands grasping below the words "XELA AID." Our first use of the newly minted logo was on our personal identification cards, and next, on stickers we made for our boxes of medicines. After our first trip and seeing it in widespread use, we topped the logo with none-other than the powerful symbol of the quetzal bird.

We planned the locations where we'd serve, found families to host all of us, sought supplies, considered transportation, made lists of what was safe to eat and drink and cultural considerations, and tended to the many other details we'd need to decide upon before embarking on our trip. There was lots of research to do about in-country safety, the need for visas, taxes to leave Guatemala (yes, there really was a "leaving tax" of about $50 at the time). And group size mattered. When there are a few people traveling, it's easy to make split-second decisions on logistics. When that number grows to forty-some, you can't do transportation, lodging, or projects on the fly. We needed to plan every step carefully and with plenty of lead time.

I contacted two other organizations that had done work in Guatemala to get tips for success, and learned we were on the right track. It was a six-month labor of love for the two Bobs,

128

Father Peter and me, and many others among the first-trip volunteers who were involved in the planning.

Like Lao Tzu's "journey of a thousand miles" that begins with a single step, our project now had a foot firmly planted.

19 - Maiden Voyage

THERE'S NOTHING QUITE as exhilarating as a group of like-minded people on a mission. Bob Rook and I were super-energized as we shared the job of leading Xela AID's maiden voyage.

When it was time to head to the airport to catch our overnight, direct flight to Guatemala, it was none too soon for me. Bob and I agreed we were as prepared as possible considering we'd never led a volunteer group before, and that we didn't know exactly how things would go when we arrived. What we *did* know was that we'd crossed every "t" and dotted every "i" we could think of, and would soon see what our efforts translated into.

I had my fingers crossed.

The sense of purpose and passion was palpable among the volunteers as we all met and mingled for the first time as a complete group at Los Angeles International Airport. Bob Rook and I visited with the various related groups of people who had joined. There was the St. Matthew's contingent led by Fr. Peter himself, and the Co-Workers of Charity group led by Brother Joseph. Then there were friends of friends of the two groups and of Bob and I. Everyone was ready for action. At 10 minutes to midnight, off we flew.

At about 2 o'clock in the morning I walked down the aisle to the bathroom. I was happy to see that most of the volunteers had managed to fall asleep. I knew that being well rested would be important since going into a new situation in a different country can be challenging.

At that time, I didn't realize just how challenging it would be.

Missing Meds

At about 6 a.m. we arrived without a glitch and filed off the plane not too much worse for the wear, considering it was an overnight flight. After folks got a chance to stop at the restroom and brush their hair and teeth ("with bottled water," I cautioned), the group perked up. It was at the baggage claim that the challenges began.

We'd carried on 40 pieces of personal luggage and checked 40 boxes full of Xela AID supplies. While by some miracle all our personal luggage had arrived, a full *half* of the boxes were missing—mostly, expensive medicines.

Bob and I located the baggage counter—a small desk with one man seated behind it—to try to track down our boxes. Almost immediately and without checking any kind of list or log, the man told us that if they hadn't come off the conveyor belt, they were not in Guatemala. We would have believed him, except that as we peered under and around the black, rubber flaps between the conveyor belt and the warehouse behind him, we could actually *see* our boxes stacked at the back wall of the warehouse!

We tried courteously to point this out to the man, but when we did, he did not even turn around to look. He insisted that whatever boxes we were seeing were "other" boxes, and not ours. This ran counter to the fact that they clearly displayed the "Xela AID" logo stickers we'd applied. He told us we'd need to check back the next day, then summarily dismissed us by beginning a conversation with the next person in line behind us.

In a state of disbelief, Bob and I retreated to have a chat. We had to remind ourselves that we were not crazy, nor were our eyes deceiving us and *yes* those were our boxes. The only conclusion we could come to was that for some reason—just to be right, or something more nefarious—the man was not going to help us get our boxes today.

Since our destination was about five hours away by bus, coming back the next day would be a challenge both in terms of time and cost. We thought about leaving one or two of us behind to deal with the boxes, but it didn't make sense since we knew they were there.

Bob and I decided we weren't leaving the airport without our boxes. Nope. But it would do no good to get mad at the man. We needed a plan.

We had arranged for Gaby to be waiting for our group in front of the airport exit doors. Bob and I had the group go ahead and exit with their personal luggage and the 20 boxes in hand, and meet up with Gaby. We would hang back. We had no idea how we were going to get the rest of our boxes, but I knew we'd think of something.

As we considered what to do, Bob and I noticed the airport becoming more crowded as additional groups arrived. The line at the makeshift baggage counter grew, and the man who hadn't helped us left frequently, apparently to look for luggage near the front area of the conveyor belt. Soon there was a long line at the little desk. We waited to put our plan into action for the moment that the man went off to deal with another client's issue. Then, we went in.

Looking as official as possible, we flashed our Xela AID I.D. cards and strode boldly through a door and back into the luggage warehouse. To our surprise, no one stopped us!

There were a number of tall metal bins with luggage and boxes stacked in them. In one of those, against a wall, were ours. A young man was stacking baggage on a large, flat dolly, and I asked if he could please help us with our boxes. He immediately complied, and for good measure, I slipped him Q20 (a bit more than $2). He smiled broadly and continued loading up our boxes.

While the loading was going on, Bob and I sweated it out hoping the man at the desk was busy enough that he wouldn't come to the back area and catch us claiming our boxes. My heart raced!

When all our boxes were on the luggage dolly, the young man wheeled them toward the public area of the airport. We told him our truck was waiting out front (we hoped it was) and he moved the packed dolly along, passing behind the man at the desk. I held my breath wondering if the unhelpful man would turn around. He didn't. The young man then took us past an area where luggage was being inspected, which turned out to be

Customs. Bob and I followed closely, aiming to look dignified and official. I was now sweating profusely.

Almost unbelievably, we exited the building—luggage and all—without incident. I breathed a sigh of relief, not only for our success, but also, because we immediately found Gaby waiting with our group and smiling ear to ear. Our happy reunion didn't last long, though. After hugs all around, she pointed out the large, hired truck waiting for us, all according to plan. She then reported that she'd had a run-in with the driver of that truck.

Bamboozled

"The owner of the truck has made an adjustment to the price," Gaby told me, obviously disappointed. When I asked her how much, she answered, sheepishly.

"Well, he's *tripled* the price."

I was outraged and felt my face turn red. Bob kept his cool, suggesting we negotiate. I agreed and took a deep breath. Bob didn't speak Spanish, so I'd do all the talking.

I made my way over to the driver, and despite my poor Spanish, we communicated. He had no explanation for the change in the price. I was not calm.

"We are here as volunteers to serve your own people who have no food or medicine!" I howled. "Why have you jacked up the price?"

The man not only did not answer, but stood with his arms crossed, wouldn't look me in the eyes, and wouldn't budge on the price.

I could feel that my face had flushed red. I took Gaby aside with Bob.

"Okay, fine. We'll play the same game," I told them. "We'll agree, then after we get there, I'll just pay him what we originally agreed to."

Gaby shook her head in disapproval. "You can't do that," she told us.

"Why not?" I asked.

"Because truck drivers carry guns and he might *kill* you," she answered, stone-faced.

Considering the risk, and feeling certain the truck owner wouldn't try anything in the busy airport setting, we agreed to another tact. It would be risky but not life threatening.

I told the truck owner, "Thank you, but your services will not be required."

His bravado turned to astonishment, then anger as he yelled after us in Spanish, "You can't cancel. We had a deal!"

That's what *I'd* thought, but I wasn't about to work with anyone who'd go back on their word as he had. It never ends well.

His closing shot was, "You'll never find anyone to transport the boxes at the price I'm offering!"

As we walked away, Gaby told me he might be right. I assured her and Bob that we would simply hire a few small pick-up trucks to get the job done. I had no idea where we'd find them, but considering the double-digit unemployment in Guatemala, I was sure we *would* find them.

And it didn't take long.

As our group waited patiently in a huddle to the right of the airport exit, Bob and I cornered everyone we saw in a pick-up truck. In less than a half an hour we found a man with a medium-sized truck who swore he could pack in all our boxes. He was willing to take them 30 minutes away to the *Galgos* bus station for about $50—the original deal we'd had with the first guy. (Yes this whole ordeal was over an extra $100, but it was the principle of the thing…)

We made the deal. The boxes were stacked higher than we would have liked. But with a bit of finessing and a tarp and lots of rope, the man was able to convince us that the boxes were secure.

We grabbed cabs for the entire group and with all our luggage and our newly hired truck driver in tow, we headed to *Galgos* to board our "luxury bus," as Gaby called it. During the ride, Bob, Gaby and I talked about our various victories in the airport, and how we were off to a good start. We were quite pleased with ourselves.

We made it to the *Galgos* station, everyone got a seat, and all our personal luggage and boxes fit nicely into the luggage compartment. Since enough had already gone wrong, we figured the odds for success were now in our favor, and that it would be smooth sailing from here on.

But no such luck…

Middle of Nowhere

I've never been on a bus that broke down—let alone broke down in the middle of nowhere. But our *Galgos* "luxury bus" did just that. The driver and other passengers acted as if it was common place, which was not reassuring. Everyone filed off in an orderly manner and surprisingly, the driver and his helper started off-loading luggage. Apparently, there would be no repairing this bus.

The Xela AID team members soldiered out of the bus, and upon collecting personal luggage and all 40 boxes, began stacking everything into a neat pile. We were at that point operating under the logical assumption that "the most reputable luxury bus company in Guatemala" (as Gaby had described *Galgos*) would send a replacement bus, and soon. When I noticed that the Guatemalan passengers, on the other hand, picked up their luggage and scattered faster than leaves in a monsoon, it occurred to me to confirm what *Galgos'* plan was to get us to Quetzaltenango. I grabbed Gaby and we cornered the bus driver.

"Don't worry," he assured me in broken English. "Another bus will be along in 15 minutes."

Satisfied, I turned and walked contentedly toward our team members to reassure them, when Gaby set me straight.

"That means *tomorrow morning*...if at all." she quietly informed me. "He's just being polite."

Well that's nuts I thought, feeling deflated and contemplating what to do next.

Gaby, Bob and I discussed options. Based on Gaby's experience with luxury busses (and busses in Guatemala in general), there was less than a snowball's chance in hell for a replacement bus. If we didn't want the first night of our volunteer trip to be spent along the roadside, we'd clearly have to find another way to get the team to Quetzaltenango. We decided Gaby and I would hitch a ride to the closest bus station of any kind to negotiate a new bus. Bob would hang back to keep the group in good cheer (they were not currently in good cheer, but he'd work on it).

We let the group know the plan and at the same time, made a few jokes about Murphy's Law and getting all the bad juju out of the way early so the rest of the trip would run like clockwork. We got only a few half-hearted laughs, but I knew this stalwart group would recover quickly, once we were back on our way.

I hoped that would be soon.

Gaby and I walked up the road with some urgency to a place where a vehicle could easily pull over to stop for us, and began to watch for a possible ride. I could see our Xela AID team members now hunkered down on our boxes, watching goats grazing across the road. As fate would have it, it started to rain. I imagined them getting drenched in the open, and felt my urgency level rise. Luckily, it wasn't long before our ride came barreling down the highway and Gaby flagged it down.

"I left with God…"

Question: "How many people can you fit into a Guatemalan chicken bus?"

Answer: "Always *one more.*"

I'd heard that joke a few times, but hadn't understood how fitting it was, until now.

Gaby and I squeezed on to the already overloaded, diesel-spouting converted-yellow school bus. It was complete with a tremendously colorful paint job that included mirror portraits of the Virgin Mary at the top and each side of the outside front window. I followed Gaby as she made her way into the bus's aisle which was already packed with people, piglets, goats and yes, chickens—thus, "chicken bus."

Incredibly, a boy of perhaps 12 or 13 was using his hands and feet while hanging upside down, Spider Man style, to crawl along two bars affixed along the ceiling of the aisle. In this way, he collected ours and everyone else's Q1.50 each.

Painted across the driver's window on the inside in bright red script was, *"Me fui con Dios. Sólo Dios sabe si regresaré. Si no vuelvo, estaré con Él."* This means, "I left with God. Only God knows if I'll return. If I don't return, I am with Him." Renaissance-style angel decals placed at each end of the phrase put a sobering emphasis on Part 3 of the painted text message: "If I don't return…" We had lots to do, and I was not ready to *not* return. I hoped this wasn't some weird harbinger of more bad luck to come.

There are no Galgos stations between Guatemala City and Quetzaltenango, Gaby informed me. We'd need to stop at *Los Encuentros*, a place where the thousands of chicken busses of Guatemala converge daily, stop for a break, load and reload. It's a kind of Grand Central Station of Guatemala that happens along a congested city street.

At *Los Encuentros*, Gaby and I were able to negotiate with a driver to go back for the group. It would cost about $35 for the initial pickup, then we would just pay for everyone the miniscule bus fare of about 5 cents. The bus would be open to the public, but we figured all members of our group would get seats since they'd be picked up first. That would be important since the balance of the journey was about two hours (if nothing else went wrong).

Despite the warnings of the prayer painted on the window of our chicken bus, we *did* return. When we arrived back at our broken-down bus, the team was a little wetter for the wear, but in very good cheer. It had stopped raining, and the goats had found their way across the street where they were now keeping the group entertained. They had moved within reach, and were nibbling grass to the amusement of the volunteers—some of whom had made friends with them, and were stroking their heads and photographing them. It wasn't what I had imagined the first few hours in Guatemala to look like for our very first volunteer group, but at least the trip was already something to tell the kids about.

The driver of our new chicken bus wasn't thrilled when he saw our forty boxes plus luggage that would need to be loaded onto the roof of the bus. He frowned as he contemplated the boxes. But our cheery group immediately began helping him and his young assistant and he was obviously relieved and appreciative.

Once loaded up, we were on our way, again.

By the time we got to Quetzaltenango, our chicken bus was bursting at the seams. In the close quarters, many of the team members had taken the opportunity to interact with local people. Those in our group who were not Spanish speakers did a lot of communicating with smiles, while Spanish speakers made comments and asked questions like: "Your clothing is beautiful." "Where are you from?" "What are your children's names?" In one case, referring to a small piglet a woman had on a tether, a volunteer asked in Spanish the well-intentioned but culturally naive question, "What is your pig's name?"

Since pigs are not kept as pets but raised for slaughter, it is not customary to name them and the question got a laugh not only from the owner, but also, from half a dozen local people on the bus who overheard it. Our young volunteer was a bit off-put since she was an animal lover (and a devout vegetarian). I had observed this interaction and thought about the difficulty she would likely have on this trip as she adjusted to the facts about local animals. The street dogs she'd see would be thin, potentially injured, and likely eating garbage and sleeping along the streets at night. She would also learn that the fate of every cow, pig and chicken she'd meet was a dinner plate.

The rest of our bus trip, happily, was without major drama. We made it to Xela before dusk. Marcos was waiting for us at the school with the "Fab Four" teachers who together had been in charge of identifying needs and finding locations where we'd work. Considering the expertise we'd put together, they had settled on medical and optometry clinics, and also, on having us build a small home for a family they'd identified as having particular need.

Gaby had arranged for each member of the group to stay with local families who, due to the many language schools in Xela, were set up to host foreigners. We agreed to meet back at the school at 8 a.m. sharp to travel together to our first group activity. (We had to agree ahead of time, because most private homes did not have phones, and cell phones were not yet widely used.) Gaby and the teachers then escorted the volunteers in twos and threes to meet their host families who would provide dinner.

I returned to Dena's home to stay with her and the kids. Gaby walked me there, and Claudia and Hugo practically tackled me after they opened the door. Forgetting I was still not a fluent Spanish speaker, they excitedly hurled commentary and questions at me which came so fast that I understood them only in part. But I had learned quite a bit more Spanish since I'd last seen them, and felt encouraged by all I could understand. We exchanged hugs and I gave them each a school backpack complete with school supplies, for which they were elated. It was lovely to see Dena, who seemed particularly emotional about my return.

When I looked quizzically at the tears welling in her eyes, she told me, slowly, "Things are not easy here…the war, you know…"

After Gaby took her leave, I sat down to speak with Dena for what I thought would be just a few minutes, and light conversation.

It was neither.

Secrets

Maya Angelou wrote, "There is no greater agony than bearing an untold story inside of you." I could sense this kind of agony as Dena led me to her small kitchen table speaking in whispers, her eyes now filled with tears. She directed the kids off to bed, then, when she heard their bedroom door close, she poured out the story of what had happened to her little family since I'd left. It was chilling.

Dena had lost her job at the phone company, a considerable blow in the awful Guatemalan job market. Hugo had nearly died of appendicitis that went undiagnosed for several days after the pain began. After he survived the emergency surgery, he got a serious infection, just like a full *half* of all people who are admitted to the general hospital in Xela. Thankfully, he recovered. And Claudia, just 12 now, had been abducted! Though returned, she had suffered some kind of abuse she wouldn't talk about.

Additional details concerning these three incidents made them even more disconcerting.

Dena had lost her job when she refused her boss's sexual advances.

Hugo had nearly died because Dena simply did not have the money to take him to see a doctor, despite his intense pain. She'd hoped it would pass. In the end, she'd relented and taken him to the emergency room, and lucky she did; he would have died without surgery. She had to borrow money from every relative who'd help to save his life, and now was taking in laundry in addition to boarders like me to pay it back and to feed her family.

Claudia had been taken on her way to school—by an officer in the Guatemalan Army, Dena knew, from what Claudia described he'd been wearing. Dena wasn't certain about all that had occurred because Claudia wouldn't, maybe *couldn't*, tell her. But she knew from a change, a deep-rooted fear in Claudia, that whatever had happened, it had been traumatic. The fact that the abduction had been by an officer assured there would be no justice for Claudia, Dena explained.

I was horrified by what I was hearing, and at one point, felt lightheaded and flushed with a kind of fury. I saw red. Dena was obviously beside herself with grief on all accounts. She cried, and I held her. But I was too angry to cry. I thought about the no-win situation of having to choose between keeping a job and your own self respect, and having no recourse for abuse at work. I imagined what it must feel like to watch a child suffer with an illness and have no means to help. I thought about the unimaginable news of learning your young daughter is missing, followed by the elation of finding her. Then, the heartbreak of learning she'd been taken and almost surely abused by someone in a powerful position, and that you have absolutely no recourse. It was a feeling of utter helplessness and hopelessness, and under that, pure *rage*.

When everything that could be talked out had been, Dena wiped her eyes and offered me dinner. I felt too sick and exhausted to eat, excused myself, and retired to my room. She told me she was grateful for my having listened, and I thanked her for trusting me with her story.

In my room, I closed the door and changed into PJs. I set my small travel alarm. Before lying down I dug into my suitcase until I felt it in my hand, then pulled it out and sat the brilliant green-and-red-beaded *quetzal* in its anointed place at the center of the dresser. This is exactly where it had been the day Gaby told me her grandmother's story of the meaning of the quetzal just six months earlier. My life had changed so much since then…

I stared at the beaded bird as I considered the horrors that Dena and her family had been through. I could do nothing to change what had happened to them but listen, and learn. But *we* could do something to ease suffering, and to help families like Dena's. If we did it in the right way, the help we provided could be significant, life-changing, empowering.

We'd have to learn what that kind of help looked like, and I knew I had *lots* to learn. I also knew that it felt right to be back, and with reinforcements.

I flopped down on the bed absolutely exhausted, and slept.

20 - Inaugural *Jornada*

J*ORNADA* IS N.G.O. LINGO[11] for a medical mission that's most often staffed by doctors and other health care professionals who treat patients for free, or at a minimal cost.

A *jornada* can be held in a clinic, in a home, or in tents in the jungle. The excitement was palpable as our volunteer team gathered in the damp-cool of the morning for our very first such undertaking. Ours would be held in a private home, while our construction crew worked to build a small home for a homeless family.

We met at the school at precisely eight o'clock in the morning to begin. When 8:10 came and went and no one from the Guatemalan contingent had shown up, it suggested we might have already run into a cultural difference.

Gaby and Marcos arrived at the school at about 8:15 and assured us the others would be along soon. Marcos clued us in to what became Cultural Difference Lesson Number 1: If you want people to come at a specific time, it's best to give a time 20 minutes earlier than you actually want them to arrive. "Here, eight o'clock *means* 8:20, or even 8:30. We actually arrived *early!*" Marcos explained.

The Fab Four teachers (Enrique, Freddy, Fernando and Nery) arrived "promptly" at 8:20, as Marcos had predicted, with two vans and a small truck. The medical team, optometry team and musicians loaded up in one van, and our construction team piled into the other. Bob, Gaby and I stayed with the medical team, while Marcos and all the Fab Four (except Nery, a musician), loaded into the other van to head to the village about 45 minutes away to begin work on the small house.

Gaby told us that we'd be holding the clinic nearby. To simplify logistics, our first *jornada* would be held in Xela rather than in a rural village outside the city. Gaby, Marcos and the Fab Four had arranged for us to work in the courtyard of a relatively large home. Gaby felt it would be an ideal setting, and that those in need would travel by foot, or by mini-bus (prevalent and inexpensive) to see us. She had just come from the location. She told us the family had hung sheets to create doors and moved personal items out to convert bedrooms into exam rooms. She was happy to tell us, too, that we'd have working toilet facilities and running water!

"This sounds like a piece of cake," Bob Rook commented to me in his inimitable, cool-guy style. In our friendship I was the nervous one and Bob kept me calm—like Labradors do for cheetahs in a zoo setting. Nothing could rattle Bob, and I couldn't imagine how we'd manage without him.

But both of us were in for a shock.

After about 10 minutes of driving, we turned a corner and saw a line of people standing on the sidewalks all along a full block. At first, we thought they were waiting to pay a utility bill, or to collect some kind of a free prize since there were *so many* of them.

Then it hit us. We were astounded to realize that there were *hundreds* of people lined up waiting for something much more obvious, when I thought about it.

Us!

I will never forget our optometrist Taylor Bladh commenting, "I hope we are not in over our heads."

"Well of course we are," I quipped back, only half joking.

After we parked, Gaby instructed us to offload and bring our supplies in. She squeezed through the crowd and led the medical and optometry teams and musicians through the press of people and into the courtyard of the home, an old adobe.

When we entered, we were impressed at how large the courtyard was. But we soon found that the home was not exactly ideal. At only about five-and-a-half feet tall, the door frames were most definitely made for shorter people. So we'd have to be careful not to knock ourselves out on the top beams! The adobe home was also well worn. Several of the walls looked like they might tumble down if we bumped or leaned against them. We agreed we'd need to be careful bringing in supplies, and that we'd need to try to remember *not* to lean on or put any pressure on any of the walls.

From inside the adobe, we could see people's faces pushing in desperation against the metal-gridded, screenless windows. In some of the rooms as we unloaded and set up, we could hear the home actually *creak* due to the press of the crowd. Gaby looked as concerned as we did, and with the help of some of the volunteers, she managed to move the crowd back and establish a perimeter a few feet away from the house without creating a riot.

We assigned volunteers to various posts as we finalized the perimeter outside. In the courtyard we set up a reception area and a pharmacy. The bedrooms would make perfect exam rooms. We set up rows of chairs that had been lent by neighbors, and created a waiting area. We set the band up in the waiting area to entertain. About half our volunteer group was at the clinic site and there was a place for everyone to help.

Once we were ready to go, Bob and I huddled with our international team of medical doctors, Jan, Diep and Juan. We also met with our optometry team, Taylor and his technicians Chris MacDonald and Joyce Downing. We asked the group how they'd like to proceed in terms of selecting patients. The medical doctors told Bob and me that since each doctor could see at tops 40 patients that day, we'd have to triage to identify the most critically ill. Taylor said his optometry team could see about 60 people that day, and to admit his patients in the order they arrived.

We opened the clinic with optometry patients who began to move through stations where the reason for their visit was noted on an intake form. They were given a visual acuity check to get an idea about what their prescription might be. From there they went to Taylor, the optometrist, and so it went.

In the meantime, we'd begun to triage for the medical doctors. We'd sent some funds ahead for supplies, and Gaby had purchased tickets—the kind you'd use for a raffle—for this exact purpose. She'd counted out 120 of them and gave 40 to each of

147

the three local translators who'd walk the line with the doctors. It would be their difficult task to select who would be seen. The translator would then give out the ticket and explain that the person should stay in line. The others, sadly, we'd have to dismiss.

Gaby and I accompanied Dr. Diep and her translator, a young girl called Jeni (pronounced, "Yeni"). To my dismay, it seemed that every person we encountered had a desperate problem. Some had painful rashes, high fevers, or *vomitos* (vomiting). Some showed signs of being dangerously dehydrated. Many were weak and with so many symptoms that it was tough to get a sense of what might be wrong. One woman we interviewed had a painful condition that sounded like a urinary tract infection. Diep and I were shocked when she said she'd had it "about one year."

"Is it always this bad?" I whispered to Gaby.

"Yes, because these people can't afford to see a doctor even when they are very sick," she explained.

My heart sank with each person we had to turn away. We told some to try again tomorrow. Some *begged* for a ticket, so desperate to end their suffering. It was gut wrenching, and it took every bit of control I had to keep from bursting into tears.

As each doctor returned to their exam room, we began moving patients through to them. The reason for their visit and a brief medical history were recorded at one station. Our volunteers took and recorded each patient's blood pressure and temperature.

After making it through the various stations, all patients were seated in order in the waiting room, and then when it was their turn, they were taken to either the medical or eye clinic. Soon, the volunteers were shuttling patients to where they belonged in a remarkably orderly fashion.

Meanwhile, the band played. The live music at the *jornada* offered volunteers and patients alike a cheerier atmosphere than they probably expected. We also handed out bottled water, and sweetbread pastries. These were small things we could do to make

148

the patients' visit more pleasant, and to transmit the idea that we really cared.

Over the next few hours, the team jelled. And of course with a group of neophyte humanitarian volunteers conducting a clinic in a war zone, that night, there was no shortage of stories to tell…

$1 Cure

Patient after patient streamed in for eye exams, and more arrived who didn't have tickets. Many reported that they'd never before had their eyes examined, including men and women in their fifties and older. Our lone optometrist Taylor and his team Chris and Joyce didn't flinch and refused to take a lunch break. Instead, they took a few sips of water and ate a few mouthfuls of food at their posts. They wanted to see every person they possibly could before we shut down that day (and in the days following, too).

For the patients who needed glasses, we'd brought about a thousand donated by Direct Relief International, and the team was usually able to find a match. For those difficult cases, Taylor wrote a prescription and we helped with costs from a small pot of "emergency" money we'd cobbled together as part of trip donations.

There were patients with painful eye infections Taylor was able to cure with antibiotic drops we'd brought. And there were other cases he couldn't help, like people who had cataracts. We quickly learned we'd need to build a network so we could refer patients— *note to selves.*

In one case, a woman with long, dark hair in two braids dressed in a stunning yellow and white huipil told the team she'd woven the beautiful blouse herself about five years earlier, but had since lost her ability to see up close—and so, had lost her livelihood. She was 48 years old. The team was able to restore her close-up vision and ability to weave and earn a living again with something as simple as a donated pair of reading glasses, value, *one dollar.* My heart skipped a beat at her successful attempt to thread a needle wearing her new dime-store glasses. I watched a broad, joyous smile come over her face. Pure joy and purpose was

149

restored with something that costs less than a cup of coffee at a Denny's. Amazing.

In all, Taylor and team examined and treated *80 patients* on the first day, about 8 people each hour, rather than the 60 they'd thought was their max. This was a crazy-high number that no optometrist should try at home, nor would want to. And in the following days, they kept up the pace.

Soft Spots

Dr. Juan called me into an exam room to show me an example of the kinds of illnesses people in the area suffered, and how we were treating them. Our videographers Rudy and Rick were nearby, Rick with his camera in hand. They followed behind me, thinking they might film.

Dr. Juan introduced me to Diego, a boy of about three years old.

"The top of his head is soft and there's some movement there," Juan said. "There appears to be something alive under the scalp and we have to remove it."

His mother who'd already received the news looked fearful. I stepped over to offer her a hug.

Dr. Juan prepared an injection of lidocaine to numb the area he'd have to cut into, and before he even injected it, the frightened little boy began to *howl*. His mother was soon crying with him. The boy began squirming and tried to run just as his mother caught his arm. It was obvious that someone would need to hold him. Dr. Juan called on Rudy. He and Rick were so distracted by the scene that they hadn't been filming. Rudy looked like a deer frozen in headlights.

Rudy agreed, hesitantly, asking Diego's mother if it was all right that he helped. She replied in the affirmative and Rudy—a native Spanish speaker—tried to coax the boy to settle down, but it was no use. Soon, Rudy had no choice but to hold him in a bear hug. The boy let out a *blood-curdling* scream, the kind that only fearful children can. Rudy's eyes welled up, as did Rick's, and mine. It was a surreal scene for a bystander like me who had little experience being around a terrified child, and none viewing a surgery, minor though it would be. My heart raced and I broke into a cold sweat.

Dr. Juan administered the injection, then readied a razor. He gently shaved off the hair in an area on the top of the boy's head in approximately a two-inch square. Rudy continued to hold the screaming child, Rudy's eyes now squeezed closed.

Dr. Juan then picked up the scalpel and he began to cut. I felt a panic and my stomach turn a somersault. The last thing this scene needed was me on the ground, so I averted my eyes and focused on other things like I had in Flor's room in the Home for Abandoned Grandmothers. Here I focused on the dirt floor and the dusty adobe walls, and hoped the surgery would soon be over.

When I thought it was safe, I looked back and found that Dr. Juan had been right about something alive. He had already extracted something, and it was moving. I involuntarily grimaced at seeing it, a plump, reddish-brown wriggling blimp of a worm about an inch long.

"This is a bot fly larva," Dr. Juan announced, setting it in a small plastic bowl on a nearby table. He squeezed at the wound and to Rudy's, Rick's and my chagrin (their faces looked like they'd just sucked on lemons), out came two more of the wiggling creatures. He then carefully examined the opening to make sure those were the last ones.

"They are already through the skull," he observed aloud as he finished his examination. "If we hadn't removed them, this little guy could have ended up in very serious trouble."

Horrifying!

Dr. Juan fastidiously cleaned the wound, then stitched it up while Diego continued to scream and weep so pitifully that onlookers had gathered at the door to make sure no one was dying inside. Rudy continued to hold on to the little boy as if for dear life, his eyes tightly closed again.

When Dr. Juan finished and told Rudy he could release Diego, the boy ran into his mother's arms. Rudy's face had drained to white. Tears were running down his cheeks as he leapt out the door. I was tempted to follow him, but could see he needed some space to recover.

Dr. Juan sent the mother and son home with antibiotics, and told her to see a doctor for follow-up in a week or so to make sure everything was healing and there was no infection. Gaby explained to me that unless it appeared to the mother that something was going terribly wrong, she most likely would not go to another doctor.

"The doctor would charge her at least 50 *quetzales*," Gaby told me. "She probably works days for that much money."

At least Diego has antibiotics, I thought.

When I asked Dr. Juan about the case, he said it was unlikely there would be any complications, and that due to the child's age, the small gap left in the skull would likely fill in. This was a relief to hear, considering that the mother would likely not be able to take the boy for follow up.

I could see that being a parent who didn't have the means to keep a child safe from disease was the norm here in the Guatemalan highlands.

How painful...

Polio, Still

Later that day, Dr. Juan brought Sandra, a girl of 10 years old, to meet Gaby, Bob and me. He pointed out that one of her legs was shorter and thinner than the other.

"This is due to the polio virus," he told us.

"She will have to live with this deformity the rest of her life, and it could have been prevented with a vaccine that costs just a couple of dollars..."

We immediately let local health officials know about the case. The man I spoke to told me it was "almost impossible" that the girl had polio, since only 10 cases had been reported in all of Guatemala in 1990, none had been in the area we were working, and the World Health Organization was "on the verge of certifying that polio had been eradicated in Guatemala." No matter what evidence I presented, he was sticking to his story.

"It is *most definitely* due to polio," Dr. Juan repeated to us. All three of our doctors asserted that this health official was wrong.

I left the health official's contact information with the Fab Four. Nery later told me he'd tried to follow up, but couldn't get a call back. If it was for the lack of time, resources, or interest, it seemed that for local authorities, the case was closed.

Our goal for our first *jornada* had been to provide as many people as we could with high-quality emergency medical and eye care in the two weeks we had to serve. By the end—and keeping what admittedly was a grueling pace—we had seen and treated more than 1500 people. We had an inkling that we might be able to have a broad, positive impact if we could return and establish some kind of ongoing presence so that follow-up and consistent care were possible. The seed of an idea for a headquarters and clinic was already stirring.

We were on to something.

21 – The Gift of Ann's Shoes

ANN FINNERAN ALWAYS LOOKED well put together. She and her husband John were St. Matthew's Church parishioners who had come on this first trip to Guatemala to lend their talents. Gaby and Marcos had told us about a family who'd been made homeless by flooding and mudslides, and had been living in a cornfield. John would co-lead the building of a small house for this family of four. Ann was a hairdresser by trade, and on this trip, was cutting and styling hair for the very poor—most of whom *never* before had the luxury of such an experience. Ann was also teaching bits and pieces of her trade to those interested in learning.

We'd split our large volunteer group so that each day while the *jornada* hummed along, our construction crew could make progress on the small house which was located in a village outside of Xela. I was anxious to go visit, but had stayed at the clinic to solve problems that cropped up—like the morning we had no running water, or the time we ran out of small plastic bags to dispense medicines. Or when we ran out of deworming medications and I had to go buy them, or had an overnight invasion of roaches... All the usual stuff for this kind of work, I figured.

This morning at the clinic I'd been singing and playing guitar with the band, Paul, Mirella, Carla and Jeff. Rudy and Rick filmed as we entertained patients in a waiting area with our largely 50s, 60s and 70s repertoire in English (think Arlo Guthrie, Beatles, Eagles, America). Of course our audience couldn't understand the words, but their smiles made me believe they could sense our enthusiasm.

At least once an hour we'd repeat the single song we knew in Spanish, *"Un Millon de Amigos,"* by 1980s Brazilian heart-throb Roberto Carlos. The song tells a story of how a person gathers friends to sing along, and in the process, this song of friendship, of sharing, of love, and peace, becomes louder and more powerful. Together, they can get lots more good things done than they could have accomplished alone. It was the perfect soundtrack for our work.

Ann had been trimming and styling the long, dark hair of women and girls waiting to see a doctor who felt well enough to be publicly pampered. And she'd been doing it fashionably dressed, with make-up on her face that looked professionally done, and every hair in place. Her style extended to her footwear—tennis shoes that, oddly, I thought, were the talk of the Fab Four and other young people who had visited the clinic. They'd smile ear to ear when they saw her distinct, Nike Air Max '93s in all their bright-white, "Just-Do-It"-*swoosh*-branded glory. It was as if these young people had recognized a famous person or got their first glimpse of the aurora borealis!

The popularity of Ann's shoes was explained to me by a 15-year-old local, and requires some context: Bill Clinton was president. Whitney Houston's "I Will Always Love You" was at the top of the music charts. And Ann Finneran's Air Max shoes were being plugged by basketball superstar Michael Jordan. In Guatemala, Jordan was almost as well known as Mickey Mouse, and by association, so were Ann's shoes.

So, strangely, against the backdrop of long lines of people waiting at the clinic, throughout the day as Ann cut hair, her shoes had been the buzz. As young people would ask her about them, she'd lift up a leg to display one, garnering smiles all around and a swell of whispers in Quiché, the local language, with the words "Michael Jordan" peppered throughout. The music and Ann's shoes provided a distraction from the harsh reality of why most of the people had come—to get relief from the infections, malnutrition, and chronic conditions that so many endured without treatment for months, or years in some cases, because they couldn't afford to see a doctor. I was glad we were there, and that Ann had worn her trendy shoes.

Karen King, a volunteer who came to Xela AID by way of the Co-Workers of Charity, was a particularly organized woman with good ideas about how to streamline the way the clinic was being run. By changing the flow a bit and doubling people up in key positions, she had patients moving in and to the various stations like clock work. With the clinic running smoothly under Karen's supervision, I felt confident that I could leave and travel to the construction site. The work was taking place in an area known as *San Martín Chile Verde*, known for its fertile soil and green chili production. Ann, too, was excited to go and see what her husband John had been up to as he co-led the construction crew. Rudy and Rick accompanied us to film.

Gaby agreed to take the four of us to the construction site, and off we went in the dented Datsun. The drive would take 45 minutes on a good day, she said, depending upon obstacles we encountered along the way. Extra-deep and problematic potholes, floods, landslides, broken-down vehicles and a spate of other issues could slow us down. Like all other infrastructure maintenance issues in rural, predominantly indigenous areas, keeping the roads in good shape was clearly not a priority for war-time national and regional governments, and it showed.

Despite us bumping along, the road to *San Martín Chile Verde* was enchanting. It passed through beautiful countryside. Lush, green fields of corn stretched across valleys and hills. Cornfields blanketed even the steepest slopes. We passed Mayan men, women and children walking along the road in colorful, woven clothing. In some cases, every member of the family carried wood in oversized bundles on their backs, necks, and even stacked on top of their heads. This included very young boys and girls.

Many women carried babies on their backs, as did some younger girls. Some women and girls carried colorful, striped jugs on their heads—water, Gaby told me. Many were barefoot. Boys and girls led skinny cows and goats. Just off the road, smoke flowed from the windows of adobe houses. Large trucks filled with sugar cane zoomed by bellowing diesel.

Sting's song "Fragile" about the cruelty of war played on the radio as we drove along. "How fragile we are…"

San Martín Chile Verde is located at about 8,500 feet in *El Área Mám*, a region of Guatemala dominated by Mám-speaking Mayan people. It is known as one of the worst poverty belts in

Guatemala, with almost all inhabitants living below the poverty line and up to 30 percent of families living in "extreme poverty" on the equivalent of about $1 per day. In most cases, this translates to dirt floors, no electricity, no running water let alone clean drinking water, not enough food, and little or no access to education or health care.

Although I knew the statistics, I was still surprised to see the state of the homes, mostly run-down adobes or shacks made of wood and tin. I was surprised, too, to see so many children and adults walking barefoot on the rocky roads, which often were strewn with garbage, trash, and in places, shattered glass. I imagined it was a parent's nightmare knowing the risks for their barefoot children, yet having no choice in the matter, which Gaby confirmed.

"They have just barely enough to eat, and eating has to come before shoes," she told me. *What a choice to have to make.*

When we arrived at the work site, I thought we'd find other small homes. I was surprised to see nothing but a cornfield stretching in all directions. Gaby explained that a flood had completely washed away this family's adobe, as well as the adobe home of their immediate neighbors. This family was particularly poor, had no relatives to stay with, and so had taken refuge here, hidden among the stalks of corn in their field.

"A mother and her five children have been living here under tarps," Gaby described, telling us we'd soon meet them.

"They all barely escaped the flood. It is a miracle that none of the family drowned."

During the rainy season from May to October, this part of Guatemala gets rain almost daily. I'd read that these can be gentle and short-lived, or downpours that turn roads into rivers and cornfields to deep, sticky mud. Given that it was June, I wondered what it must be like for a family to live under a tarp in a muddy field. It was difficult to visualize, and distressing to imagine people living in the dirt, like animals. *Dogs in the States have it better than this,* I thought.

We walked through the muddy cornfield between what seemed to me to be exceptionally tall stalks. They were a healthy green with tinges of purple and brown and were heavy with large ears of corn that bulged, looking ready to pick. I'd never seen such tall corn, which, using my height to measure, must have topped 14 feet.

We followed a path through the corn mounds and then came upon an area that had been cleared by our team. Construction was in full swing. John Finneran was merrily working away with his buddy Mike Valles, and Murphy Tammaro, assisting. All were St. Matthew Church parishioners. John and Mike both worked in construction while Murphy admitted he was "not too handy," showing us his swollen and partially bandaged left forefinger which had somehow gotten between a hammer and a board, by his account. Murphy had been a long-time friend of Brother Simon and had joined our team in honor of our fallen monk friend and mentor. This day, and throughout the trip, Murphy offered touching toasts and prayers in remembrance, challenging us all to serve with the kind of gusto Brother Simon had. He'd left huge shoes to fill.

The remainder of our volunteers and a collection of local residents who'd come to help mingled together at the site. They had dug a footing, and filled the foot-wide trench with rock. They had built a wooden frame around the footing, and some were now leveling the ground around the wooden frame where cement would be poured to create a pad for the house.

There was lots of wood cutting and nailing going on. Due to language barriers (English, Spanish, Mám), there wasn't much talking between groups. There was, however, an amazing amount of cooperation using body language, and plenty of smiles and laughter that bridged our diverse groups.

One of the volunteers introduced those of us who'd just arrived to the mother and her children who were the recipients of the house. The mother, Catarina, was dressed in local, indigenous clothing, including a skirt and top that were in need of washing. Her general state was as you might imagine for someone living under a tarp, and mussed, black hair framed her broad, sunburnt face. Still, she managed a smile and shyly shook our hands. A little girl of perhaps 8, cuddled her two little brothers. The woman's other two children were older boys, Gaby told me, and were working in the fields.

The mother and her children were all barefoot. The family watched intently while our team measured, sawed, and nailed boards together. The little girl had an ear-to-ear smile that, when Mike looked at her, made him smile, too. (I saw him wipe a tear away as he worked.)

Soon, Rudy and Rick had set up their camera to capture the process on video. It was a joyous, busy scene with everyone humming along like bees in a hive putting that little house of hope together.

Construction went on for the rest of the day, and the progress was impressive. In the late afternoon, the little wooden house was completed. We all gathered in front of the single-room dwelling, along with Catarina and the three children. Then, together, the four of them opened the door and looked in. They walked through to the back door, looked out, then strode out, all smiling.

The mother then addressed the group, speaking eloquently and breaking into tears several times as she expressed her gratitude. Many of us cried with her.

We'd brought some tropical fruits and juices (a big treat in the village) and distributed them to celebrate. With a fresh slice of papaya and an orange juice in hand, Catarina commented on Ann's handsome tennis shoes. In a split second and coming as quite a surprise to the group, Ann sat down on the ground in the damp dirt in front of Catarina, and began taking off her coveted shoes, followed by her socks. She then knelt before Catarina, and lifted up one of her bare feet. Catarina placed her hand on Ann's shoulder for balance as Ann tenderly slid her very own socks and shoes onto Catarina's feet!

When Ann finished tying the laces of the Nikes, she told Catarina, "¡*Para ti!*" (for you).

Catarina at first covered her mouth, astonished. Her eyes welled up with tears, as did Ann's. Then Catarina spoke aloud a blessing to Ann.

"¡Que Dios le dé muchos más zapatos!" (May God give you many more shoes!)[12]

The two women shared joyful, mirrored smiles as they looked at one another then embraced in the aftermath of the gift. I felt a lump in my throat. I realized that in full-hearted giving, the line between giver and receiver vanishes and both lives are transformed.

The gift of Ann's shoes came on our last day in the village. It was one of those unexpected, deeply touching moments that make you want to pinky promise your best friend to never forget. It was a well-deserved emotional payoff for everyone in the group, since they'd worked lock-step for two weeks without a break.

Some days had been an emotional roller coaster. There is most certainly a sea of human suffering, and it would be easy to drown.

We'd been frustrated on some counts. We lacked some medicines we needed, and were short on prescription glasses. Our emergency fund quickly dried up leaving some people with unfilled prescriptions they may not have the money to fill. We saw people who needed various types of surgeries, and had no referral network in place. And then there were just the sheer numbers—all the people we had to turn away.

We were fortunate to have Father Peter and Brother Joseph on the trip for words of inspiration and comfort. Father Peter told us one night that he was amazed at how much we were accomplishing despite the stress of the new place, culture, and lack of some things we needed, "We are all undertaking the challenge in such a good way. Something blessed is bound to come of it."

"God never gives you anything you can't handle," Brother Joseph assured the tired group one evening. "Everything is possible with love."

When our two weeks had come to an end, I was both exhausted and satisfied. I was satisfied that we'd done the best we could with what we had, and that we had done a good job considering our level of experience. I was satisfied, too, that we had learned from the experience, and would be even more prepared next time.

For my part, I would meet with long-standing, successful help groups that worked in Guatemala such as the Peace Corps and the Red Cross. I would save time and precious resources by learning from their mistakes. Even before leaving Guatemala I'd added those meetings to my to-do list.

In the airport, a weary member of our group asked if I thought we had really made a difference. I remembered Mother Teresa's words about how she made a start by "picking up a single person from the gutter," and how that first action had led her to eventually rescuing 40,000 people from certain death in the gutters of Calcutta. I shared that story with the group.

"We're picking up our one person right now," Bob Rook jumped in, bubbling over with enthusiasm. "So, yes, we are making a difference.

"Am I coming back?" he asked aloud, rhetorically.

"You bet I am!"

22 - The Big Bite

You've abandoned your history books
Expecting easy money with your saddened looks
But those looks will buy no pity
With no detours to the city...
You will squeeze yourself of breath
And only bribe yourself to death

—Alfred Ramos,

Excerpt from *"La Mordida"* (The Bribe)

T HE WORD *MORDIDA* TRANSLATES, literally, to "The little bite." But it means a *bribe*. I learned early on working in Guatemala that some "little bites" are not so little.

In the States, securing donated medicines wasn't as difficult as one might imagine. The supply of antibiotics, aspirin, cough syrup and many other extremely useful medicines available to be donated is driven both by overproduction by pharmaceutical companies, and by shelf life. Medicines that are within less than a year of expiration are routinely retrieved from store shelves, and along with overproduction, slated to be destroyed.

Help organizations like Direct Relief International, Brother's Brother, and M.A.P. ("Medical Assistance Programs") International had figured out that they could gather up oversupply and short-dated medicines and distribute them for use in markets where the same medicines were not being sold, such as in developing countries. And to our good fortune, Dan Smith had added our young Xela AID project to the list of long-standing organizations approved to receive medicines from DRI. It was a real coup.

After we'd successfully distributed a first shipment of DRI-donated medications to Guatemala, Dan had been on the lookout for more medicines we'd need. He called me one day about a very large shipment to a war zone that had been cancelled due to safety concerns, and asked if Xela AID could use the medicines. They were short-dated, but included lots of antibiotics.

"Yes!" I replied enthusiastically.

"It's quite *a lot* of medicine," he emphasized.

"We'll take it!" I assured him. I was unsure about what "a lot" meant, but figured that given the lack of *everything* I'd seen in Guatemala, we'd find a good use for all of it.

With my unequivocal "Yes," Dan had prepared the shipment. No need for us to hand-carry anything. He slated it to arrive by ship to Port Quetzal on the west coast of Guatemala to coincide with the arrival of our second Xela AID group. There would be 36 of us who'd be doing both medical and optometry clinics, and beginning construction of a school in a village called *Loblatzán*.

Our recruiting efforts yielded someone to help us with our medical mission, as if on cue. Jim Mramor was a tall, good-looking, good-natured, can-do kind of a guy. He was a career nurse, and just what the doctor ordered as we worked to grow our medical missions. Jim was well organized and agreed to take on logistics for our next *jornada*. He had daily contact with doctors, and since we were looking to sign one or two up, he'd have opportunities to recruit. He also had connections for medicines, and I reasoned it would be good to have a back-up plan in case something went wrong with the DRI shipment. There had to be many things that could go wrong, I thought—things I couldn't even imagine.

Jim made contact with Gaby who helped him figure out exactly what was needed. She advised that we focus on antibiotics, deworming medications, anti-fungal creams, non-prescription pain relievers (like aspirin and ibuprofen), and cough syrup as top priorities. Jim was on it, and began collecting sample medications from doctors.

With the civil war raging on, Dan had clued me in that there may be some issues getting the DRI medications safely out of port. Shipments of goods coming from port by land were being hijacked and stolen by vigilante groups. Heeding Dan's warning, I did what any reasonable person would do, I thought. I called the Presidential Palace to arrange to talk to the President of Guatemala to ask him for help. Remarkably, the person I reached told me that a meeting could likely be arranged, and to come to the Palace when we arrived in Guatemala. So that's what I planned to do.

Jim had great success getting sample medicines. So much success, in fact, that his garage, as well as Sam's and mine, were overflowing with boxes. Not only had he managed to collect medicines, but he'd also gathered stainless steel surgical tools like those we'd gotten donated from a hospital on a previous occasion—many boxes of them. As another bonus he'd found incubators, three of them, that although in working condition were being tossed after a hospital had upgraded theirs. These would save lives if we could figure out how to get them to Guatemala. In the meantime, into our garage they went.

Where the medicines were concerned, we'd learned our lesson when we'd traveled with boxes on the first trip. They had second priority over personal luggage. And if they did arrive with us, they might end up in the airport's warehouse. At the suggestion of our friends at Taca airlines, we packed all our supplies in luggage, rather than in boxes. We packed a bag of medicines for each volunteer to check along with their personal bag, which would be in keeping with the two-checked-bag allowance. Both bags would have priority, and hopefully, would get to Guatemala and be delivered to us without incident this time.

I was excited to be returning to Guatemala. I was anxious to see Gaby and Marcos, but also, to see how much better we could do with our *jornada* after all we'd learned the first time around. Jim was a great addition to the team, not only because I had no medical background, but also, because with him focusing on the medical mission I would have more time to consider the project as a whole, and what we may want Xela AID to become in the long run.

The overnight flight was without incident, and I actually got some sleep as did Jim, and Bob Rook. We made our way through the airport with the group, then to the luggage carousel to see what we would find. Bob and I had told Jim about the first luggage debacle, so we had braced ourselves for the worst. We began gathering up luggage and were pleasantly surprised when, like we'd been told by Taca it would, all our luggage arrived together and was delivered without a snag. At 6:30 a.m. after an overnight flight, this was a great relief.

While Bob and I had dealt with the box issue on the first trip, our volunteers had gone through Customs, which had been tricky. Agents had made a fuss about random things they'd come across—like a hair dryer, a can of spray-on deodorant, a pair of tweezers... There seemed to be no rhyme or reason to their concerns, and they'd asked to see passports over and over again. I had since learned from Gaby that asking for a person's passport was a not-so-subtle hint that the Customs agent wanted to find a dollar or two discretely tucked into one of the pages. On the second trip, I was stubborn enough that I had planned to ignore these hints and withhold this *mordida*, and told the team to do the same since we'd eventually get through. In the meantime, our luggage was picked over from bras to undies and everything in between. In some cases, suitcases were opened and examined multiple times. Rather than a few minutes in Customs, it took our group more than an hour to pass through, but in every case, we did manage to escape the "little bite."

After making our way through Customs without handing over a cent, we poured out onto the street level and found Gaby and Marcos there to meet us as promised. They were in good spirits and excited to welcome Bob and me back, and to welcome our group of new recruits. Not wanting a repeat of the truck and broken-down bus issues, this time, we'd sent money ahead for a private bus which Gaby and Marcos had inspected, found in good condition, and arranged for us to rent—with not only a driver, but a driver who also was a good mechanic.

The reconditioned school bus that pulled up to meet us looked rather like the one that had taken me to elementary school, and was likely as many decades old. It must have been newly retired, since it had not yet been converted into a full-fledged, fully decorated Guatemalan chicken bus and still bore the yellow color and labeling inside in English.

When we boarded we found worn, green bench seats narrowly spaced from row to row, obviously, for small school children. But our private transportation, albeit a school bus for kids, was preferable to our situation the prior year. We'd clued this group in to our first-trip missteps and how bad it *could* go, perhaps to lower expectations. Nothing was guaranteed.

Gaby and Marcos had picked a place for a breakfast stop for the group before heading on to Quetzaltenango, but Bob and I had an appointment. We left Jim in charge of the group with Gaby and Marcos, and the two of us grabbed a cab.

"El Guacamolón," the cab driver stated to Bob and I when we asked to go to the Presidential Palace.

"Big *guacamole?"* I said aloud, translating for Bob and having no idea what the cab driver had meant—that is, until I saw it.

The Guatemalan National Palace is situated on one side of a large, traditional Spanish colonial plaza. You couldn't miss it, not only because it's the largest and most architecturally interesting building in the square. But also, because it's green, like *guacamole.* Thus, it's moniker.

Next to the building's color, the most eye-catching feature were the numerous young soldiers dotted along the face of it carrying very large guns. I still hadn't gotten used to seeing armed soldiers on the streets, and Bob commented that he didn't know if he should feel "threatened or protected." We convinced ourselves to feel the latter.

The cab dropped us off in front of *El Guacamolón,* and after asking several people for directions (including one of the armed soldiers), we found our way to a reception area and made contact with a woman stationed there. After a relatively short wait, the same woman who had greeted us ushered us to an office toward the heart of the complex. She opened the door to reveal a large, clean, space with little in it. There was a simple desk with a chair behind it and two chairs in front of it covered in sand-colored velvet. Against the wall there was a matching velvet couch, a bit worn around the edges, with a wooden table sitting in front of it. There were no paintings or any other adornments on the walls. There was a large cream-colored plastic mobile phone sitting at the very center of the desk, and on the top, right-hand corner of the desk, a polished wooden block with a writing pen sticking out of it. The phone had an antenna extending out of the top, making it two or three years older than the unit that had recently been deployed to me at work. I noticed how it had been arranged exactly at the desk's front and center, trophy-like.

A young woman smartly dressed in a business suit with her hair pulled back in a bun entered the room. She was followed by a well-groomed, older blonde woman in heels and a tailored navy-blue skirt suit with gold buttons.

"I present you to the First Lady of Guatemala," the young woman said in a loud formal voice, as if a declaration. She followed by presenting the two of us by name, in a conversational voice, to the First Lady. Then, she took her leave.

It wasn't the President, but there was a good chance the First Lady would be able to help us, I thought.

The First Lady motioned for Bob and I to sit down in the two chairs in front of her desk. We then proceeded in *Spanglish*. The three of us did the best we could, given that none of us were fluent in the other's language. It soon became clear that she knew exactly who we were and why we were there.

The First Lady listened intently, thanked us for the work we were doing in Guatemala, and said she and her husband could help. She also told us about her charities, and particularly, her focus on orphanages. She explained that in Guatemala it is customary for First Ladies to dedicate themselves to charity, and we congratulated her on her efforts.

The First Lady then made a brief call on her mobile phone and the young woman who had introduced us before, apparently her aide, entered again. Not sure what would happen next, we stood up, and as we did, a gentleman entered.

The aide then announced, "I present you to the President of Guatemala."

Surprised, Bob and I each shook his hand.

The President, too, had been briefed. He knew about our project, our shipment, and our concerns about getting our medicines safely to Quetzaltenango. He told us he'd already made preparations to help us.

"I have an armored truck, a trusted driver, and other personnel waiting for you outside," he said reassuringly, and in impressive English.

This red-carpet treatment was something I hadn't expected, and I told him we were sincerely grateful.

He offered a few words of praise for our Xela AID projects at a time when, he commented, "the Guatemalan economy is particularly depressed." He mentioned that monies coming in from the United States to the poorest Guatemalan families represented a large part of Guatemala's gross national product, and that he, personally, was grateful for this influx of funding. He asked that if at any point I had the opportunity to advocate on the Guatemalan people's behalf with those in power in the United States, that I take it.

I told him that I was not involved in politics, but that with our new project, I spoke often about the state of the Guatemalan economy and the great need, especially in its rural areas. The President seemed satisfied, and again thanked us for our work. He said the aide would take us to where the truck and personnel were waiting, shook our hands again and took his leave.

The First Lady then said her goodbyes, and asked us to wait in her office. We sat back down in the sand-colored velvet chairs. Bob shot me raised eyebrows like, *Wow, we just met the President and First Lady of Guatemala.* I shrugged my shoulders and smiled like, *Wow, yes we did!*

A few minutes later, the aide reemerged and this time, sat behind the First Lady's desk. She'd brought with her some paperwork which she began explaining. It was a familiar inventory list of the medicines in our shipment, topped by a cover sheet. I'd received a copy of the inventory from DRI before we left, and was surprised that the aide had a copy. *It must have been FAXed from the port*, I thought. I pulled out my matching copy.

The inventory sheet from DRI detailed everything in the shipment. I began to read the cover sheet and saw that it bore a stamp from the Office of the First Lady. It contained a small amount of text followed by a detailed list of medicines. These, the aide explained, were the ones that had been selected for us to "share" with the First Lady's orphanage project.

I must have looked as stunned as I was, since the aide said, "We are grateful for your collaboration," followed by the statement: "It *is* your intention to collaborate..."

I was dumbfounded and momentarily mute. Bob knew something was up, but I hadn't yet translated for him. The aide had presented the list and made her statement so matter-of-factly that I was completely caught off guard. I couldn't have imagined we would be asked to donate medicines to the government, and particularly, not the quantity and value of what appeared on this list.

My mind raced, thinking alternately in English and Spanish. If the first shock of learning we'd be "collaborating" hadn't been enough, when I looked over the list in more detail, I got a second shock. Products for children that would have been appropriate for orphanages—such as cough syrup, deworming medication, baby aspirin and baby shampoo—didn't appear on the list at all. Instead, it contained line after line of the most powerful and expensive medicines in our shipment, including Rocephin, a heavy-duty antibiotic often used to treat life-threatening infections.

Even someone with little understanding of medicines, like me, knew that what appeared on the aide's list was not the bread and butter of what would be used in an orphanage.

I felt as if I'd been kicked in the stomach. Was this what it seemed? Were those among Guatemala's richest and most powerful people stealing from the poorest and most disempowered? I felt flushed, and dizzy. What to do…

Bob and I exchanged glances. Not knowing how much English the aide understood, I could say little. Without telegraphing my distress, I told him that I was just looking over the list of what we'd be "sharing" with the First Lady's orphanages. An understanding came over his face and he played along seamlessly, shaking his head in agreement as if it had been part of the plan all along.

I pulled out a copy of a load sheet I had, which included values, and compared it to the First Lady's list. It was the first time I'd paid close attention to the actual value of the donations. The value of the full shipment was shock number three. It exceeded *$3 million!*

I showed the list to Bob and pointed at the total dollar value. I then pointed to the First Lady's list. We had a coded discussion masking our dismay as we both did an approximate calculation of the value of the aide's "collaboration" list. Unbelievably, of the total value of the shipment it represented at least a third—about *$1 million in medicines!*

I did mental somersaults to come up with a scenario in which we could avoid losing these important medicines, but there wasn't one I could divine. The warning from Dan Smith about the danger of physically moving items of value from Port Quetzal hours away to Quetzaltenango had been echoed by Gaby and Marcos. If they were accurate, we could be in for big trouble without the President's truck and driver, who I imagined would be savvy and cautious. I was stumped as to what to do, and couldn't overtly ask for Bob's help in front of the aide.

With a gulp and a mental holding of my nose, I signed the papers. In just seconds and with one swipe of a pen, *a million dollars* in life-saving medicines for those with stunning need was gone, most likely to be sold for personal profit on the black market.

I felt sick.

The aide, Bob, and I exchanged niceties. Bob and I were led downstairs. We dared not speak within the confines of the palace about the extortion that had just occurred, but shared disapproving glances. There would be words later.

In this case, it had not been classic *mordida*—a few dollars lining a palm. This was a BIG bite, and both of us were feeling the sting.

23 - Boys with Guns

BOB AND I WERE STILL REELING from the realization that in just a few moments we'd lost a million dollars in medicines, but we held our tongues as we followed the Palace aide to where we'd been told a truck would be waiting. Bob reached over and squeezed my hand and I squeezed back tears as they welled in my eyes. It was all so wrong, but there was nothing either of us could do, at least at that moment.

Shake it off, I told myself.

The aide led us to a place within the confines of the Palace to find, just as the President had said, a truck and a driver. That was a relief. That our "collaboration" had yielded the needed help to get the rest of the shipment to safety was of some consolation.

I noted that the truck wasn't just *any* truck. It was a Mercedes *armored truck* that looked sturdy enough to drive through a mountain if it had to. A man appeared from behind the truck and the aide told us he would be our driver. He looked to be in his late 50s, or perhaps early 60s, and was about five-feet five-inches tall. He introduced himself to Bob and I as *Kike* (KEY Kay), "Personal driver to seven presidents including this one."

Kike confirmed with us that the destination was *Puerto Quetzal,* and then back to Quetzaltenango. Agreed. In broken English he continued, telling us he was at our service and ready to head out at our leisure.

The first leg would be about two hours, he said, and our second would be four or five. He said he had room for one person in the cab with him. Since I spoke at least some Spanish and Bob did not, and speaking Spanish could be important if some unexpected circumstance arose (and it seemed they always did in Guatemala), we decided I would travel with the driver. Bob would return to the group, and I would catch up with everyone in Quetzaltenango.

Bob said he'd take a cab to where the group was eating breakfast. We said our goodbyes and with a *yeah we'll talk about all this later* look, Bob left with the aide. There I was alone with Kike, or so I thought.

It occurred to me how many interesting stories Kike must have, being that he had been, after all, driver to seven presidents. I decided that during the ride, I'd ask him. He pulled a portable step from behind the driver's seat of the truck. As he walked me around to help me get into the passenger's side of this high-riding cab, I asked him what kinds of trouble we might face picking up the medicines. And would the armored truck be sufficient to protect us?

"No, it won't," he answered to my surprise, stepping back from the door he'd opened for me.

"*Venga,*" he said, motioning me to follow him. He walked me around to the back of the truck where he then unlatched the heavy doors.

"What the armor doesn't protect us from, *they will,*" he said, motioning with his hand toward the truck bed as he swung open the doors.

There, sitting on the far-wall bench seat and on the floor, were soldiers—lots of them.

"Twenty," Kike told me.

"They are our back-up plan," he continued, smiling and adding as he pointed a forefinger skyward, "*Ojalá*" ("If God is willing").

This was a surprise. As I scanned their faces, I realized that these soldiers were little more than boys, perhaps 14 or 15 years old. Each held a rifle. They smiled, and several waved. I smiled feebly and waved back. It was surreal.

Kike closed the door. He walked me back to the cab and I used the step he'd put down to hop up. This was going to be an interesting ride.

It didn't take me long to ask Kike to share some of the most interesting experiences he'd had in the service of presidents. But my hopes of learning about such adventures were soon dashed.

"Confidentiality," he began. "It is part of loyalty, and there is nothing more important."

Then, he stopped talking. It was going to be a long, *quiet* ride.

Over the hours we managed to chit-chat about Guatemala—how beautiful and green it was, that it had 37 volcanoes and was a land of many diverse and interesting traditions. But truly, Kike was a man of few words and as soon as I stopped making conversation, he stopped talking. He did, however, turn on the radio, which we listened to for several hours.

At one point, news came on. "It is the First Lady talking," he pointed out. "It is about your project!" he declared with glee.

Unfortunately, between the static and how quickly the First Lady was speaking, I couldn't understand. Kike translated roughly the following:

'She is happy to welcome Xela AID. Your project is close to her heart. She is talking about the many government projects she and the President do to help the poor. She was "*encantada*" (roughly, "delighted") to add Xela AID to her long list of successful projects,' Kike said, smiling.

Though completely untrue that Xela AID was her government's project—beyond them lending the truck, driver and soldiers—it was all very educational. The way she promoted Xela AID as an extension of the government (no doubt to gain favor with voters), the hefty price we'd paid in medicine, and the trade-off of getting two thirds of the medicines to those who really needed it, were all things I had to digest.

When we rolled into the town of *Escuintla*, I had to use the facilities. I could only imagine what the bladders of the boys bouncing in the back of the truck must feel like. I asked Kike to pull in to the first place possible so that all of us could make a pit stop and get some water, too. As he was about to drive by a hotel that appeared to have some kind of a small restaurant attached, I implored him to stop, but he hesitated, and suggested we could stop later.

"I really need the bathroom, and I bet the soldiers do too," I protested. He relented, and pulled in. It didn't take long for me to see why he had resisted stopping here.

Kike parked and I jumped out to go locate the restroom. As I entered the apparent restaurant, I found women sitting on men's laps, some scantily clad and wriggling in ways that could only be interpreted as lap dances (or at least what I'd heard of them). A woman of about 30 years old immediately approached me and put her arm around my waist, apparently trying to start some kind of intimate interaction. There was no doubt in my mind that I'd unwittingly convinced Kike to stop at a house of ill repute! I gently removed the woman's arm, telling her, *"No gracias."* While I was slightly intimidated, it didn't stop me from finding a restroom.

When I returned to the truck, I found that Kike had not let the soldiers out, and refused to.

"I don't want trouble here," he told me. I could imagine that it wouldn't take too much for trouble to find us considering the boys' young age and the persistence of the ladies. We were quickly on our way.

Not too far down the road Kike found a *gasolinera* to stop at. When he opened the back doors, the soldiers jumped out like firemen on a mission, heading straight for a wall—an acceptable *baño* under the circumstances, apparently. Kike explained himself clearly, making sure I understood that he had avoided the awkward and potentially dangerous situation at the last stop. I conceded he'd been right.

It wasn't long after this pit stop that we reached Port Quetzal where I was impressed by how the red carpet was rolled out for Kike. Two guards appeared who obviously knew him, or knew of him, and immediately took us to our shipping container amidst many rows of similar ones. The guards opened it, and we were presented with an interesting challenge. The contents—stacks and stacks of medicines—were tightly wrapped in plastic on pallets that filled the container to the ceiling. The problem was that pallets are normally loaded and unloaded by special vehicles. No such vehicles existed at the port, not even for the President's driver.

"We will have to cut off all the plastic and take the boxes off the pallets a few at a time by hand," Kike declared.

On top of that, we'd need to separate out our "collaboration," Kike reminded me as he presented me with a copy of the list of items the First Lady's office had checked off. Considering the number of pallets and boxes and the work it would take to verify what was in all the boxes and match contents to the list, I could see this was going to take a while.

The soldiers, Kike and I began unloading by tearing the plastic off the large boxes. When we opened them, we found dozens of separately labeled small boxes inside. We had to read the label on each one to separate out the portion for the Palace, and there were hundreds of small boxes. *Argh.*

As we de-palletized, Kike checked that we had found every single item on the First Lady's list and had set it aside. We would load those items intended for the Palace into the truck first. This painstaking exercise alone took hours.

When we were done loading the Palace medicines, Kike worked with the soldiers to rope them in place, separating them from the rest. We then began loading the balance of the medicines box-by-box, trying to put the largest, heaviest boxes on the bottom. This took another hour and a half.

When we'd finished, Kike and one of the soldiers roped the balance of the boxes in place, and at the same time, fashioned places for the soldiers to sit. I was amazed we'd been able to fit in all the boxes and make a place for every soldier to sit. There was room to spare!

As we readied to leave, I considered my options. I could spend another who-knew-how-many-hours in silence in the cab with Kike, or learn about the soldiers. I told Kike I'd decided to sit in the back of the truck on the way to Quetzaltenango. Surprised, he helped me jump up and into the back of the truck before shutting the door.

The soldiers smiled quizzically and immediately offered me a preferred "seat" among the medicine. Each sat with a rifle across his lap, which creeped me out. I wasn't accustomed to seeing weapons, and especially not in such close proximity. I wondered if they were in some kind of safety mode. *Probably not.* Soon after the door shut, lights came on. I was relieved. At least I wouldn't be riding along in the dark with 20 loaded weapons.

At first, the soldiers were not talkative. I had to begin all conversations, and did so first by thanking them in my broken Spanish for coming to help with the medicines. Many of them laughed nervously. A bit later, I asked a young man sitting next to me how it was that he'd come to be a soldier. His name was Johnny. He told me he'd been at school playing ball with his friends when the soldiers came. They'd taken him—and many of his classmates—with them. At the time, he was just 13 years old.

"Do your parents know where you are?" I inquired.

"I don't know," he replied, shrugging his shoulders.

This had occurred, he said, about two years prior. Several of the other soldiers told me similar stories.

Although each boy spoke carefully in front of the other soldiers, I imagined that many, if not all of them, must be lonely and homesick. What 13 or 14-year-old wouldn't be? The boy sitting next to me had rosy cheeks burned from the sun and a look of seriousness on his face beyond his years. A faint pout and furrow of his brow belied his youth, and an unspoken sadness. I had an overwhelming urge to put my arm protectively around this young man, but under the circumstances, staved it off.

The journey was many hours. We stopped several times at *gasolineras* to use the facilities, and Kike gave me updates. It was pouring rain. He told me that we were moving along slower than expected because of the rain, crashes, and thus, traffic. I had assumed we'd arrive in Xela before nightfall, and I was sure Bob had, too. Each time we stopped, I tried to use a phone to call the school, but I couldn't get through. I was anxious about not being able to let Bob, Jim, or anyone at the school know we were running late, but were safe.

By the time we neared Quetzaltenango, it was almost 9 p.m. The rain had turned fierce and pounded down on the metal of the truck shell to the point that, inside, we couldn't hear each other speak. It had also gotten chilly inside. I was relieved when Kike opened the back of the truck to get me out. He needed me to join him in the cab to navigate to our final destination. He had stopped along a main road on the outskirts of Quetzaltenango.

I jumped into the cab and soon began to recognize landmarks. When I saw *"La Marimba"*—a large statue of an indigenous woman with Guatemala's national instrument of the same name, I knew we were just about 30 minutes out. We wound our way through an industrial area, and then into the heart of Xela and toward the Spanish school.

I figured that although we were late, at the very least, Marcos, Gaby, Bob and Jim would be waiting at the school. There could be others, too—maybe locals. I thought about the soldiers in the back with loaded guns, and how those who were waiting to greet us might be put off by this—even afraid. I asked Kike to pull to the side of the road, and told him I wanted to talk to the soldiers before we arrived. He obliged.

Kike opened up the back of the truck and I asked the soldiers to get out. The young men looked at each other, obviously not knowing how to react. They then looked at Kike who nodded at them to do as I asked. I walked to Kike's open driver's side door, and pointing to the rather large space behind the seats, asked the soldiers to please put their *armas* there.

Again, the soldiers looked hesitant, confused. All eyes were once again on Kike, who hesitated.

"Their guns will scare my friends," I told Kike. "They don't have to protect the medicine where we are going. There is no more need for the guns."

179

Kike paused momentarily to consider what I'd requested, then nodded his head to the soldiers who immediately obeyed. One by one, they walked almost ceremoniously to the cab and surrendered their weapons, carefully stacking them behind the seats. As they did, I made eye contact, smiled and thanked each one of them.

After the last rifle was in the cab, I felt relieved. Kike again loaded the soldiers and closed up the back of the truck, and I joined him in the cab. I guided him to the language school and the very large room just across the street where I was staying.

When we pulled up, Gaby, Marcos, Bob and Jim were all waiting with a number of volunteers from the group. They were sheltered from the pouring rain just inside the Spanish school door, and greeted us excitedly.

"Great to see you, Les!" Bob exclaimed. "We were beginning to think something might have happened…"

I told Bob and the others about how we'd had to de-palletize the shipment, about the road conditions, the weather, and then, about the soldiers…

"Soldiers!" Marcos exclaimed.

I added that they were not armed, currently, and just in time as they filed out of the back of the truck. Marcos was obviously startled. He eyed them momentarily, then seemed to accept their presence as they began to help us off-load the boxes.

The room where I was staying opened directly on to the street and we stacked the boxes inside. The process took more than an hour in the pouring rain. When we reached that roped-off section of boxes, I told the group that they were not to be unloaded.

"Why is that?" Marcos immediately inquired. Bob had not told Marcos about our "collaboration," and wisely so. We'd both seen that Marcos had a temper, and a disdain for the government. His attitude was understandable, given the brutal war and the living conditions for most rural Guatemalans that had fueled it.

I told Marcos I would talk with him later about the medicine we'd left in the back of the truck.

While we were unpacking, Marcos told me he and Gaby had been listening to the radio and had heard a speech by the First Lady during which she'd mentioned Xela AID as part of a government effort to bring medicines to the poor. I didn't mention that I had heard it, too.

Marcos was seething about the deception. Gaby, too, was clearly annoyed.

When the last of our boxes was piled into my room, we all thanked Kike. Bob and I shook the hand of every soldier. I felt a lump in my throat saying goodbye to them, thinking about how I would feel if I had a child who'd gone missing as many of these boys had. This was a situation I could do nothing about. But we *could* help others, and would. I was seeing the value of staying focused on where we could help.

After unloading, we were all soaking wet and exhausted. Bob, Jim and I arranged with Marcos and Gaby a time to meet with the group in the morning, and I was hoping to go straight to bed. But Marcos hovered, accompanied by Gaby, and the two followed me into my room. Marcos began to ask questions about the medicine we had not unloaded. I felt I had no choice but to tell them about having "collaborated" at the request of the First Lady's office.

Almost immediately, Marcos became enraged, and Gaby, silent.

"They'll sell the medicine to private hospitals to finance another mansion or trip to Europe while they take credit for helping the poor," Marcos railed. "This is the corruption that has ruined Guatemala!"

Marcos went on for some time. I listened respectfully. He had a right to by angry. He implored me to share the story of what he called "the extortion," with the press. To do nothing, he argued, would be to allow Xela AID to be used to nefarious ends. He would arrange an interview.

"It is the right thing to do," he urged.

On the long road from the port to Quetzaltenango, I'd come to terms with the whole ugly affair of the "collaboration." I had taken the pragmatic view that getting the lion's share of our donated medicines to those who needed them most was better than getting none of them through, which would likely have been the alternative. There's always in life a price, and a prize. The collaboration, the *big bite,* had been the price. The medicines we got through were the prize. And likely, the shared medicines would save lives anyway, even if they made someone a buck in the process.

"I'll need to think about it," I told Marcos, explaining my reasoning. But he was completely irate and continued to try to convince me.

"While one hand has stolen medicine, the other is using Xela AID as a tool to gain favor and stay in power. This bolsters the popularity of the corrupt government and damages the peace process," he continued. "It would have been better if you hadn't brought any medicine at all!"

Gaby had taken several steps back and was looking at the ground. I wondered about her opinion on the subject, but got the sense she would not disagree with Marcos—at least while he was in this agitated state. Perhaps she did agree?

I had vowed we would steer clear of politics, but somehow, had ended up smack dab in the middle of it over the medicine. Marcos continued on, now livid.

I tried to understand what it might be like day after day, year after year, to be faced with injustices such as this. Watching the richest and most powerful politicians of the country not only turn a blind eye to the basic needs of the poor, but *stealing* from them, and truly, murdering them. By the time I'd arrived in Guatemala, mass graves were being discovered and there was significant evidence that confirmed Marcos' claim that at least 200,000 Guatemalans had been murdered, mostly Mayan people, at the hands of the Guatemalan military.[13]

Marcos and Gaby were *Ladinos*, Spanish speakers with both Spanish colonial and indigenous roots and relatives. They were members of a very small middle class straddling the line between those who had enough to eat day to day and the 80 percent of the nation's rural population who lived without clean water, enough food and other basics. I thought about how these betrayals by Guatemalan leadership would have impacted Marcos on a personal level—the family and friends who had suffered and died through neglect and persecution. It helped me understand his rage.

But I couldn't agree with Marcos' prescribed course of action in this case. I wanted Xela AID to be able to operate in Guatemala for the long run, and didn't believe that aggravating those in power would help. It would certainly hinder. I explained my view to Marcos, but for him, there was only one right reaction, and one course to take. His view was black and white.

Marcos left before Gaby, still angry. Before she left, Gaby added. "It is a complicated situation here. He really cares. I know you care too…" She then took her leave.

I stretched to imagine myself in their place, and tried to understand. Despite best intentions, it's not possible to walk in another's shoes unless you've actually had them on.

I hadn't.

24 – The Press Conference

AFTER THE FALLING OUT with Marcos and Gaby, I didn't sleep well. I hoped the issue wouldn't keep Gaby from showing up to our *jornada* today. I got up and made a conscious decision that today would be a great day no matter what, preparing myself for what I dreaded most: *triage*.

It's the act of finding those in the most urgent need of health care and prioritizing them to be seen by a doctor. This results in having to turn other people away—people who might have a life-threatening condition detectable only upon closer examination. And the more successful we were at getting the word out about our *jornadas*, the more turning away we had to do. We couldn't help everyone. I tried to stay focused on who we *could* help, but still felt unnerved each time we had to turn someone away.

During this trip we would again hold our clinic at a private home. When we arrived, I was pleased to be greeted by Gaby who, despite the previous night's disagreement, appeared to be in good enough spirits. That was great news.

With all the medicines we'd procured, we had decided to do a joint medical and eye mission. As had happened before, far more people showed up than we'd be able to serve. We had two medical doctors and two optometrists, and at most, could squeeze in 120 people each day. The first day, our triage resulted in about 180 urgent cases, and we were determined to see them all. We went to work.

The clinic moved along without distraction until Jim came in to the break room we'd fashioned out of a bedroom. I was busy preparing cups of coffee and simple snacks to distribute when he told me there was trouble.

"Five police officers are standing in front of the clinic," he described. "If I understood correctly, that includes the local Chief of Police who is asking to see our 'permission papers...'"

I went out to speak with the officers, and Bob joined me.

We showed them a letter from the Consul General of Guatemala. It was a letter of invitation "To Whom it May Concern," that recognized us as an invited help group, and authorized our related help activities. When that didn't seem to phase the officers, I told them we'd been sanctioned by and were working with the First Lady of Guatemala (a true statement). The lead officer turned out to be the Chief of Police himself. He told me that while having the permission of the national government was well and good, we also needed "local permission." I was stumped. Thank goodness for Gaby, who pulled me aside.

"All they want is eye examines and some medicines to take home," she explained.

"Give them that, and they will be happy and leave us alone."

La mordida, "the little bite," had struck again.

"But give it to them in a way that is not noticeable, and not in front of the other people here," Gaby cautioned.

This time, I wasn't inclined to be stubborn. For the relatively small value of what we would give them, the "bite" wasn't worth fighting over.

"We would love to include you in what we are doing here," I told the Police Chief. Gaby reiterated what I'd said in better Spanish and a smile came over the Chief's face. He immediately walked to the front of the long line with his men, which irked me, and I couldn't resist.

"We are very happy to accommodate you, but see all these people here? They've been waiting in line for many hours. I'll need you to explain to them why you are going in front of them," I told him, while Gaby cringed.

The line, made up of humble people standing in their worn, colorful clothing, stretched out of our waiting area and down the road. I momentarily regretted what I'd done, thinking I had backed the Chief into a corner and might bring down his wrath.

But to my surprise, and Gaby's too, the Chief took off his hat. Awkwardly, his men followed suit.

"Me and my men are working to protect you and other people in this area, but we all need to have our eyes examined. We don't want to take too much time off the job, and would like to go first, if that would be all right with you."

Gaby looked stunned.

The Mayans looked around at each other and an old, withered man—perhaps the eldest in the front part of the line—took off his tattered Western-style hat and began to speak to the Chief.

"We understand that you are very hard at work, and we would be happy to allow you to go in front of us."

I was relieved. *Note to self: Think before I speak next time.*

After the officers were in line, I retreated back to the break room, Gaby in tow. I could tell she was miffed.

"I can't believe you did that. You are lucky the police didn't take you away!" she admonished.

"We weren't doing anything wrong here. We had all our permissions in order and it irritated me," I argued. I admitted, too, that I had gone too far in making a point. I told Gaby I would practice more self-restraint the next time.

"It doesn't matter whether or not you're doing anything wrong. Here the police can do whatever they want without anyone's permission. I think you must have an angel watching over you," she said.

I think she was right.

During that day's clinic, we saw all patients we'd selected at triage—many more than was reasonable. We'd started at 8 a.m., and finished at 8 p.m. Everyone who'd worked at the clinic was exhausted, but we were satisfied. Jim asked the team how many people they wanted to see the next day, and every single person working at the clinic agreed to keep up the pace. Amazing.

To deal with "little bites," Gaby suggested that for now and in the foreseeable future we should set aside collections of aspirin, cough syrup, Pepto Bismol, tooth brushes, toothpaste and other relatively inexpensive medicines. These would be our "collaboration boxes" for the occasion of future visits by police and other local officials. They were useful. The very next day, a new batch of police officers showed up and with a simple gift of boxes, and without any kind of exam, they left happy.

But the police who arrived that next day were not the only surprise, unfortunately. Press showed up, too, and not just from a single local paper. A television reporter, radio reporter and reporters from two newspapers appeared, along with Marcos. I feared the worst, that he had propagated the story about the "collaboration" with the Office of the First Lady. There was little question in my mind. As the situation unfolded, it was my turn to be miffed, as this was a full-on ambush.

Since I'd been a reporter myself, I knew what to expect. But my mind raced, thinking about how crucial the next few minutes could be to the future of Xela AID. At the same time, I stuffed down feelings of betrayal by Marcos, for now, so I could focus and choose my words carefully. I hoped Gaby had not known about the press conference, but that was unlikely…

During my PR career I'd often told clients it was important to "never do or say anything you wouldn't want to see as a headline." And also, that you must always tell the truth to the media. With a TV camera rolling, a radio reporter's microphone in my face, and print reporters poised with their notepads, I took a deep breath and began taking questions.

The first questions were softballs about Xela AID's efforts, how many volunteers were there working, how many people we'd seen, and how Xela AID raised funds to do our work. It was a television reporter, a camera-ready young woman perfectly put together, who, obviously primed by Marcos, dropped the bomb. She asked me directly if we had to "leave any medicines at the Presidential Palace that we hadn't expected to."

I paused and thought carefully before speaking. I looked past the reporter, and saw both Gaby and Marcos standing not too far away, listening intently. Xela AID's future passed before my eyes. How could I be truthful, if innocuous? I chose my words carefully.

"Besides the medicines we are using in the villages, we have shared some specialized medicines with the First Lady and President. Their help was crucial in making it possible for us to get our needed medicines out of port and to Quetzaltenango to do the work we are doing today."

Questions were asked at high speed and by multiple people at the same time, and I didn't completely grasp any one of them. I continued. "We understand that the medicines we've shared will be used for the good of those in need. Thank you."

I ended the interview.

I glanced over and saw that Marcos was biting his lip, fuming. Gaby was on his arm and expressionless. I had a knot in the pit of my stomach. I hated disappointing Marcos, and potentially Gaby, too, but I had spoken all the truth I could speak without poisoning the water for Xela AID and by extension, those we were serving. Getting us blacklisted for entry back into Guatemala or thrown out of the country now would not have served anyone.

I began to head over to have a word with Marcos, but before I could reach him, he whisked Gaby off down the street. I thought to follow, but did not—better to let this one lie. Gaby looked back at me momentarily just before they slipped into the couple's pickup and pulled away.

I didn't see Marcos or Gaby for several days. When they showed up at another *jornada* we were running, Marcos at first avoided me, and when we did talk, the conversation was difficult.

"I understand your decision not to speak directly about the medicines, but you will be here a short time then go back to the safety of your home in the United States," he said.

"We can't go back with you. We have to live with what you leave behind, and the impact may not be what you had in mind."

Marcos explained that letting officials get away with what he deemed as outright theft, rewarded them for bad behavior. It also made them more powerful with the funds they'd earn from sales of medicines on the black market.

"You are being complicit with their behavior," he accused.

I understood his point of view and his concern. At the same time, people we were serving needed medicine, and *now*. There were lives to be saved *in this moment*, and I told Marcos as much. We clearly had different priorities and had reached an impasse.

Marcos composed himself and changed the subject. He told me that he, too, needed medicines.

"I have friends who are sick and suffering," he said. "I would appreciate your help."

Without hesitation, I walked into the room where we'd stored medicines for this set of *jornadas* and packed up a box with a variety of antibiotics, pain relievers and other medicines in it. I delivered it into Marcos' hands and at the same time, expressed concern.

"I appreciate your passion, but sometimes I feel you may be involved with something that might endanger our team," I stated as a half question. "Our volunteers didn't sign up to join a revolution."

Marcos paused, then chose his words carefully.

"I wish the lines between humanitarian aid and political action could be as clear in our country as you think they are in yours."

Marcos then reached out and we shook hands. It was a stark departure from our normal, friendly hug. It was with such finality that I felt it a parting of the ways. *It is for the best,* I thought—*at least for now.*

Gaby told me as she departed that she'd keep helping us as long as we needed her to. I was relieved to hear that.

It was our last day of clinic, and when the last patient had been seen, we packed up and returned to the school and our host families. Bob, Jim and I went back to my room across from the school and sat down to review and assess the tumultuous past two weeks. Jim was frustrated about the medicines we'd sacrificed.

"It seems outrageous to have to make payoffs and beg to do our work in a country where an aspirin is a luxury!" he railed.

Bob and I didn't argue. We all had a little steam to let off, and we let each other rail. It was cathartic.

That evening we rededicated ourselves to doing whatever we could to stay out of politics and stay focused on serving those with critical needs. (Xela AID would stick to that important practice throughout the decades.)

The medicines we ultimately delivered on that trip were valued at $1.8 million. The precise value of the medicines that got away was $1.2 million. No matter what we felt about it, we understood that in Guatemala in the 1990s, there was a cost to serving those with great need. It was a fact.

This didn't mean that I hadn't heard Marcos' concerns. I most certainly had. From that trip forward, we would be prepared for the local, "little bite," but would make every effort to guard against our project being leveraged by politicians. This meant no more container loads of medicine, at least for the time being.

We would only bring in as much medicine as we could carry in personal luggage, and come as tourists. We would do our work in Guatemala quietly, and without fanfare. And in the years that followed, that's exactly what we did.

25 - Finding Luis

IT WAS OUR LAST DAY in Quetzaltenango after a successful two weeks of *jornadas*. It was a free day for the volunteers to stroll in the town square, explore the *"tipico"* shops, or visit the local meat market to see all the things we from the U.S. usually don't see at the butchers, let alone eat—like bags of chicken feet, cow tails or platters of turtle eggs. It was not, however, a free day for Bob, Jim and me as we faced the last major challenge of our second trip to Guatemala. The thousand-plus people we'd seen over ten clinic days had barely made a dent in the stacks of boxes of medicine in my room. Many of the stacks were still ceiling-high.

In the civil war climate, there was such poverty and so much suffering that people were commonly mugged for just their shoes and clothing. I sat there dwarfed by the boxes of medicines valued at many hundreds of thousands of dollars wondering how to make sure they would get to those with the greatest need.

We could take it all to the General Hospital, but I'd been warned by Gaby that there, the expensive medicines would most certainly be stolen and sold, in some cases by doctors no less. That was depressing to hear.

I could try to make peace with Marcos and see if he and Gaby would be willing to dole the stash out as needed through their school. It occurred to me, though, that such a valuable stockpile could do nothing but bring bad luck to the school. It would attract thieves and put the school's students in danger.

It was a puzzle, but I felt strongly that the missing piece was just within our grasp if we thought about it. Jessica Bubolo was key to solving the puzzle.

Jessica was a young, energetic volunteer who'd wanted to work in an orphanage during her Xela AID experience. Gaby had arranged that. At the orphanage, Jessica had met the proprietor, and couldn't stop talking about him.

"You *have* to meet this man," she'd told me, bubbling over with enthusiasm. "He is *amazing!*"

I remembered Jessica's excitement about this guy who'd not only founded the orphanage she volunteered at, but was also an emergency room and surgical nurse, and a social worker.

"And he knows *everyone!*" she'd described after spending a few days working with him.

Just *maybe*, I thought, this guy might be able to help.

I walked with Bob and Jim to where Jessica was staying and found her at home. I asked her to introduce us to this "amazing" guy, what was his name?

"Luis!" she exclaimed, and enthusiastically borrowed her house-mother's home phone to call him. Luis agreed to come our way for a visit.

We returned to my room to wait for him. He arrived about 30 minutes later.

Luis Enrique de León, a man of perhaps 30, was quite a bit younger than I had expected considering the impressive resume Jessica had imparted. She said that besides running an orphanage, he'd worked 20 years at the General Hospital in Xela. That turned out to be true. As a youngster, he'd started doing odd jobs there, and eventually, had become a certified nurse.

Luis was of medium height and weight and had thick black hair, a mustache, and a look of surprise as he surveyed my room stacked high with boxes. He perused each box, reading what little information appeared, and looked more closely at the medicines and medical supplies in the boxes that had been opened.

"This is *quite a lot* of medicine," Luis finally observed aloud. "We appreciate all that you and your group have done for our people who have great need."

He spoke thoughtfully, and at the same time, seemed somewhat amused.

"Excuse me," he finally said. "Can you tell me what your plan was to keep all these medicines from being stolen?"

I thought about his question for a moment, then replied sincerely.

"My plan, was to find *you*."

He smiled at my answer, appearing flattered.

It was not meant to flatter, and it was not a flippant answer. I meant it wholeheartedly. Up until this point, every person we'd needed had come along at just the right moment. Why not now? There had been so many coincidences. I guess a little of Sister Thomas Moore's faith had rubbed off on me after all.

Luis saw that I was serious. He then began thinking aloud about options for the medicine. He confirmed that given their high value, they would likely be stolen if delivered to the General Hospital. Considering the current desperation in Guatemala, the school could become a target if the medicines remained in this room, he pointed out. His solution was a clever one. We agreed.

Luis borrowed the school phone and called trusted friends with trucks. He asked them to meet us at my room, but at dusk to avoid drawing too much attention. While we waited, I filled Luis in on Xela AID and our future plans. I asked if he would consider becoming involved, and he answered "Yes" with no hesitation. Little did I know then what an important moment this was for the project's future.

At dusk, a small cadre of Luis' friends arrived. One drove a half-ton pick-up, a rarity for Quetzaltenango, and three drove smaller pick-up trucks. Bob Rook, Jim, Jessica, the Fab Four, the drivers, Luis and I loaded all four trucks with medicines, managing to stuff each of them to the brim with everything that was left in my room. Luis and I jumped into the cab of the truck he would drive. Our comrades piled into the other truck cabs and followed us caravan style.

We drove for about 20 minutes and pulled up in front of a hulky old building. On it, carved in wood, was a large, red heart with a crown on it. Next to the heart, I could make out an outline where letters once had been, reading "Hospital." I was confused. Had Luis decided to leave the precious medicines at a hospital after all?

Luis jumped out of the cab and approached the aged, oversized wooden doors of the building. A large, iron, lion-shaped door knocker was mounted on one, which Luis promptly used to summon those inside. After a minute or two, one of the doors began to slowly open inward, revealing a woman. She wore a traditional nun's habit in navy blue and white. I could not hear Luis and her talking, but saw her point and motion around to one side of the building. She then closed the great door.

"They'll make sure nothing is stolen," he assured me upon jumping back into the cab. He put the truck in reverse, then led the caravan behind the building where we would unload.

"Every single pill will end up with those who need medicine the most and can't pay," Luis assured me. I believed him.

From that moment on, I trusted Luis implicitly.

I still do.

26 - The School at Loblatzán

INSPIRED BY THE SUCCESS of the little wooden house, even before our first trip ended, our construction crew was in search of a project for our next trip. Our videographers Rudy and Rick obliged, and made a touching video to raise funds with.

The two had been walking around the outskirts of *San Martín Chiquito* when they crossed into a hamlet called *Loblatzán*. There, they came across the village's only school—a dilapidated, single-room chicken coop. Inside, about a dozen young children, perhaps up to seven years old, knelt in the dirt in front of large rocks they were using as desks.

The children were being taught by a young man who told Rudy he was just volunteering, and that he and local parents were able to provide only *one pencil* per child for the school year and a *single sheet of paper* for each child each week.

"With a school house of a certain size, the government must provide a teacher and some supplies," he told Rudy as Rick filmed what was happening inside and outside. "This school is just not big enough."

When Rick later showed our volunteer group the footage, we were stunned at the conditions. And as the image of tiny children sitting on the ground in front of rocks as their school desks tugged at our heart strings, the kicker was what was happening outside. For each child inside the rickety structure, two or three more peered through the glassless windows watching, listening, *wanting* to be inside.

"Would you like to go to school?" Rudy asked one little girl. Shyly, she had nodded *yes*, and began to cry.

This encounter moved Rudy, a 40-year-old self-proclaimed "macho man," to tears—caught on film.

"I have a little girl at home about her age," he told me. "Having the opportunity to go to school is so easy to take for granted."

While building a proper school at Loblatzán had been a project too big for us to take on in that moment, we hadn't forgotten the need. Rudy and Rick turned the footage into a short film to raise funds and invite volunteers to come help build a new school on the next trip. At the heart of the film were the children in their brightly colored woven outfits sitting in front of their rock-desks writing on their rationed single piece of paper with their rationed pencils. They smiled and giggled at the camera. How could anyone say "no" to sharing a few dollars to help them?

Over the next few months, Rudy, Rick, Bob Rook, Bob Rhein and I used that 10-minute film to recruit volunteers and to raise funds to build the new school. We set our return for Christmastime, giving us about six months to prepare. In the meantime, Luis and I did some research. We confirmed the size the school had to be to obligate the government to provide a teacher, and for good measure, planned ours to be a foot longer and wider.

We were able to quickly raise $2,500—half of our need by our best calculations (yes, a stunningly low amount). I was sure we would find the rest of the money quickly. After all, there is an ocean of good-hearted people who want to help others, just waiting to find a way…

At just the right time, we received a letter from a builder who owned his own company in the States. Bruce Riley of Rock Formations said he'd heard about Xela AID's work and wanted to join us. A rock artist whose amazingly life-like work has been featured at zoos and theme parks around the world, we thought he was quite the sport to agree on his very first trip with Xela AID to lead this construction project. And not only would he lead, but he pitched in the additional funds needed. It's amazing how quickly people and resources appear once you've set your intent.

❖

We arrived in Loblatzán on a cool December morning, the air wet with fog. Luis had contacted the leaders of the community who had rounded up parents of children already studying, and those who wanted their children to be able to go to school. Several dozen had arrived to help our volunteer crew.

Heavy machinery is uncommon in rural Guatemala. Without it, construction is undertaken quite differently than in the States, with digging done by hand, for example. When Bruce realized this, he suggested we find a local contractor he could work with. Since our budget was set, it would have to be someone who would volunteer, or donate much of their time. Even Luis felt that given the sagging local economy, this seemed a tall order. Community leaders recommended we talk to Don Carlos Mendez, a big-hearted local who'd long been retired. They told us where to find him and wished us good luck.

After getting lost several times, Bruce, Luis and I finally found Don Carlos' home. We knocked on his door and he invited us in to sit in his living room, which was sparse, and cold. In contrast, Don Carlos—a well-weathered man perhaps in his mid-60s—was warm and welcoming. Luis explained our predicament, and almost immediately, he signed on to help—*for free*. He humbly told us it would be his honor to be of service. And it was a good thing he'd signed on.

We soon learned we would have had a tough time navigating local block construction without Don Carlos. Luis translated as Bruce explained the dimensions we had in mind, and he told us what and how much we needed to buy. We left cash with Luis who told us not to worry, and that everything would be there in the morning (which frankly seemed highly unlikely to us, or even impossible in so short a time).

Bright and early the next morning when we arrived on site, we found that Luis, as promised, had managed to pick out all our supplies and get them delivered to the site overnight. I was beginning to see that Luis specialized in doing the impossible!

Don Carlos arrived with his son, an *albañil* (block mason) who immediately began the tedious process of measuring, cutting and hand-bending rebar. Don Carlos put the rest of us to work, first, leveling the decrepit chicken-coop classroom, which I found to be seriously satisfying. We then had to level the land—by hand. We did it armed with nothing more than shovels. It took a dozen of us the better part of the day.

Late in the afternoon, volunteers Bob Rook, Bob Rhein, Bruce Riley, Ralph McGee and I dug the footing for the building. In my case, villagers smiled and laughed when we made eye contact. Traditionally, women wear skirts, even when they are farming the fields. Not only was I *not* wearing a skirt, and instead, jeans and a t-shirt, but digging a trench was work reserved for men in this community. I was happy to model a new possibility, and entertain at the same time.

When it was time for us all to leave, Don Carlos left his son to sleep at the site to protect the supplies—something we wouldn't have thought of.

We arrived early the next morning to find a small, hand-cranked cement mixer onsite provided by Don Carlos. Locals had gathered around it, many not having seen one before since concrete is most often mixed by hand on the ground. Don Carlos' son led the task of adding all the materials to make the concrete, then began churning the creaky beast, while onlookers watched, amazed at the contraption. After awhile, he had a look inside, tested the consistency and blend with a stick, and signaled that it was ready. Local volunteers joined Xela AID volunteers in using buckets to transport wet concrete to fill the footings we'd dug.

One little girl dressed in a yellow outfit picked up a relatively large stone and held it carefully with both hands. (I cringed imagining her dropping it on one of her little feet, but no parent intervened to stop her and I quelled my parental urge.) She walked to the concrete-filled trench, confidently threw the stone in, then looked up grinning—so proud of herself. All eyes were upon her, and there wasn't a single person who wasn't smiling. It was the kind of moment that made me remember how much I loved being there and being part of important projects like this one that could have a stunning, positive impact on the future of this community.

Don Carlos was a champ. The block schoolhouse was finished in just four days. Bruce was one happy guy, and the rest of us were grateful to have found him and Don Carlos just when we needed their help.

The School at *Loblatzán* opened days after we left, and tripled the number of children who could go to school in that community to 36, initially.

Within a year, the community raised funds to add another two classrooms, and a few years after that, we added yet another classroom by way of a gift from volunteer Dr. Flora Johnson.

At this writing, the School at *Loblatzán* serves about two hundred students.

27 – Pirates

SAM HAD GONE TO GREAT LENGTHS to get time off work so, for the first time, he could accompany me to Guatemala. On this trip, after our *jornadas* in the highlands, we would hold a clinic at Lake Atitlán. I'd discovered the lake as the perfect place to bring volunteers for R&R after a week or more of seeing patients and other tough, sometimes emotionally draining work.

Arguably among the most beautiful landscapes in the world, twin volcanoes tower over the crater lake which is more than a thousand feet deep and spans just over 50 square miles. Towering, craggy green hills girdle much of its rim and are mirrored on the water. It is breathtaking.

We had found a little inn where our groups could stay at the Santa Cruz stop on the lake. The views were amazing, and they made up for the cold-water-only showers and the sinister-looking scorpions that appeared on the walls or ceiling of the rooms from time to time. It's there, at Arca de Noë, I met Karen and Guido. They were the official innkeepers of the Arc.

On each visit, the couple welcomed our groups warmly. Karen and I jelled and became quick friends. I learned from her that despite the inherent beauty of the place and the healthy tourist economy, poverty gripped the lake communities. She had asked if Xela AID would hold a *jornada* at the lake. Of course I agreed. She and Guido were in charge of turning hotel rooms into exam rooms, and finding patients. The response had been tremendous.

"Expect crowds!" Karen told me when I called a few days before we were to arrive. I passed her message on to Nurse Jim and the team, and we were all excited to serve in a new region.

The team would take a 6 a.m. launch from the village of Panajachel, the main point of entry to the lake, to Santa Cruz, one of the first stops. We'd start seeing patients at 8 a.m. I wanted to get a jump on the setup to make sure we'd be ready on time, so a few of us would travel to the lake and set up the night before. I left Bob Rook and nurse Jim Mramor in charge of the larger group, and Sam and I and several volunteers caught a shuttle to the lake. Mike Valles was a Spanish speaker and our tough guy for security, just in case. Janamia Thompson, also a nurse, would lead set-up.

Besides our personal luggage, the four of us carted along six large duffels of supplies. We'd made a point of bringing only one personal bag each, but even then, we stood out like sore thumbs with all that cargo. I'm not sure how we could have called more attention to ourselves unless we painted red targets on our backs. Truth be known, the duffels were stuffed with more than $50,000 in medicines and supplies, the equivalent of 50 years of income for many families!

We left Xela with plenty of time. But a sink hole along the Pan America Highway and several traffic jams delayed us, and we didn't arrive at the lake until dusk. Gaby and Marcos had warned me as we left Xela that we should not travel on Lake Atitlán after dark. We could have avoided that by staying in Panajachel. But if we did, we'd end up on the 6 a.m. boat to Santa Cruz with the rest of the team. This would defeat the purpose of having come early. Without setting up the night before, we'd never be able to start our clinic at 8 a.m. Delays meant we'd see fewer people, and have to turn more people away. I didn't like that scenario.

It was growing darker, but Santa Cruz was only about a 30-minute boat ride from Pana. What could go wrong? So despite warnings, Mike, Janamia and Sam and I loaded our heavy duffels and personal luggage onto a ferry, the only boat left at the dock that late in the day.

We set out on the placid lake just as the moon was peeking up. I figured we'd spend two or three hours setting up, then still have time to get a good night's sleep. My thoughts turned to the Arc de Noë and the greeting Karen and Guido would have for us— maybe some hot tea and a home-made bowl of soup. I noticed that except for the captain and his crew mate, the four of us were the only people on this rather large boat. Since fuel costs so much, boats usually don't leave the dock until they have at least a dozen customers. I found it a little weird they'd set out with us as their only passengers.

"We're going to Santa Cruz," I told the captain in Spanish.

He was just a few feet away and should have been able to hear me, but he didn't reply. Nor did he look my way, but just straight ahead out onto the lake. I noticed he was wearing dark, mirrored sunglasses despite the dwindling light. *Even weirder.*

The three nights prior, we'd held clinics in a far-flung village. It had taken two hours to walk there, and we had slept in tents with zero amenities. Sam, Mike and Janamia were talking about hot showers, TV, and the bliss of a night without bugs the size of dinosaurs. I knew from my previous visits that the Arc was comfortable, but modest, and had to break the news about the cold showers and that there were no televisions in the rooms. There would be no *cucarachas,* at least, but there *would be* the scorpions, as well as fist-sized spiders that sometimes vied for territory on the room walls. For this announcement I earned three stares of disapproval. I didn't mention how strange it was that we were the only passengers, or the unresponsive captain. *It was probably nothing.*

We saw the outline of the magnificent volcanoes against the darkening sky. In the fading light, men in dugout fishing canoes returned to their villages with their catch—mostly small fish and crabs, I'd been told. People descended hillsides carrying bundles on their backs, in most cases, their harvest of coffee or corn. Women gathered up washing they'd done in the lake and headed home.

We hadn't yet reached Santa Cruz when we made a stop at a small, private dock. We waited there a few minutes as darkness took hold. Two men appeared on the dock and boarded, but did not pay, apparently friends or colleagues of the captain. Once they were on board, the captain got under way again. Our group continued to talk, revisiting some of the experiences from our *jornada* during the prior days. Sam was not particularly at home on the water, and spoke fondly of our arrival at the hotel—cold showers, scorpions, spiders and all.

When I realized that more than 15 minutes had passed since we'd gotten under way the second time, I thought we might have passed Santa Cruz.

"Excuse me *señor*, but our stop is Santa Cruz," I reminded. "Have we passed it?"

The captain took his time, again, as if he hadn't heard or understood me. Finally, and although I'd addressed him in Spanish, he replied in broken English.

"No espanich (sic). *Tzutujil*," he said firmly.

I understood this to mean that he spoke *Tzutujil*, one of the two most common Mayan languages used around the lake. At first I figured he must not understand where we wanted to go. I tried several ways to make our destination and my concern known. It now became clear that the captain was ignoring me.

I let the others know that not only had we likely passed our stop, but that it seemed to me something was off. Mike, a fluent Spanish speaker, tried his hand at talking to the captain but couldn't get a peep out of him.

Suddenly, the two men who'd boarded the boat after us appeared alongside of the captain. They squeezed between Mike and me, and the captain, making it clear that no further communication would be allowed. We retreated a few feet away to where Sam and Janamia were sitting.

"What's happening? What are they saying?" the two asked nearly in unison.

"The men are acting as if they don't understand us," I replied, sensing now that something was very wrong. "They don't seem to want to take us to Santa Cruz."

"So, where are they taking us?" Sam asked. I couldn't answer, but only shrugged. The four of us talked together trying to figure out what could be going on, and hoping it was nothing nefarious.

About five minutes later, a clanging began. Soon, smoke bellowed up from below the deck. As the sound of the engine died down, the boat came to an abrupt halt on the dark water. Silence.

Sam shook his head in disbelief. Charitably, he said nothing. But I could imagine what he was thinking. We'd had a very strenuous few days of clinics. Now, we were stranded in the middle of a huge, deep lake in the pitch dark with four men whose intentions were unclear. It was not the introduction to Xela AID trips I'd wanted for Sam.

The captain and his crewmen walked to the center of the boat, then opened a door in the deck. The captain and one of them went below, apparently working to solve the problem. The four of us sat silent as the ferry creaked and bobbed on the water. Several times, we heard the engine struggling to turnover, but with no luck.

"I'm going to see if they need help," Mike declared after some hesitation, taking out his flashlight. He walked to where the two men had been and disappeared below, and the remaining men let him pass.

The three of us waited, whispering. Water sloshed against the hull. Sam, who'd grown up inland on the plains of Texas and wasn't a strong swimmer remained understandably uncomfortable with the situation.

"I think we should get off as soon as we can, no matter where that is," he offered.

I didn't disagree. I strained to hear what, if any conversation Mike might be having with the captain and his buddy below. I was surprised when the mystery men who had placed themselves between Mike and me and the captain walked over and sat down on a bench seat just a few feet away. These two most definitely spoke Spanish, and had a conversation in low tones, just loud enough for us to hear.

"We could kill them now and throw them overboard, and no one would ever know," one said to the other, who laughed.

"Yes, good idea," the second man said. "But we should give them a chance to pay instead…"

The two men looked over at us, waiting for a reply.

"What are they saying?" Sam asked. I didn't dare tell him, or Janamia.

I ignored the two men, for the moment.

As suddenly as it had died out, the engine sputtered back to life. The boat began to move again, but very slowly. It continued its journey to wherever it was going, which most certainly was *not* Santa Cruz. We were headed directly *across* the pitch-black of the lake to the other side, at least 40 minutes away at our snail's pace.

Mike rejoined us and told us about the engine's many issues. He mused about the ingenuity with which the captain and his helper had jerry-rigged it into partial compliance. He then noticed the two men sitting near by us. He gave me a, *Hey, what did I miss?* look while the two men stayed put, staring.

"We have an awkward situation," I told him, to which he nodded his head. I had a sense that the best reply to the men was no reply at all, which was working—at least for the moment. The men didn't say another word, and neither did we.

Creeping along under the power of the malfunctioning engine, it was nearly an hour before we reached the far shore. It couldn't have been any further away from Santa Cruz if we'd wanted it to be. We didn't arrive at a town or normal dock, but on an isolated stretch of shore. It was clear we were expected to disembark here. We all breathed a sigh of relief at being back to solid ground. The two men who had made threatening remarks took our duffle bags and luggage off the boat and threw them onto the ground.

I was wondering what to do next, and most importantly, how we'd get back to Santa Cruz, when a vehicle drove up. The late-model half-ton pick-up truck seemed to come out of nowhere. Two men got out.

The captain and other men from the boat greeted the men who'd arrived in the truck as we stood by our luggage and supplies piled high. After they'd conferred, one called out to us in Spanish.

"I hear you have a problem," he said.

"We were going to Santa Cruz and the boat didn't stop," I answered.

"Too bad you missed your stop," the man replied.

"I can get you there for, oh, I'd say, two thousand *quetzales*—five hundred each for your safe return."

Two thousand divided by eight *quetzales* to the dollar translated to roughly $250. I winced. Lots of little extra expenses had come up on the trip. Sam and I had chipped in to cover those, and he'd been a good sport. But we weren't rich by any stretch of the imagination, and this would hurt. I further figured that since the going rate for labor was only about 25 *quetzales* per day (just over $3), these pirates were trying to extract more than two month's wages from us.

"The original fare was only *three quetzales*," I pointed out.

"Yes, and there will be a three-*quetzale* boat going that way tomorrow morning around 8 or 9..." he answered. "You can stay here tonight and wait for it if you want to."

I felt relieved to hear this, since it at least telegraphed that they weren't planning to kill us. But it didn't bode well for our *jornada*. We had all the supplies, and the team would beat us to the Arc. We'd be delayed many hours getting started, and would have to deny help to people who rarely had the opportunity to see a doctor and may be critically ill.

Mike gave me a *we are out of options* look and shrug of his shoulders, and I glanced at Janamia who looked as anxious as I felt. Sam was stoic and stone-faced. If we wanted to set up tonight and start on time in the morning, we had just one viable option.

I took a deep breath, and told the man in Spanish, "It is kind of you to offer to help us at this late hour."

To Mike's surprise I then asked, "Might you be able to help us for, say, *twenty quetzales* each?"

The man eyed me, then shouted a few phrases in what I assumed to be *Tzutujil* to the captain. The two had a brief discussion.

"I'll get you there for *fifty quetzales* each," he countered (about $6 per person, rather than the $60-plus he'd first demanded).

"*Está bien*," fair enough, I agreed, and let him know that our money was at the hotel and we would pay his men when we arrived. He nodded his head slightly in agreement.

Mike translated to Sam and Janamia what had occurred. I knew Mike well enough to know that although he was holding his tongue, he was furious. Janamia was going with the flow. Sam, while keeping composed, was at the end of his rope, I guessed.

After our negotiation, I asked the crewmen for help reloading our luggage and supplies. To my surprise, they complied.

"You have *cojones*," Mike whispered.

But the next surprise was ours. We each picked up our personal bag and followed the men who picked up our duffle bags and walked *around* the ferry we'd arrived on. There, they placed the duffels not on the ferry, but on an open, 15-foot launch.

"What's this?" Janamia asked, aghast. "What about the big boat?"

It seemed the ferry was not available.

"There are no lights on this boat, and no life preservers," Sam pointed out. "How do you know they're not going to take the money we have on us and dump us in the middle of the lake?"

It was a reasonable question, and all of us had reason for concern. But at that moment, my mind was fully on the crowds of people who would begin to line up well before dawn to be seen by a doctor beginning at 8 a.m. sharp. A return from across the lake on a public launch (if we were lucky and one stopped at this remote location) would delay us getting set up and started by several hours at the least. We had four doctors who would miss seeing up to four people each hour we were delayed. Sixteen patients per hour, 32 for two hours, 48 for three…

There was also the problem of sleeping on the ground all night. It probably wasn't safe. Even if humans didn't bother us, the elements would. The lake is famous for its heavy winds and epic downpours, and we'd also be bunking with biting flies, mosquitos, and scorpions. Sleep deprived, we wouldn't be much use the next day.

And lastly, if we stayed, we'd have no way to contact the rest of the team. They'd be standing around the next morning wondering what had happened to us.

I couldn't spend the night here, and I told Sam so.

"You won't be able to do anything for anyone if we all die on the lake!" he admonished.

I felt sure that this would not happen (perhaps naively). I also felt the responsibility for the team and the clinic we'd promised, weighing heavy. I was clear about what I needed to do.

Mike and Janamia climbed into the launch, and I followed them. For a moment, I had one foot on the launch and one foot on the shore where Sam stood his ground. I told him that I supported him staying there, if that's what he needed to do, but that I must go.

"I'm sorry," I told him, and I was, truly. I hated being in a position where I had to choose between the sensibilities of someone I loved and a mission I was passionate about. It was a horrible feeling, like a rag-doll being pulled in two directions, the seams beginning to tear.

Without speaking a word, Sam got into the launch. One of the crewmen followed him and the other pushed us off onto the lake, then jumped in. The motor revved and with a roar we sped off into the darkness.

We arrived safely at the Arc. The crewmen helped unload our luggage on the dock, and I paid them as promised.

Karen was distraught when we told her what had happened. She said that encounters like this with what amounted to pirates on the lake were becoming more common, and that recently, there had been a spate of robberies. She was relieved we were unharmed, and quickly got us to our rooms. She followed up with the hot tea I'd been looking forward to. But no amount of hot tea could sooth the frayed nerves and angst that fueled the difficult and emotional discussion Sam and I had in our room that night. He was reflecting not only on the dangers we'd faced that night on the lake, but thinking about what else could happen to me in Guatemala in the future.

I mostly listened. I couldn't defend my actions. I couldn't convey how deeply I'd been touched by the people in the communities we were serving, and the intensely gratifying feeling of the work itself. I couldn't communicate what it all had come to mean in my life. I was at a loss for words.

The conversation went in a direction I had not predicted, but maybe should have. Sam told me he could no longer live with the uncertainty, and related, the intense worry that he was experiencing because of my work in a war zone. I saw his point, and understood it completely. I imagined I would have the same worry and feel the same way if the tables were turned and it was my spouse working in the same conditions. At the same time, I was clear about my commitment to this work. It had already become, and would remain, a cornerstone of my life. We were at an impasse. My heart ached in my chest.

We chose separate beds and laid down to go to sleep. I felt miles away, in a kind of altered state—shell-shocked, like a bomb had just gone off and I was still assessing if I still had all my parts or if something was missing. I laid there thinking in circles, feeling clear about my future, and at the same time, feeling confused, sad, and sorry for myself.

By the time I dozed off to sleep, the dust had settled. I *heard* Sam—he could not live this way. I knew I couldn't live any other way. It had sunk in that I couldn't have both my life with Sam and my work in Guatemala, and that quite unexpectedly, my life would be changing.

Not long after that night, Sam and I parted ways, amicably. Life is too short to make new regrets or enemies. He is a kind and caring human being, and I recall our time together fondly.

Years later, my therapist friend Dorothy Satten shared her thinking on why, even when people love one another, their marriage can fail. "For a marriage to work, you must not only love one another, but also, be able to build a life together that both of you want."

Such a powerful insight. I filed that one away for future reference.

28 - Snails to Boil

URING OUR VOLUNTEER GROUP'S RESPITE at the Arc about a year after the pirate incident, I met Rosa. I sat in a hammock and watched her. She was a wisp of a little girl, maybe five years old. She crouched on a rock on the shore and peered down into the water, the tips of her long, black hair dipping in as she reached for something. What she plucked from the water, she then put into a small bucket she was carrying. I wondered what she was collecting. Was it a child's game, or something more important?

Curiosity soon got the best of me and I walked over to her, made eye contact and smiled. I introduced myself, and she said in Spanish that her name was Rosa. I asked what she was collecting, and she showed me the inside of her bucket which contained what appeared to be a pile of little black stones. She spoke very seriously as she explained to me in detail what she'd been fishing from the water.

"This is what we'll have for dinner," she said, holding the bucket closer to my face. I saw that the black objects were not stones at all, but black snails, slightly smaller than dime-sized.

"My mother will boil them to make a soup," Rosa explained.

It didn't sound particularly appetizing, but I could imagine it—snails are protein, after all. I wondered how many she'd need to feed the family.

"There is my mother and father and my brother and me, so I have to fill up half the bucket," she said.

Not wanting to deter Rosa from her task, I moved along the rocks with her as she sought out more snails.

"What do you want to be when you grow up?" I asked.

"I will be a weaver like my mother and my grandmother," she answered, with clarity beyond her years. "There is nothing else to be."

I told her that it was wonderful that she'd be a weaver—an artist—like her mother and grandmother. She nodded yes, and gave a slight smile at the encouragement.

I asked her about the lake, and what her life was like here. In reply, I got more than I'd expected.

"The lake is where the world began," Rosa told me. Her people, the *Kaqchiquel,* and all other people on the earth, were born from the waters of Lake Atitlán. It happened *"very* long ago" she emphasized, when "a great volcano exploded and the lake was born." She said that one day, the world would end in the same way—with a great, volcanic explosion right there on the lake. Everyone—her mother, father, brother, and everyone else she knew, like me, and people she didn't know, too, were all going to die that day.

"Because we're all going to be together that day, I am not afraid," she told me bravely.

Rosa was so enchanting that I returned to the hotel to get our filmmakers, Rudy (who was fluent in Spanish) and Rick, who had joined us once again. When I brought them to meet her, she was happy to share her stories again.

The two men were as enchanted by Rosa as I had been. During the filming, she expanded on the plans for her crawling catch. Her mother's recipe included *"aqua, sal, yerbas y fuego"* (water, salt, herbs and fire). She repeated the creation and end-of-world stories that had been told to her by her mother, she thought, but wasn't sure. "Everyone here knows the stories," she assured us. "It could have been anyone who told me…"

Near the end of the filmed interview, Rosa announced that she was not in school, nor would her parents send her even if she wanted to go. "School is only for boys—that's what my father says," she concluded.

That didn't sit well with me, Rick, or Rudy who was the father of not just one but four daughters.

We eventually said goodbye to little Rosa who then began up a steep, dirt road that led to her home in the hills above in the village of Santa Cruz. But she wasn't out of mind.

Karen Edwards was a social worker from Canada who'd founded a half-way house for women recovering from addiction. Colleen Dodds was a retired school teacher and stained glass artist, among other talents. My two Canadian friends had joined us to run an optometry clinic. (They later became regulars on our trips, and joined the Board.) When Karen and Colleen came to breakfast, Rosa was the topic. Rudy and Rick shared the footage they'd shot of her speaking, and the two women fell in love with the little girl. When Karen saw the footage of Rosa repeating her father's claim that "School is just for boys," she was outraged.

"It's great that she's picking up snails to help feed the family, but that little girl should also be in school!" Karen effused, matter-of-factly. She was a smart, accomplished and powerful woman with a huge heart and strong opinions she wasn't shy about expressing them. There weren't many arguments I'd seen her lose. *Lord have mercy on Rosa's father if Karen ever gets ahold of him*, I thought.

Being a retired school teacher, Colleen had her own strong views about the need to educate both boys and girls. The two spoke privately together, then came to an agreement: they would sponsor Rosa to be in school, assuming that we could find her again, get her parents to agree, and that Xela AID would agree to distribute the funds to her. Deal.

Finding Rosa wasn't too difficult. We knew a local boatman named Fidel, and after I described Rosa to him and shared her name, he sent word up the hill to the village. We were still sitting at the breakfast table when Rosa materialized. I translated for Karen and Colleen who were thrilled to meet her. Rosa was a delightful little girl who radiated sweetness and quickly warmed up to the two women. If she could grow up to do any job in the village, she would be a teacher, she told them.

When Karen had heard enough, she began to lecture. "You should be in school following your dreams and we're going to make that happen!"

When I translated, Rosa's face lit up with an ear-to-ear smile. It was time to go meet dad.

The path to the village of Santa Cruz de Laguna, more than 300 feet above the shoreline, was muddy, and steep. Karen, Colleen and I trudged up following Rosa who seemed impervious to the slipping and sliding that challenged us. On the way up, we saw spectacular views of the volcanoes Atitlán, Tolimán and San Pedro rising from the crater. Below, fisherman floated in their dugout canoes, women washed clothes and children played. The sky was crystal blue with no clouds except for white wisps that gathered around San Pedro's peak. The day was flawless.

Sweating from the steep, hour-long climb and panting from the altitude (5400 feet above sea level), we finally reached the village. We passed a few modest homes made of wooden planks and emerged at the town square—a beautifully aged, Spanish-colonial white church at the backside of a small soccer field. It was flanked by a school, a municipal building, and homes on the four sides. The far side was dotted with simple wooden houses that were elevated, reached by a path up. Rosa pointed across the soccer field at one house in particular.

"Where the birds are flying in and out of the holes beside our door," she said.

The family raised pigeons, she explained. I wasn't sure what they did with the pigeons, but thought they must eat them. I didn't ask. (This assumption was later confirmed.)

We passed through the square in front of the church which was, according to our hosts Karen and Guido at the Arc, built in the 16th Century. I climbed concrete steps up to the massive wooden doors which were wide open. Natural light streamed through to light the old building's well-worn interior. The altar featured a woman with her arms outstretched and a half dozen candles at her feet. She looked half-sized, had been skillfully carved, and was beautifully gowned.

"She is Saint Elena," Rosa told us, wistfully. "She is beautiful."

Rosa's gaze was adoring and her tone reverent as she spoke of the carved likeness.

"Is your family Catholic?" I asked. Rosa paused for a moment and thought.

"No," she finally replied. "My mother and I are weavers and I don't know what my father is."

So much for religion when you're five.

Sunlight through small windows of the church bathed the old wooden pews, and along the walls, carved icons of long-dead saints and conquerors were illuminated in sepia tones like a very old photo. The church alone was worth the climb.

We exited, and made our way to the path to Rosa's house. We followed her up about ten thin, steep stairs to the wooden door which she opened and walked through, motioning us to follow. I didn't want to startle her parents by suddenly appearing in the family's home, and suggested we wait outside until she brought her parents to us. Rosa agreed and disappeared inside, leaving us momentarily to watch the comings and goings of the pigeons through the row of openings in the house's front wall.

I'd heard about lung disease associated with keeping birds in a confined area, and wondered about the family's long-term health.

A minute or so later, a woman appeared with Rosa who she introduced as her mother. When her mother spoke, it was in *Kaqchiquel*, rather than Spanish. (Rosa, like many children at the lake, a tourist destination, regularly interact with visitors and so become bi- and even tri-lingual while still very young.)

Rosa's mother was a woman of about five feet tall with skin the rich brown tone of her daughter's. She wore her hair up, neatly wrapped around her head in stunning blue fabric, like a halo. Her red *huipil* had a flower design on the top half—emblematic of the community of Santa Cruz.

After exchanging greetings, I translated Karen and Colleen's intentions from English into Spanish for Rosa, who translated them for her mother from Spanish to *Kaqchiquel.* Her mother listened politely, then told us we'd need to speak with her husband regarding this subject. While she remained stoic, a slight smile shown briefly at the corners of her mouth, making me think she was happy at the prospect of Rosa going to school, something she herself had never gotten to do.

We stood on the steps a bit awkwardly after the initial exchange, then Rosa's mother invited us in to speak with her husband. We followed her into the house with anticipation.

The family's home was modest—dirt floors, a combination living room-kitchen-dining room, and what looked like a single bedroom off the main room. There was no electricity in use that I could see. Laundry hung on lines that took advantage of the sun streaming through where the tin roof ended. Along an entire wall, pigeons nested in cubbyholes, cooing intently. Their roosting space filled a quarter of the "living room" space of the home.

There was a rustic kitchen where piles of vegetables dotted the countertop. There was a well-used wooden table and a few chairs, where Rosa's mother invited us to sit down. A young chicken strolled through, which Rosa quickly caught and cradled in her arms. I was delighted to be in her home getting a taste of real life (as compared to tourists' life) on Lake Atitlán. It was eye-opening.

Rosa's father was nowhere to be seen, so I reasoned he must be in the apparent room off the combination living room-pigeon coup. Just as we sat down, he appeared in the doorway of that room, and the three of us stood back up to greet him.

Rosa's father, like her mother, was thin. He looked to be perhaps ten years older than his wife, and moved stiffly, as if in pain. I guessed that he was not a well man.

When he arrived at the table, Karen reached out to shake his hand with full enthusiasm as was her style.

"I'm pleased to meet you," I translated to Rosa, who translated to her father, and then translated her father's reply greeting to me and me to Karen as the entire conversation would go.

The three of us took our seats again. Rosa's father and mother stood. Rosa kneeled next to us on the dirt floor, still cradling the chicken. Her father did not initiate any questions, nor did Rosa's mother share any information with him. He waited for us to speak. It was going to be an interesting discussion.

Karen quickly got to the heart of the matter of why we were there. When Karen was convinced that through our translation loop Rosa's father fully understood her and Colleen's intent to sponsor Rosa to go to school, she stopped talking and waited to hear his reply. He was quiet longer than I expected, and his answer was even more unexpected.

"It is kind of you to offer, but Rosa doesn't need to go to school. If you would like, you can sponsor my son, Adalberto."

Rosa looked down at the chicken and spoke in a dull tone as she translated to me in Spanish. She was clearly disappointed, and so was I. In my short time in Guatemala I had several times come across the attitude that girls didn't need to go to school since they were being raised to work in the home and have babies. 'Everything a girl needs to know, she can learn from her mother at home,' came out of the mouth of a young male teacher at the purportedly progressive Spanish school I attended, no less. I was hoping we could change that idea, at least in this case.

Before I translated this to Karen and Colleen, I glanced at little Rosa. She was now fixated on the floor and silent. There were so many negative messages contained in "Rosa doesn't need to go to school," and in her father reserving that privilege for her brother. I wondered how I might have been impacted if I'd heard my own father talk about me that way. I felt an uneasiness in my stomach. Such words coming from my own father might have made me feel less valuable and capable than a brother, or than all boys. I was hoping that Rosa had some fight in her and was still young enough that she hadn't fully bought in to her father's storyline.

After I'd translated, Karen brought her right hand to her chin and rubbed it between her thumb and forefinger. She exchanged a few words with Colleen, which I did not translate, then her eyes narrowed and communicated, *I have something very serious to say.* She asked me to translate her proposal word for word:

"Sir, we would be happy to sponsor your son," she began, causing Rosa's father to crack a subtle smile. "However," she continued, "We will sponsor your son *only* so long as Rosa is in school.

"If this is agreeable to you, we will also sponsor Rosa," Karen concluded.

Rosa's father was quiet for a moment, then repeated, "You will sponsor our son Adalberto as long as Rosa is in school, and you will sponsor her too…"

I affirmed that was the deal.

Another silence ensued as her father considered the proposal. I looked at Rosa who was still looking down at the chicken, motionless.

Breaking the silence, her father finally replied, *"Estoy de acuerdo"* (I agree).

Rosa jumped up as if resurrected, startling the chicken which clucked and fled. She smiled, if slightly, and hugged her father around his waist briefly before moving on to her mother. Shyly, with what seemed like some prompting in *Kaqchiquel* from her mother, Rosa thanked the two women who beamed enthusiastically.

The First Two Kids

On girls reading books, Nicholas Kristof of the *New York Times* wrote, "There's no force more powerful to transform a society."[14] Adalberto and Rosa were the first children to receive Xela AID educational scholarships, and Rosa was just the first of many girls. Little did Karen, Colleen or I know that day in Santa Cruz how significant this moment had been, and what it would begin.

29 – Oscar

DURING A VOLUNTEER TRIP IN 1994, Luis had arranged for a plastic surgeon we'd brought from the U.S. to see burn patients at Xela General Hospital. On this, our last day in Xela, Dr. John Padilla made a point to catch me after our group dinner and make a request.

"There's a young man I saw today who I can't treat here," he told me. "Do you think you can arrange for him to come to the States?"

I told John it may be possible, and if so, could take awhile. I would look into the requirements for a medical visa once I had details about this young man. I would need a treatment plan, too, which John agreed to supply.

"How long of a stay will he need?" I asked.

John thought for a moment, then said, "More or less—about *ten years.*"

He was dead serious.

Dr. John then strode off to his room, leaving me with a thousand questions. Luis filled me in later that evening.

The young man was Oscar de León Xicará from the barrio *La Cuchilla* on the outskirts of Xela. Luis had been contacted by Oscar's mother on the morning of our last day in Xela, and had put him on a waiting list to be seen if there was time. John had a few minutes to spare, and squeezed him in. I couldn't have known then how fortuitous this moment would be for my life...

Xela AID had been operating for just a few years, but through Luis' contacts, had already fashioned a small local network of doctors to refer patients to for low- or no-cost follow up. Oscar's was a rare case where a local referral was unlikely, if not impossible.

Dr. John had done some research, and hadn't found plastic surgeons or doctors with a reconstructive specialty in Xela. He'd found only a handful of specialists in Guatemala City, four hours away. Even if we could have located a local burn specialist, without some connection, we'd have a snowball's chance in hell to get services donated. Paying was not an option, since our young organization was fueled primarily by volunteers, donations and good will and had precious few financial resources. Among the many uncertainties, one thing was clear—Dr. John was committed to helping Oscar for the long term.

After some inquiries, I figured out that all we'd need to make this happen for Oscar was for the U.S. Embassy to agree to issue a visa, to find someone to sponsor his airfare, to find a host family in the States for a long-term stay, to find an anesthesiologist willing to donate time and a hospital willing to donate facilities; and, to get a few more stars to align as obstacles came up. I took it as a personal challenge to make it happen, if that's what Oscar, his parents and Dr. John wanted. I felt it was important for me to touch bases with Oscar's parents, Rafaela and Marco Sr., to hear their wishes first hand.

I visited the couple at their small block home in *La Cuchilla* on the outskirts of Xela. I sat with Rafaela in the warm kitchen where she served me steaming hot tea and *paches*, a delicious, savory *tamal* steamed in leaves. She looked squarely into my eyes and shared the story of her journey with Oscar. It was a story that would become deeply personal to me.

A fallen candle set off a fire in the family's home. Oscar, then just six month old, received first-degree burns to the right half of his body, including his hand, arm, and face. There were no doctors specializing in burns at the local general hospital, so the family had to travel four hours to a public hospital in Guatemala City.

Oscar's burns were extensive, and his recovery, slow. After a number of months, his parents were able to bring him home. But his prognosis was a mixed bag. Oscar needed surgeries that might restore vision in his right eye, release scar tissue holding his head to one side, improve the use of what was left of the fingers on his right hand, and improve his breathing which was impaired by scar tissue in his nose. His father Marco Sr. earned a modest income sharpening knives for a living. Rafaela cleaned houses and took in laundry and ironing to add to the family's income. The back-breaking work they did from dawn to dusk each day was barely enough to put food on the table, let alone pay for costly surgeries. The two were desperate to find help.

Rafaela had sought help from every doctor she knew, and from friends, churches, and help groups she heard about. Her efforts paid off, and as a youngster Oscar underwent numerous procedures and spent many months of his life back at that hospital in Guatemala City with other children who had suffered burns. Progress was made, but when he was released, more surgeries were needed. Over the years that followed, his mother's persistence won him several follow up surgeries, including a stint in the U.S. at age 8. But all the surgeries fell short.

"I never gave up hope," Rafaela told me, her eyes filling with tears. "My prayers were answered with Xela AID!"

Rafaela's story of persistence moved me deeply, and her declaration raised a lump in my throat. I hoped we'd be able to make the difference in Oscar's life that Rafaela had been praying for. From our conversation it was clear that she and Marco Sr. understood that they'd have to entrust their son to strangers for a decade. They were willing to do whatever it took to ensure him a better life. As far as I was concerned, it was a go—if we could manage to work through the maze of requirements, that is.

Surprisingly, it took Dr. John and me stateside and Luis in Guatemala just a few months to make all the arrangements. It was a relative piece of cake considering the jungle of bureaucratic red tape we'd sliced through in the past to operate and grow our project in Guatemala. It was the beginning of a life-changing journey for Oscar, and for me.

Arrival

On a sunny day in March, 1995 (my father's birthday as a sweet coincidence), Oscar arrived in California. He was escorted by none-other-than Luis. This was the first time I'd actually met him. He was a thin, shy, 14 year old, about five-feet-three-inches tall and as polite and humble as could be. The day he arrived, the Los Angeles Marathon was in full swing. I had a family member running in the race, and thought it would be an interesting place to take Oscar as his first field trip.

"I've never seen so many people in one place," he observed with some trepidation. He was right. That year, there were about 200,000 participants and spectators at the Marathon. Xela's entire population was only about 145,000, and surely he'd never seen them all in one place.

After the event, I drove us towards the Pico-Union district of Los Angeles where the Guatemalan family who would host Oscar lived. He and I chatted—or mostly, I talked—while Luis filled in the blanks for Oscar when my Spanish failed me. Luis also clarified Oscar's responses to me, although they were mostly "yes" and "no" with little explanation. (Teenage boys are the same the world over.)

When we reached the home and got out of the car, I could see Oscar had something to say to me. He was timid, but determined. The baseball cap he never took off cast a shadow across the scarring on his young face, but it couldn't hide his kind expression. He looked straight into my eyes, then took my hands cupping them in his. He declared slowly and with resolve, *"Muchas gracias por la ayuda"* (thank you for the help).

I immediately choked up at both the tenderness of his words, and the irony. It was such a joy to be able to help that I felt it was me who should be thanking *him*.

The host family situation started out rocky. We arrived to some kind of fierce argument between spouses creating a lasting tension that was palpable. I was concerned from the beginning about leaving him there, but was heeding the advice of a social worker friend who said it was best that Oscar stay in a Guatemalan home. I vowed to visit weekly.

On my first visit with Oscar, I learned there was a religious mismatch. In Guatemala, he was growing up in an Evangelical Christian home. We had unwittingly placed him with a devout Mormon family. I told Oscar I'd find a church compatible with his family's beliefs, and come and take him each Sunday. He marveled at the hundreds of choices in the phone book located near his host family, and finally picked one out with a name similar to his church back home.

Sunday came. The church was in a strip mall. We were welcomed warmly. I have to admit I was startled by the altar, a full-wall-sized painting of a cross in flames on its side speeding across the backdrop of a dark universe. Oscar seemed comfortable enough, so we stayed. The service was four hours, and I was happy to see Oscar fidgeting—I wasn't the only one.

At the end of the service, converts living up to their promise to evangelize pressed me about my beliefs. I explained that I had a personal and private relationship with God. Since Oscar was enthusiastic, I agreed to be "prayed over" with him. About twenty people encircled us and began whispering their individual prayers, simultaneously, and with passion. The resulting barrage that went on for many minutes was both unintelligible, and observably heartfelt. Not my cup of tea, but our weekly visits were well worth Oscar's spiritual well being.

After a few months, Oscar's church in Los Angeles became a moot point. It became evident that the father of his host family had a drinking problem. I wasn't about to leave Oscar in that situation. After all, I had a spare bedroom.

As my house guest in Anaheim, Oscar was a dream. I'd never met a 14 year old as courteous or thoughtful. He called me "Doña" Leslie, a title of respect I quickly squelched. Leslie would do.

Oscar picked up after himself, and asked if he could help me with work around the house. He wanted to learn to do his own laundry and, since I worked a hectic day-job, I quickly obliged. He had no complaints about anything—his small room, the strange food, my lousy Spanish, the long hours he had to spend at the Boys and Girls Club where I had to leave him when I was working. He went out of his way to show me he was grateful, although it was entirely unnecessary. His gratitude kept me in a constant state of feeling over-appreciated, and humble.

We tried a few local churches in Orange County, but over time, Oscar seemed content to pursue other interests on his Sundays, like studying English and karate, bicycle riding and skating with his friends. It was exciting to see his curiosity piqued and his interests broaden. His world was getting bigger.

As a patient, Oscar was brave beyond his years. At the beginning of his treatment, I had no idea of how intense the process would be. The damage to the tissue on his face had been so extensive that Dr. John opted for a process that would grow new skin, like a pregnant woman does as her belly grows. In the first treatment phase, he implanted a medical "balloon" in Oscar's neck to inflate with water injections. The plan was that when the balloon reached full size—roughly, a half-basketball proportion—he would use the newly grown skin to replace the burned skin on Oscar's face. He would leave a portion of the new skin attached for blood flow. After the new skin had taken hold, Dr. John would sever it where necessary, and would make adjustments. The whole process would take five months.

Oscar was game, and we moved forward. What I hadn't expected, was that since we lived more than two hours from Dr. John's office, the twice-a-week water injections would be done by me. Giving an injection was the last thing I ever wanted to learn, and I was pleasantly surprised when I didn't faint. I tried to keep a poker face so I didn't telegraph my horror to Oscar, who had the patience of a saint. With practice, we both got through that part.

Oscar never complained about the physical discomfort of the goiter-like appendage growing under his chin, nor did he say anything that belied the emotional effects of the unwanted attention he drew when in public. But I could tell it bothered him, and my heart went out to him. Through the surgeries by Dr. John and later, by an ophthalmologist to reveal his right eye and restore his eyebrow, he was hero brave. I so admired his resolve.

After the first six months of Oscar's treatment were complete, the results were impressive. But as Dr. John had predicted, he now confirmed that the treatment plan for Oscar would span a *decade*. I couldn't allow Oscar to continue missing school. After all, we were interested not only in his physical well-being, but also, in his overall development as a person. But getting him in school would take some doing. There was also the challenge of medical insurance. I was living on a modest salary. If Oscar took ill or was injured, how would I be able to care for him?

To get insurance, enroll him in school, and represent him as a minor in so many other situations, I would need legal status. But pursuing it wasn't for practical reasons only. From our first weeks together, Oscar began to ease his way into my heart. He was relentlessly positive, and witty. (He'd crack us both up pointing out my mistakes in Spanish. Like the time I wanted to say I was embarrassed, but instead said I was pregnant, *embarazada*.) For these and so many other reasons, I quickly grew to love him.

Oscar's parents understood the need, and were grateful for any steps made that were necessary for his long-term well being. Six months later, we appeared in family court, arriving to find a bright-blue teddy bear sitting on the chair intended for Oscar. We appeared before a judge, each stated our desire, and Oscar became the son I would now be able to properly care for stateside and share, gratefully, with Rafaela and Marco Sr. I became his local mom.

As a strange coda to this story, within weeks and without warning, Oscar fell ill. It wasn't like him to complain. After he said he was in pain and I found he had a high fever, I took him to the emergency room. There it was confirmed that he had appendicitis, and needed emergency surgery. The survival rate for this surgery at a public hospital in rural Guatemala—due both to a propensity to wait too long to operate, and a high chance of infection—was only about 50 percent. I thanked my lucky stars that Oscar hadn't suffered this infection in Guatemala, or two weeks earlier before I had health insurance for him.

Shifting Old Narratives

Of all the challenges Oscar and I faced together as a result of a blue-eyed English-speaking *gringa* adopting a brown-eyed Spanish-speaking medio-Maya *chivo* (a Guatemalan from the highlands), navigating the school system was among the most difficult.

Oscar had finished sixth grade when I went to enroll him with young people his age in ninth grade. The school principal had assured me that this would be the best strategy for Oscar's success, and that with a little extra care at school and some tutoring at home, he could succeed. A counselor working at the school didn't share the principal's enthusiasm, it seemed. She presented me with the study plan she'd prepared for Oscar, and it was aimed at high school graduation, only, rather than college preparation. It failed to include even a single college preparatory course.

"We just try to graduate these people from high school and hope they can get a job—any job," was the defense Mrs. Gapa offered when I questioned her plan. "They don't make it to college."

I was astounded at hearing this. Not only because I had every intention of seeing that Oscar was prepared to go to college, if he wanted to, but also, because it was coming out of the mouth of a Latina! Her assumptions so underestimated and limited the potential of migrant students that I found it unconscionable to let the matter go. I reported it.

To his credit, the principal took immediate positive action. He personally created a new college-track plan for Oscar that would assure he'd have the opportunity to complete the prerequisite classes he needed to go to college. The principal took a wholehearted interest in Oscar's success and gave him a pep talk about being able to catch up to his grade level. At first, Oscar did not share the principal's enthusiasm.

"I don't think I can do it," he shared with me on the morning of his first day in high school in the United States of America. I asked if what was bothering him was that he'd only gone through sixth grade and was skipping to ninth, the new school and not knowing anyone, the fact that he spoke little English, or something else. His answer, was "Yes."

I felt my tiger-mom kick in.

"You may not know that you can do it, but I know you can," I told him, recognizing the same words of encouragement I'd heard so many times from my own mother and father as they slid off my tongue. "Go just this one day, and let's see how it goes. Just do your best."

Oscar had such a positive nature that he couldn't resist the challenge of doing his best, just for this one day, to start. He went to school and that first day wasn't so bad, he decided. And so went our conversation each morning for the first few weeks of ninth grade, until like magic, a full school year had passed.

When a new school year was about to start, we had a similar conversation. I reminded him that at one time he thought he couldn't make it through his first day at high school, but he had. "Do your best, just today..." I reminded him.

This sequence continued through high school. After that, he knew the drill—he could do it. *¡Sí, se puede!*

The narrative we get about ourselves from those we love, those in authority, the media, and the world at large can be incredibly powerful—for better, or for worse. That said, Oscar's success was by no means rooted only in the positive narratives of others, let alone mine, which came relatively late in his life. He was fortunate to have grown up in the embrace of his mother's positive persistence and the stubborn resolve of a father who'd served in the Guatemalan Army and lived to tell about it. Most importantly, from the challenges of his own childhood, Oscar had become a survivor. He had developed his own unique spirit, a vibrant personality, and had found a method to thrive. He'd come to his success through his own hard work and persistence.

On the eve of Oscar's high school graduation he readied to go to bed and I asked him if there was something special he'd learned. Upon reflection of the past, sometimes-difficult four years, he commented, "I never knew what I never knew." With that kind of insight, I thought, *this young man will live an examined and purposeful life.*

Oscar proved Mrs. Gapa wrong on so many counts. Through his own determination and the grace of several teachers who lovingly tutored him, Oscar graduated from high school on time. He had applied to two colleges and one university, and was accepted to all three of them. Oscar graduated from the University of La Verne with a Bachelor's Degree in journalism, then graduated with a Master's Degree in Leadership and Management. He went on to find meaningful work as a journalist, translating, and managing events for cities (so far). While running his business as a farmers' market manager, he helps others to make a living. What a waste of human potential it would have been if, as his high school counselor had planned, Oscar's education had ended there.

To celebrate his first college graduation, Oscar's parents and brother Marco Jr. came to the States. Dozens of other people who loved and admired Oscar gathered with us. I couldn't have been more proud of him.

A President Got to Meet Him

In the early 2000's I again visited Guatemala's Presidential Palace. Customs agents had stepped up pressure for *mordida* on the donated goods we were bringing in, and I'd gone to ask the sitting president to issue us a document we could use to dissuade this. President Alvaro Arzu agreed to meet with me and to provide us with a personal letter. During our meeting, I told him about Oscar.

As it happened, the President would be in Los Angeles within months of our meeting in Guatemala to run the L.A. Marathon and attend a cultural fair afterward. He invited Oscar and me to join him in the booth where Guatemala would be represented. I asked Oscar if he'd like to go.

"I'd get to meet the President of Guatemala?" he mused, wide eyed.

"No," I corrected him. "The President of Guatemala would get to meet *you*."

Oscar looked at me quizzically, then a smile broke out across his face. From that moment forward, this twist became part of our insider banter.

After his meeting with the Guatemalan President, Oscar became a fearless celebrity magnate. He not only runs across celebrities more than anyone else I've ever known, but he isn't shy about asking for an autograph. Since the proliferation of cell phone cameras, he's never missed an opportunity to get a celebrity to join him in a selfie. His star-encounter list after President Arzu, has included singer Vikki Carr, civil rights leader Dolores Huerta, comic actor Will Ferrell, UFC fighters Tito Ortiz and Ronda Rousey, *Modern Family* sensation Rico Rodriguez (Manny) and some others I'm too old and uncool to recognize. When I can beat him to the punch, I ask, "Oh, so-and-so got to meet you?"

For me, the twist was no joke. What a joy it is to share Oscar's life—a testament to the power of positive thinking and persistence. He is an inspiration to so many, and always, my star.

30 – The Dead of Night

LUIS' FAVORITE SAYING IS, "There are no problems, only solutions." His maxim would be tested on this particular night.

Like Lake Atitlán after dark, the road passing just below the town of Santa Maria de Jesus in the Department of Quetzaltenango was one of the many places during Guatemala's civil war that sane people didn't go. We were bound for Xela, but had set out to return later than we should have. We found ourselves in a jungled area about three and a half hours southeast of Xela. Just like in a scary fairytale, it was a dark and stormy night, just before midnight...

Luis and I were traveling by car to Xela with volunteer Wolfram Alderson, and on assignment from the *Los Angeles Times,* reporter Tracy Weber and photographer Gail Fisher. Wolfram was a strapping, outdoorsy, let's-get-this-done type of guy with bushy blonde hair, a beard to match, and a positive, bigger-than-life personality. Tracy was a tall, fit, 30-something award-winning investigative reporter and feature writer who'd taken on tough and dangerous assignments like drug smuggling and exposing corrupt politicians. Gail was small of frame, fit, and like Tracy, fearless. The heavy camera bags on each shoulder had accompanied her into many an extreme situation—including war zones.

The two journalists had joined us to report on the activities of Xela AID during this summer's volunteer trip. And now, we were returning late from Guatemala's tropical West Coast where we'd just turned homes into exam rooms and held a medical clinic. Luis was driving.

That day we'd been barraged by hopeful patients. Well over three hundred people had waited in long lines under a baking sun in hopes of seeing one of our two doctors. To honor their great effort and treat as many people as we could, we had stayed as late as possible. When we finally began closing down the clinic, I sent the rest of the team back to their accommodations to keep them off the road at night where accidents were twice as likely to happen. But someone had to stay and pack up, and that someone had been Wolfram, Luis and me, and Tracy and Gail who'd also stayed to help. Instead of a roomy bus, a hot shower and a delicious dinner that night, their reward was a small, over-packed car traveling along dark, bumpy roads in the rain and thunder with nothing to eat but that afternoon's cold tortillas.

Tracy and Gail were inquisitive and we'd been talking up a storm about Guatemala, the people, and the war. We'd been on the road for about an hour when Tracy finally asked Luis if he'd heard of any trouble in the area. To my displeasure, he let loose with a scary bunch of facts to the backdrop of the pouring rain and windshield wipers on high, *greeching* in both directions.

Luis described the almost daily battle that had been taking place *in these very hills* we were driving through. It was an epic battle of bullets between the *guerrilla*—the revolutionary, freedom fighters—and the Guatemalan Army, and it happened on an almost daily basis.

"Many, many people have been killed here!" Luis recounted, shaking his head with regret.

"*Muy triste* (very sad)... "

At just that moment we entered a tunnel, the Santa Maria Tunnel, named for a nearby village.

Luis added, "*Fíjate* (think of it), on the other side of this tunnel just about a week ago there were seven people found dead...*beheaded!*"

Stunned, no one said a word in reply.

As I imagined the horror Luis had just described, we slushed and bumped through the dark tunnel, and just before popping out, were jarred to the point of coming out of our seats from what felt like a giant pothole we'd hit. At the same time, a sound like two gun shots rang out in a nerve-rattling *POW POW* that caused us all to gasp in unison.

236

When we emerged from the tunnel, Luis pulled off the road to the right. Gail, Tracy and I had our heads down, buried in our laps. Wolfram and Luis were talking in Spanish faster than I could understand and had figured out what was going on before the rest of us.

"A flat!" Wolfram exclaimed as the rain continued to pour down and the wipers continued, *greech, greech, greech.*

We sat up cautiously as Luis and Wolfram hopped out into the rain to further assess the damage.

"*Two* flats!" Wolfram called in through an open window, correcting himself.

Luis explained that we'd hit a deep rut, "probably dug by the *guerilla*" to detain vehicles. The two then got back inside.

What now? I thought.

It was sinking in that we were stranded in a storm in the dead of night in a place we shouldn't be. As the five of us sat there discussing what to do next, none of our options seemed appealing. We could stay in the car and wait until morning when it would be safer to walk along the road and easier to find a repair shop open. That would mean a long, uncomfortable wait for six hours or so. Who knew who else may be wandering these roads, and come upon us?

We could leave the car and together, try to find a ride to the closest town. But we had no umbrellas or rain coats and the rain was relentless. Also, walking on this road in a group at night could attract unwanted attention. It could even be mistaken as a show of force, Luis explained, and put us at serious risk. Besides, we hadn't seen a car come by for at least an hour. And if one did come by, what were the odds that anyone reputable would dare stop to pick us up? If they did, what were the chances they would have a vehicle that could accommodate all five of us?

Leaving the car there, too, was risky.

"If we all leave it, the car probably won't be here in the morning," Luis counseled, "Or at least *most of it* won't be…"

When we'd discussed our options, Luis decided to check the spare. Returning to the driver's seat dripping wet he declared, "Flat, too."

He got in and quietly thought for another moment, the rest of us now stewing on what to do. He then declared, "We'll take off the flat tires and I'll go get them fixed!"

What repair shop would be open at the midnight hour? And how far might it be? What about the danger? Luis's plan seemed like a long shot, to me. But since Luis had come up with it, we hadn't come up with anything better, and he was the local authority, we agreed it was the best idea on the table.

Luis hopped out of the car and Wolfram followed him, telling us to get out so they could take off the flat tires. The three of us stood in the rain and nervously scanned the dark for something dangerous. Wolfram gathered large stones. Luis jacked up the driver's side of the car where both the front and back tires were flat. As he pulled each tire off, Wolfram placed a stone to set the vehicle on. When the two wheels were off and the driver's side was secured, Luis told us to get back in the car, lock it, and wait.

Reluctantly, the four of us obliged.

We watched in dismay as Luis walked down the rain-soaked road with a tire in each hand. He walked away from the tunnel toward Xela, in the same direction we'd been going, having decided it was his best chance to find a repair shop open. I wondered how many hours it would be before we'd see him again, if even before dawn, and if we all would be safe.

Just as we began to settle in, a most amazing thing happened. It hadn't been two minutes since Luis had set off, when we saw light and a vehicle emerged from the tunnel. It slowed to a near stop to pass through the giant pothole that had foiled us at the tunnel's end. It was a white panel van with no windows. It passed us, then slowed to a stop when up ahead Luis flagged it down. Someone opened the side door. Luis and the person spoke for a moment. Luis then handed the two tires to someone inside the van and ran back to us. Wolfram rolled down a window and Luis called in.

"The driver is a friend of a friend of mine," he said. "He'll take me to get the tires repaired!"

We were impressed. Luis seemed to find a connection with everyone he came across. This could be mistaken to be the predictable circumstance of a normal professional who'd spent his whole life in the relatively small community of Xela. But here we were, hours away, and still, he had friends of friends.

With this, Luis was off. We were left to wait.

It was a wet wait. We'd all been drenched by the rain, and now, our seats were soaked too. Luckily, temperatures in the Santa Maria de Jesus area during the rainy season of May to October were mild, so we were chilly, but not *freezing* cold.

An hour went by, then two. Then the rain stopped. Wolfram, Tracy, Gail and I began to fixate on what would happen if someone who wanted to steal or strip the car found us inside. We wondered if we'd be safer outside the car, hiding. Losing the car would be better than losing our lives, we reasoned. It looked as if there were lots of good hiding places in the landscape, albeit wet and jungly.

We decided to take our chances outside the car with spiders, snakes and whatever other jungle creature's habitat we would invade. We walked away from the car through the mud, and eventually, settled on a location where we could still see the car. We stepped carefully into a tangled thicket watching for wildlife as we nestled ourselves in so we were thoroughly obscured by vines and other vegetation. Wolfram, ever resourceful, gathered up palm-sized stones which he assembled into a pile—an ammunition store, of sorts, just in case. We hunkered down and waited for Luis's return, taking turns as lookouts.

Hiding in the forest at midnight with a *Times* reporter and photographer was not the way I'd hoped this trip would go, but the two women took it all in stride. They stayed calm and kept a sense of humor. Wolfram, too, showed character. In fact, he seemed to be thriving in this situation as he watched attentively for any sign of danger with a rock in hand, clearly the protector of our lair. There was something very cavemanish about the whole set up. We all admitted we were glad he was there.

Between legitimate worrying about our safety, we did a lot of laughing (some of it nervous laughter) at the situation we found ourselves in. Gail likened it to a cemetery she'd photographed where warring factions were holding ceremonies for their dead, simultaneously, just yards apart. She'd been in situations like this one before, and some even more dangerous. That made me feel a little less foolish.

Many hours went by. It was beginning to get light when what looked like the van that had taken Luis away, reappeared. Sure enough, Luis stepped out, both tires in hand. The nice people in the van had taken him to the shop of a kind soul willing to repair tires after midnight. They had also waited, then returned to drop him off. Given the late hour, the rain, and that Luis was merely a friend of a friend, I found that extraordinary.

Luis thanked the driver, then each of us took a turn. This is the generosity of the Guatemalan people I came to experience on many occasions. And of course, this situation was influenced by Luis with his sheer force of personality. I was glad he was on our side.

Thanks to Luis and Wolfram, in about half an hour, our vehicle was back in driving order. Roughly three hours later we were safely back to our hotel rooms in Xela, exhausted. I thanked Luis for having been our guardian angel that night. He brushed off the compliment.

"There are *real* guardian angels, *fijate*," he said, glancing upward briefly, crossing himself, then kissing his thumb as he did every time he drove us past a Catholic church. If guardian angels are for real as Luis wholeheartedly believes, that night, ours were working overtime.

And then there are the angels right by our side…

Out of great need

We are all holding hands

And climbing.

Not loving is letting go.

Listen,

The terrain around here

Is

Far too

Dangerous

For

That.

—Hafiz

❖

31 – Nat

BEFORE HE WALKED INTO MY OFFICE at Harvey Mudd College in Claremont, California, I had no idea who this man was. He was a tall, portly fellow wearing a dark business suit and a tie, and was perhaps in his mid-sixties. He shook my hand, smiled pleasantly, then closed the door to my office before he sat down in front of my desk. I was intrigued, and a bit uncomfortable.

He told me his name, which meant nothing to me. He said he held a post at the college, and had heard about Xela AID and our work in Guatemala. He was interested in learning more about the project. But first, he said, he was interested in my background— how I'd come to work as the communications director at the college, and how I'd ended up in Guatemala.

I am not suspicious by nature, but this man's visit came out of the blue. It was odd. I gave him the short version, including my college credentials and a few words about my previous life as a writer and editor. I told him I'd gone to Guatemala to learn Spanish, and saw help was needed. I then asked him how he'd heard about our work, and about *his* background. Where a moment earlier he'd seemed sincere and charming, he was noticeably evasive at the first question, and the second.

"A friend mentioned Xela AID," he said, but didn't elaborate.

To the second question, he answered vaguely, "I worked in the diplomatic corps in Guatemala, but have long-since retired."

I couldn't gauge if he was just being humble, or trying to hide something. He quickly circled back to me and to my connection to Guatemala. The line of questioning that followed made me feel alternately like I was being interviewed for a job, or accused of a crime.

243

He told me that what he knew about me (and what was that I wondered?) convinced him that I was "intelligent" and "well educated," and that I came from a family with "good values."

"Are you a patriot?" he asked, catching me off guard.

I wasn't sure what to think of his question. I felt put on the spot at being asked so forcefully. I kept calm and asked him in return what he meant by his question. He said he wasn't talking about my party affiliation, if I had one. From that moment on, he got right to the point.

"Do you believe you must always act in the best interests of the United States?" he asked, any sense of warmth having entirely drained from him.

I was clueless as to where this conversation might be leading, but was feeling increasingly uncomfortable. It seamed like a trick question that no matter how I answered was going to lead somewhere I didn't want to go with this stranger. Realizing that I was only in the hot seat if I agreed to be, I asked him instead what his point was. He wasted no time getting to it.

"You should not be meeting with foreign heads of state," he replied bluntly. "Presidents, First Ladies, or anyone else who holds a significant post in a foreign country."

I'd first met a Guatemalan president when we needed help getting medicines out of port. I'd met another to ask for formal exemption from paying taxes on donated medicines we were bringing in. I hadn't hidden these meetings from anyone, and had no sense I'd done anything wrong. But I was not broadcasting what I was doing in Guatemala, or with whom I was meeting. How had this man known?

"Why is that?" I asked, wondering to myself why this "long-since retired" once-member of "the diplomat corps" could possibly have an interest in me or Xela AID.

The memory of the helicopter attack flashed across my mind.[15] Perhaps I was on this stranger's radar because I'd been somewhere I shouldn't have been?

My heart raced. Was I a loose end, a witness to something I shouldn't have seen? I was actually relieved at the next words the man spoke, because his concern seemed to have nothing to do with my presence in the mountain village under fire.

"When large quantities of valuable materials are being shipped into a country, it's important to work in coordination with the U.S. Embassy," he said matter-of-factly, looking me squarely in the eyes.

I wondered if this mystery man thought I was a political activist taking sides in Guatemala's internal conflict. I decided to explain to him that Xela AID's mission is strictly humanitarian, and for that reason, I'd avoided the Embassy whose mission, as I understood it, was political.

"We stay out of politics," I assured him. His comeback was unexpected.

"Rewarding Guatemala with aid at this time works against our national interests," he said, expressionless.

I hadn't the faintest idea of what he was talking about, and asked him to explain. His description was the first I'd heard about the "Helms-Burton Act." First passed in 1961, its purpose was to strengthen the United States' long-standing embargo against Cuba. It accomplished this by authorizing the U.S. government to penalize companies and countries that chose to do business with, trade with, or in any other way support Cuba.

"The Act was reinstated in 1992, and Guatemala is in violation," he told me. "I have a list of countries approved for aid I can share with you."

So Xela AID's efforts to relieve suffering, it seemed, were bolstering up what the U.S. government was now classifying as a nation disapproved for humanitarian aid because it traded with Cuba. *What kind of punishment might Xela AID expect if we didn't comply?*

I didn't ask.

This was a lot to take in and I needed time to think. It was curious to me that our little project had come to someone's attention, and that I was being asked to withdraw humanitarian aid to villages full of suffering people as part of a strategy to squeeze Guatemala into compliance in the United States' quarrel with Cuba. My thoughts returned to the village where Xela AID was now operating. Estrella Vasquez lived there. She was a little girl with a big dream of becoming a nurse and helping people someday. Another child, Luis Miguel Lopez Vasquez, wanted to grow up to be an architect and make beautiful buildings in his village. Juana Gomez wanted to become a teacher, and to help other children learn to read and write. These children came from very poor families, lived on dirt floors, and sometimes missed meals. They were just three of the many children in Xela AID's educational sponsorship program who, if we left Guatemala, would lose the chance to go school and radically change their lives. Why should posturing between governments lay waste to their precious dreams?

The more I thought about it, the more incensed I felt. But I was also painfully aware of the great disadvantage I had since I knew virtually nothing about whom I was talking to. I believed this conversation could be an important one, and decided the best strategy was to bring it to a close as soon as I could, do some research, and reconvene if need be. I tried to appear nonplussed.

"I appreciate that you brought this to my attention," I said. "I will consider the options."

Having decided the meeting was over, I took a deep breath and stood up, then moved toward the door.

The man stood up and looked down at me.

"I strongly suggest you reconsider your work in Guatemala," he said. "I can arrange U.S.A.I.D credits so you can ship supplies to any approved country, at no charge...

"I also suggest that you work through the U.S. Embassy," he continued. "Working around the Embassy won't keep you safe."

Was I being threatened? I felt a chill run up my spine, but didn't react.

We politely shook hands, and as we did, he looked at me deadpan and added, "But certainly, you don't have to take my advice…"

He then took his leave.

I sat back down at my desk to absorb what had just happened. *Had* I been threatened? I didn't know anyone in government, and if I had, I don't know if I would have called them. I did have a friend who'd been a political activist, someone I could call.

Paul Baker[16] was a man I'd met while coordinating volunteers for the Missionaries of Charity. He spent years as a Trappist Monk in Scotland, but gave up monastic life to advocate for human rights. He'd fashioned a guitar from discarded wood at the monastery, learned to wield it, and made powerfully relevant folk songs his weapon of choice. We'd played a few small concerts together to raise money for causes. He'd also authored a book about the plight of a young woman who, in the 1980s, was followed to the U.S. by death squads from her home country of El Salvador.[17] I thought that if any of my friends would know something about this man who'd just left my office, it would be Paul.

He did.

"Alarmed" would be putting it mildly to describe how Paul reacted when I called and told him one *Nathanial Davis* had been in my office.

"Holy Mother!" he'd said with a gasp. "Stay right where you are!"

Within an hour, Paul had made it from Los Angeles to my office and was asking for details of Davis' visit.

In his fifties, Paul had kind green eyes and a short gray goatee and mustache like that which might grace the face of a Lord in Elizabethan times. Usually a soft-spoken man, this news of Davis' visit had made Paul far more animated and agitated than I'd ever seen him.

He'd brought with him a book called *Missing*, the basis of a movie of the same name. This book, Paul told me, was based on a true story detailed in another book, "The Execution of Charles Horman: An American Sacrifice" by Thomas Hauser.[18] [19] Both books chronicle the plight of Edmund C. Horman, an American businessman who goes to Chile during a military coup, "orchestrated by the United States," Paul added. Horman was seeking the whereabouts of his son, a reporter and filmmaker who'd been living in Chile and had disappeared.

This coup was news to me. It was another example of a U.S. intervention overseas, a major event that had not been included in any of my high school or college history or political science curriculum.

Paul told me that in *Missing*, the U.S. Ambassador being portrayed was, in real life, none other than Nathanial "Nat" Davis—*the man who had been in my office hours earlier*. Paul then read passages to me wherein the Ambassador denies U.S. involvement in the coup, or in the reporter's disappearance.

Ed Horman asks, "What is your role here? Besides inducing a regime that murders thousands of human beings?" The U.S. Ambassador (Nat) then answers (as Ed Harmon claims Davis did): "There are over three thousand U.S. firms doing business down here. And those are American interests. In other words, *your* interests. I am concerned with the preservation of a way of life."

Paul then shared a vast knowledge of Davis' history with the U.S. foreign service, including his "disappointing human rights record" in Guatemala and other countries where he had been posted. Paul encouraged me to seek out additional details for myself, and to "be alert and very careful when dealing with Mr. Davis." Noted.

He encouraged me to keep him posted on any further contacts with Davis. I agreed.

When Paul left me that day, I was even more shaken than I had been before he'd arrived—but nothing like I would be after I researched the history of Nat Davis.

✣

In the days that followed, I did my homework on Davis, and on U.S. actions in other countries—especially in Latin America. What I found reported by various reliable publishers and peer-reviewed journals offended me as a patriot. Page after page of ugly truth telling confirmed Davis' role, and additional details about the CIA-backed coup in Guatemala first revealed to me by Marcos during his talk at the Spanish school.

Davis' record of foreign service was stunning: diplomatic posts in Florence, Rome, Moscow, Caracas; work with the Peace Corps, the National Security Council, advisor to U.S. Presidents, and Ambassador to both Guatemala and Chile. In the best of framing by various sources he was a gallant protector of U.S. interests. In the worst, he was complicit in mass murder.

Nathanial "Nat" Davis was Ambassador to Guatemala from 1968-71. The George Washington University National Security Archive[20] documents that he worked to support the homicidal military government that had evolved after the CIA-orchestrated coup that unseated democratically elected Guatemalan President Jacobo Arbenz in 1954. Ultimately, this action by the United States resulted in the disappearance and killing of more than 300,000 indigenous people.[21] It is not a part of American history that I am proud of.

From Guatemala, Davis moved on to become U.S. Ambassador to Chile (1971-73) where, according to the afore-mentioned books and movies and later, declassified documents,[22] he supported the bloody coup that felled democratically elected president Salvador Allende and empowered General Augusto Pinochet. The action resulted in Allende's death, the detention of 40,000 people who had supported Allende and protested against the coup, the torture of countless among them, the exile of 9,000 people, and the murder of some 4,000 Chilean citizens.[23]

While teaching at the Naval War College in 1983, Davis and several others filed a libel suite of up to $120 million[24] against individuals and companies involved in the *Missing* books and movies, claiming they had falsely suggested that the plaintiffs had "ordered or approved the order for the murder of (journalist)

Charles Horman" who had stumbled upon evidence of U.S. involvement in the coup in Chile. During the proceedings and under oath, Davis admitted U.S. support for the bloody *coup d'état*. Although their legal action kept *Missing* out of print for several years, ultimately, Davis and the other plaintiffs lost the lawsuit.[25]

While accounts of Davis were a mixed bag, nearly all describe him as a career diplomat dedicated to advancing U.S. interests. What is for sure is that his visit to my office, and all I learned in the aftermath, shaped how Xela AID would operate going forward.

Quietly.

32 – The Phantom Baxter

ABOUT A MONTH AFTER THE ENCOUNTER with Davis, my assistant answered a call on my Harvey Mudd College office phone line. It was from a gentleman who said he was from the Peace Corps. His name was Baxter—"*just* Baxter," he told me when I asked for his last name. "I work with the diplomatic arm."

I didn't know much about the Peace Corps at the time, but I noticed during my research on Nat Davis that he'd been assistant to the director of the Corps from 1962 to 1965. I found this odd considering his prior posts: He served on the Soviet Desk at the State Department as the Cold War was raging. He then served in Venezuela where a socialist movement linked with Cuba and worrisome to the United States had been gaining steam. It struck me as odd that a man of his expertise would end up working with an ostensibly humanitarian branch of the government. That raised some questions in my mind about the nature of the Peace Corps.

Baxter said that he'd "heard about Xela AID..." *Where*? I wondered, as I had with Davis. He wanted to meet with me about how we may be able to "partner."

I was suspicious.

"What kind of partnering do you have in mind?" I asked.

There was a momentary pause. He then said he would prefer to discuss it in person. I pressed that before I could commit the time, I wanted to understand a bit more about what the Peace Corps was proposing.

Perhaps realizing there would be no meeting unless he revealed additional information, he said, "I would like to talk with you about an opportunity for you to do more for your country..."

I felt a chill. The incident with Davis had me on edge, and I fought the urge to hang up the phone. Instead, I responded neutrally. I told him I'd like to call him back at a more convenient time, and asked him for his phone number. He did not offer a phone number, but said instead that he would call me back.

After the call, I researched the Peace Corps. It had been formed in 1961 by President John F. Kennedy following the urgings of Connecticut Senator Brien McMahon. He'd proposed a decade earlier that the U.S. should send "an army of young Americans" to act as full-time "missionaries of democracy" to "aid in the struggle for free-men's minds."[26] According to various sources, Kennedy and others saw placing thousands of young American aid workers in strategic foreign lands as a way to combat stereotypes of Americans as "imperialists"—well earned perhaps by U.S. military interventions such as the CIA coup in Guatemala and many others well-documented in later years.[27] [28] By 1966, more than 15,000 Peace Corps volunteers were serving in 44 countries.[29]

In my research I came across accusations that the Peace Corps had, on some occasions, been a well from which to recruit spies.[30] Learning about the connection between the Peace Corps and spying was another stinging disappointment for this startlingly naïve, "hope-springs-eternal" young patriot. This accusation has persisted in modern headlines.[31] [32] Since Peace Corps workers (and other humanitarian workers recruited by the U.S. government) have been detained[33] [34] [35]and even killed[36] based on the belief that they are spying, it is interesting to note that as of this writing (2019), the Peace Corps website stipulates, "If you have ever worked for the Central Intelligence Agency, you are not eligible for employment at the Peace Corps in any capacity."[37]

Post Baxter call, I again sought the counsel of Paul Baker. We met for coffee in a little café in downtown Claremont. As we sat in that college town surrounded by bright young minds steeped in hope for the future, Paul gave me a dark history lesson about foreign aid, also known as "soft power"—part two of the *one-two punch* of American foreign policy. The gist was that wherever

America fought a war on the ground, it followed with rebuilding efforts and humanitarian aid to fill the void and minimize opportunities for unsavory anti-American groups to recruit local people. At the same time, the efforts acted to recruit locals to America's side.

It wasn't that the humanitarian benefits provided through such actions weren't real, he explained. They were. They improved, and even saved lives. It's just that those efforts shouldn't be misunderstood as selfless acts of compassion or human decency. They were, and are, implemented as a means to the end of advancing U.S. self-interest and are undertaken only for as long as they accomplish that, Paul concluded. (In 2017, commenting to a Congressional Committee, then Secretary of Defense General James Mattis drove this point home when he said, "If you don't fund the State Department fully [think diplomacy efforts, foreign aid, "soft power"], then I need to buy more ammunition...")[38]

The U.S. government's humanitarian efforts such as the Peace Corps, Paul explained, were organized under the U.S. Agency for International Development (U.S.A.I.D.) which President John F. Kennedy had formed alongside the Peace Corps by executive order in 1961. Its mission was "to partner to end extreme poverty and to promote resilient, democratic societies while advancing the security and prosperity of the United States."

U.S.A.I.D. works in collaboration with the Secretary of State, the National Security Council, and reportedly the sitting U.S. President. The "Foreign Assistance Act" (also enacted in 1961)[39] tasked U.S.A.I.D. with having oversight and being the organizing body for foreign aid. Almost since its inception, U.S.A.I.D. was in the news as much for being a cover for U.S. spying operations, as it was for delivering aid. (These allegations continue today.[40] [41] [42] [43])

As I listened to Paul's revelations, I found the practice of withdrawing humanitarian aid to *punish* countries that faltered in their support of the ever-changing U.S. agenda particularly repugnant. This, because those punished would not be the politicians, but in most cases, the very poorest of people with the greatest of needs.

Paul's history lesson was depressing to hear, but necessary in my training so I would better understand, and hopefully, find a way to stay clear of the cloak-and-dagger politics that had the potential to impact Xela AID and those we served. He advised that I take the meeting with Baxter, in a public place, and see what he was proposing.

I agreed to do this.

A week went by, and Baxter did not call. A few days later, I called the national headquarters of the Peace Corps looking for him, and was transferred to various departments. An operator looked through a directory of affiliate offices.

"Maybe it's a nickname. Didn't you get his full name?" she admonished.

A dozen transfers later, I still couldn't find him. In fact, no one I could find at the Peace Corps head office had ever heard of anyone named "Baxter" among their ranks, as a first or a last name.

Baxter never called back.

Father Peter, Bob Rook, Brother Joseph and I talked over my encounters with Nat and Baxter. We were clear about our mission, which at that time, was simply to care for the sick and educate the young. Our various moral compasses informed us.

For Father Peter and Brother Joseph, the Gospels were clear. "For I was hungry, and you gave me to eat..." (Matthew). For Bob Rook, compassion was king: "There is nothing more rewarding than helping others who are struggling mightily to beat the odds."

And I'd given my word, and my heart.

Coming from our different points of view we all arrived at the same conclusion. We would continue supporting those in Guatemala with great need over playing politics. We would *not* work through the U.S. Embassy which, with its political mission, would only continue to pressure us to leave Guatemala when that suited its political end game.

But we also knew better than to spit into the wind.

Our first post-Davis-Baxter-encounter service trip took place about seven months later. For that trip, and all those that followed, we went about our business more quietly than ever. We abandoned the idea of ever arranging for another shipping container full of large quantities of medicines, due to the fanfare it would generate. We would stick with what we could hand-carry—one person, one suitcase of medicine at a time. We made it a policy to source in Guatemala anything we could not hand carry, or anything like high-priced medicines that might draw attention to us.

Besides side-stepping the U.S. Embassy, we cut ties, too, with the Guatemalan Consulate and kept our name out of the news. These were unfortunate but necessary measures to keep our independence and stay out of harm's way—if we were lucky.

33 – Kidnapped

I HAVE NO IDEA IF WHAT HAPPENED in the summer of 1995 had anything to do with the encounters with Nat Davis or the phantom Baxter and our unwillingness to deprive a Guatemalan community of life-saving aid for political ends. I prefer the explanation that no one delivered members of the Xela AID team into harm's way, and that what happened on a major thoroughfare between towns could have happened to anyone driving along it that day.

It's impossible to know for sure.

We arrived in Guatemala as quietly as possible, 30 volunteers. As per our revised mode of operation, each of us carried one bag of personal items and one full of Xela AID supplies. We declared our donated medicines, nothing of high value, and easily passed through Customs.

For our *jornadas* during this trip we set up tents along the Pan American Highway where a muddy dirt footpath intersected it. The path wound up through the jungle, a two-hour walk ending at a shack-village with no-running water known as *San José Más Allá*. The residents were refugees from the road-accessible *San Jose*. Their town had become a war zone, so they had fled into the jungle and reestablished it in the *"más allá"* —a double entendre meaning both "further over there" and "the other world" (or afterworld). We would run the clinic at the base of the road for four days. On the first day, more than 500 people arrived for help. Given that we had only two doctors and two nurses, we felt we would be able to treat only about 100 people each day—and that was pushing it.

A nurse, a translator and I walked the rainbow line of hopefuls who spoke both Spanish and Mám. We looked for people who were the worst off, with life-threatening sickness or injuries. The sick feeling I got when we were forced to turn people away, to choose, to play God, grew in my stomach. It was now all too familiar.

Among the most memorable cases was a woman standing on a single crutch who moved her right leg out from under a long skirt as we approached. Her leg was so swollen that it looked like a continuous thigh—her knee and ankle had completely disappeared. We learned that her husband hit her with a metal rod and broke her leg *a full month earlier.*

"*Bolo,*" the woman whispered while holding up her thumb and little finger, making a tipping motion toward her mouth that meant her husband had been drunk. The leg had never been set, and infection had settled in. This was something our doctors could treat. When the translator told her she'd been selected, she burst into tears and blessed us repeatedly as she hobbled to the head of the line.

We continued to walk the line, and I noticed how the bellies of so many toddlers bulged. This was from malnutrition and parasites. The nurse noticed a little boy squinting, his eyes blood-red and tears running down his cheeks. His mother told us his name was Eduardo, that he was 10 years old, and that he continuously sobbed with pain in the light of day. This had been going on for at least *a year.* Eduardo was selected.

During this painful daily routine I tried to stay focused on those we *could* help, and to feel satisfied. It was the only sane perspective to have, for the moment. The frustration of having to turn so many people away was also the impetus for thinking ahead to what Xela AID could become. With infrastructure, a full-time presence, we wouldn't have to turn anyone away. *Some day*, I thought.

For those we could help, the work was exhilarating. In some cases, we got to see instant relief. Like the joy on the faces of both Eduardo and his mother when a single antibiotic drop in each of his eyes immediately alleviated his suffering. The total cost of the treatment was about $10.

258

Farmers spend long days planting and harvesting crops under the hot sun. As a result, they can suffer daily with headaches and body aches. One day we gathered a large group of farmers from the line, all with these same symptoms. A nurse sat them in a circle and gave each an aspirin and water, then asked that they stay and wait a few minutes. It was wonderful to watch faces etched with pain ease and turn to smiles as the pain diminished. Many in this group cried with joy and gave us so much thanks and praise you would have thought we'd saved their lives. We sent each of them off with a bottle of aspirin, and suggested they wear hats under the hot sun.

It felt wonderful to help, but sad, too. Everyone should have access to tools as basic as a hat or an aspirin, but they didn't. It was telling that the gift of a two-dollar bottle of aspirin was received as if it were a bar of gold.

On the third day of our *jornada*, we were running low on medicines. I planned a trip to stock up in *San Juan Ostuncalco* about a half-hour back towards Xela. I asked two of our volunteers to come along. Gretchen was a first-time volunteer with Xela AID and was also on her first trip outside the United States. She had accompanied Dr. John Padilla, our plastic surgeon. Gretchen had been skittish about coming to a developing country in the first place, and also, had so much anxiety about flying she took medication to calm down. In country, she'd been a trooper and fit in well with the group. Jim Ehlers had traveled with us before and had joined our Board of Directors. He was an old hand at international travel, so the two were a balanced pair.

Gretchen and Jim hopped into the back of a well-used pick-up truck we were borrowing. I climbed into the cab to drive, which was something that always made locals smile; in Guatemala, it was still uncommon to see a woman behind the wheel of a car, let alone a truck.

Finding medicine was easy in Guatemala. There were a half-dozen wholesale pharmacies and we didn't need a prescription to buy most medications. Medicines were also inexpensive by U.S.

standards—just pennies for common antibiotics. I was looking forward to a quick trip down the pot-holed Pan American Highway to buy just enough medicine to finish out our last day-and-a-half in the area. But a quick, uncomplicated trip was not in the cards.

I was the first to see them. Three ominous figures stood in the middle of the road ahead. The men wore camo gear and black ski masks. Each carried an automatic weapon. As we approached, they lifted their guns and pointed them *directly at the truck*. I continued driving toward them, but slowed. Through the open back cab window I called to Jim and Gretchen, "I think we may have an issue."

The two were sitting in the truck bed facing the scenery behind us. Gretchen whipped around and when she saw the masked, armed men, gasped and covered her mouth. Jim saw them, raised his eyebrows, and calmly, commented, "O.K."…

The men motioned us to pull over. One approached the truck. I felt my face flush and my heart speed up. *Perhaps this would be the last moment of our lives. Had I failed to keep the team safe?* I took a deep breath as I faced the man, now at the window, which I rolled open.

"*¿Hay un problema?*" I asked.

"You'll have to come with us," he answered in Spanish.

As if in a dream, I replied in Spanish, thinking of the others waiting for us to return with needed supplies. "We're very busy right now. Could we join you another day?" (The things people say in life-and-death situations.)

The masked man at the window repeated to the two men behind him what I had said. Then, the three looked at each other and *laughed* beneath their masks.

Composing himself, the man said to me sternly, "Drive down this road." He motioned toward a dirt path with his weapon. "And don't turn back or we may have to shoot you!"

O.K. Got it.

Gretchen began hyperventilating and reinforcing her most intense fears about being kidnapped, or worse, by saying them out loud. Jim worked to calm her, as did I.

"Take deep breaths," he told her.

"You can do this," I offered.

Although Gretchen had needed a Valium just to get on the plane to *travel* to Guatemala, with only a little bit of prompting, she was able to compose herself and put on a brave face. I was proud of her.

We soon reached the town square at the village of *Concepción* which was filled with people who, like us, had been forced to assemble there. The village had only one road in and one out, and was the perfect place to stage a mandatory public meeting. Armed revolutionary soldiers (*guerrilleros*) stood in groups in rag-tag uniforms sprinkled throughout the crowd of about three hundred people. The Commander, a light-skinned man wearing a beret, spoke as we all listened. These were his messages:

Corrupt politicians have taken away our land and our children's future. We want to work, but there are not enough jobs. We want to learn, but there are not enough schools or teachers in our rural villages. We need medical care, but there are only a few clinics and even less medicine. All we have left is the hope that we can take back what is rightfully ours.

The crowd clapped softly, fearful of taking sides, I imagined. Stories (later confirmed as true)[44] had circulated about the Guatemalan military commonly massacring citizens who sided with revolutionaries such as this speaker and his troops.

The three of us, fair-skinned and tall, were standouts in a crowd of dark-haired, coffee-colored people who were generally no more than 5 feet 4- or 5-inches tall. Almost immediately, the Commander spotted us. He began to make his way toward us and was joined by a half-dozen associates.

I greeted the Commander with a firm handshake, and looked him directly in the eyes. Jim followed suit. Gretchen hung back, thoroughly and justifiably frightened, but standing tall.

"Pleased to meet you," I said. "We are humanitarian workers."

He said he knew exactly who we were, and what we were doing in the area.

"I know you understand our suffering," he continued. "I have people in these mountains who are fighting for the rights of the poor and who need medicine. Will you help us?"

This was a terrible moment. If I said yes, our entire team could be in great jeopardy since it was well known that government brutality had not been restricted to locals. It had also been waged against foreign aid workers who purposely, or even inadvertently, helped the *guerrilla*. If I said no, perhaps the three of us would die that very day.

I paused to think, and studied the Commander's face. On pure intuition, I opted to speak my heart.

"Sir, you are the commander of a group of people whom it is your duty to protect. In the same way, I have to protect my people.

"If we give you medicine, *los militares* may believe we're affiliated with your group. This would make it unsafe for us to stay to help the poor—the same people you're helping." Then, I stopped talking, and waited.

The Commander didn't reply at first. He pursed his lips as he thought, apparently undecided about whether to treat us like friends or enemies. Several young men stood at his side. Each sported a battle scar—one, a slash across the top of his hand, and the other, a full arm wrapped in a blood-soaked bandage. A third had a deep slash across the cheek of his young face. The state of these young men tugged at my heartstrings.

I was moved to add, "We never ask who comes to our clinics. They are open to everyone... *Toda la gente.*"

The Commander's gaze was intense, as if he were searching my eyes and the nuances of my expression for the truth of my heart. I had spoken in earnest and offered the best compromise I could muster. This situation was now out of my hands.

The Commander motioned his soldiers to follow him, and they convened to speak just out of earshot. Jim, Gretchen and I stood by, unable to do anything but wait.

When the Commander returned a few minutes later, I noticed immediately that his eyes had softened, and I was dumbstruck to see what looked like tears welling up. After a short pause, he said the following to us.

"God bless you for the work you do helping our people in need. You are free to go. But go quickly," he warned. "There will soon be an *enfrentimiento*" (a confrontation with the Army).

We were stunned and somewhat relieved, and after thanking him, moved quickly back to our vehicle. Jim and Gretchen squeezed into the cab with me, and I powered our small truck around the crowd, now dispersing, and toward the dirt road out. We watched local citizens and revolutionary soldiers alike disappear behind our dust. After about two minutes, we heard shots in the distance. I picked up speed.

For some time, none of us spoke.

When we arrived back at our compound of tents, Dr. John ran up to the truck to meet Gretchen who began to tell him all about our delay. Jim and I shared sighs of relief, each of us remarking about how very fortunate we were to get back unscathed, albeit without medical supplies.

Luis ran up to our vehicle, obviously shaken that we'd been missing for a number of hours. When I told him what had happened, he turned white, then flushed red. He took me aside.

"Don't tell *anyone* else that you were taken by the *guerrilla* and then *let go!*" he said, emphatically. I didn't understand.

263

"The military will believe they let you go because we are helping the *guerrilla*. They could come after you, after *us!*" he railed, now beginning to pace. "Don't tell anyone else, not *anyone*," he repeated. He told me to make this clear to Jim and Gretchen, too. I did.

Later that night, alone in my room, I felt like I was coming unglued. I began to sob and had a hard time stopping. It was in part a delayed reaction to the kidnapping. Hell, we could have all been killed! I cried, too, for the people I'd seen suffering amidst the cruelty and injustice of this civil war. I thought about the Commander. The same injustices had moved both of us to tears, and set us into action. They had set Marcos, too, on his revolutionary course. Maybe I had more in common with Marcos than I had once thought.

❖

Between my encounters with Nat Davis, Baxter and the Commander, I began to understand Marcos' insistence that no matter how dedicated Xela AID was to staying out of politics, actions that empower those who challenge power *are* political acts. This is because the reverse of the axiom, "The enemy of my enemy is my friend," is also true. *The friend of my enemy is my enemy.*

Xela AID was helping the rural poor who were 99 percent indigenous. These were the same people against whom the Guatemalan military was waging war—or more precisely, full-on genocide.[45] As the friend of the poor Maya, we were by default an enemy of the military, the government, and potentially, a target.

I'd been naive, and now, I knew it.

34 – Plowing Ahead

RAWING ON SOME COMBINATION of stubborn focus and youthful naiveté, I shook off the kidnapping and never looked back. Jim, too, took it in stride, stayed involved, and made other trips with us. Gretchen decided that development work and the inherent risks of a war zone were not her cup of tea. While it was the last we saw of her, I had a sense she'd been in exactly the right place at the right time. When we returned to our *jornada* after surviving the experience, she stepped out of that pickup truck a bolder, more confident woman— changed forever, I'd bet.

Fortunately, Xela AID tended to attract people with a certain sense of adventure. They were the type who framed an experience like ours at gunpoint as a blip in the bigger picture. Because of this, our stream of volunteers kept flowing to us, and it didn't take long to cobble together a passionate leadership team. We began holding monthly planning meetings. Soon, we had two and sometimes more volunteer groups going to Guatemala each year.

After a few years in operation we could see that access to health care and education was making a massive, positive difference for the people we were serving. The work had the potential to help lots of people create lasting change in their lives, if we did it right. We listened carefully to what local people wanted and needed, and together, shaped programs, set goals, assessed how we did, and made tweaks so we could continuously improve. Soon our programs were serving well over a thousand people each year.

Our educational sponsorship program grew and flourished, first under the watchful eye of Ana Maria Flores, a social worker who had volunteered on an early trip. To Rosa and Adalberto, the children Karen Edwards and Colleen Dodds had sponsored, and a bright young boy named Gregorio sponsored by Jim Mramor, Ana Maria added several dozen more children who wanted to go to school but hadn't been able to.

We attracted a number of specialists to travel with us. Among the first was Brad Farrow. He owned a prosthetics company. He replaced missing limbs with high-quality prosthetics that allowed people to be mobile, and to work. His tireless efforts and generosity completely transformed their lives.

Over the years we were joined by volunteers who brought with them hearing aids that Luis quickly found homes for. It was thrilling to see children, some of whom had never heard more than a faint whisper, hear clearly for the first time. I never knew anyone could smile so big.

After a few years in my garage, we were finally able to deliver the three donated incubators to a Guatemalan hospital. A month later we got word that the devices had saved the lives of six infants born prematurely. In the U.S., the high-quality, working-but-aging machines had been tagged for the dump.

We got ahold of a large shipment of intraocular lenses and donated them to an eye-care hospital. Later, we reveled in reports of how they'd been used to restore sight after cataract surgery—in some cases, for children who hadn't seen for years, or ever.

In so many instances, we were turning things that had been considered "trash" in the States into *treasure* for real, flesh-and-blood people. They were people who, just like us, had hopes and dreams for their lives. They also had unmet critical needs that shackled them. While we weren't operating under any illusion that we had a magic pill to cure all that ails, we were making a significant difference in people's lives and it showed. It was incredibly satisfying work.

Trip by trip, we were piecing together and honing in on elements of what would one day become Xela AID's formula to successfully collaborate with our new friends towards lasting, positive change starting in one corner of the Mayan world.

Over the next three decades, we learned a few things.

266

PART V ✚ INSIGHTS

35 - Sacred Ground

"This work transformed me. I feel as if I've walked
on sacred ground..."

—Pat McElroy, Xela AID Volunteer

PAT MCELROY IS A THOUGHTFUL, well-spoken woman in her fifties who volunteered with us. When I asked about her experience, she described it with delight, and with reverence—like a great meal she'd partaken of on a spiritual retreat. She'd tasted poverty, hope, and lots more in between. She'd let her joy and sorrow simmer together, savored it, digested it, and she'd grown because of it. Seeing through fresh eyes like Pat's reminds me of why I do this work, and the honor it is. I rely on these new perspectives to continue to learn and grow.

Twelve years into Xela AID's evolution, another volunteer came along with lots to teach me. In Mel Dinkel, I was reminded of what it means to work selflessly, tirelessly, and with great love.

Lucia barely came up to Mel's waist when she wrapped her arms around him. Her 24-year-old daughter Maria wasn't much taller. Lucia looked ancient, with her colorful, hand-woven *huipil* and skirt in the style of San Martín hanging loose on her gaunt, stick-frame—the result of sometimes eating "no more than a single tortilla morning, noon and night," Luis had told us. Theirs was a dire situation.

Both Lucia and Maria had sun-weathered skin and kind eyes. We relied on Maria to interpret for her mother who spoke only her Mayan dialect, and not a word of Spanish. A few trips into this project, they both had wide smiles every time they saw Mel, and with good reason: They'd seen him work from dawn to dusk for days straight in rain, wind and cold, leading the teams of volunteers whose heartfelt work would change the two women's lives—make it so they would live like human beings again. Their gratitude was palpable.

Xela AID's "Leaders in Training" youth group had identified the pair's need, putting the women on a list with other families living in "extreme poverty." This list represented the poorest of the poor and those who had the most urgent need for housing. These were the people in the area who were *so* poor that they fell through the loose weave of any safety-net programs. Lucia and Maria's case had fit the bill. They owned their land, so whatever improvements we helped with could not be taken away. And their need was urgent.

Lucia and Maria were living in a dangerous adobe they'd been forced to continue to call home even after an earthquake had almost completely collapsed it. They'd propped up just enough of the debris so that they could crawl under and sleep in it, and pile in a few belongings. Their toilet was outside, a hole dug behind a bush. A pipe sticking up from nowhere with a faucet on it provided water at certain times of the day. A dog to safeguard them, all bones, was tied close by. His small block shelter covered in a rusting tin scrap was in better shape than where Lucia and Maria slept.

"No one should live like that," was all Mel could manage to say the first time he saw the adobe and the bathroom, his voice cracking with compassion. Other volunteers, too, had needed to take leave of the group to shed a few tears in private. Mel's questions to Luis—all about logistics and how soon we could get started—telegraphed his passion for getting the women into safe, dignified housing. An engineer in earlier years, Mel had quickly converted his initial disbelief, sadness and controlled outrage into fuel and was revved to get going. Once he started, he never stopped, and his boundless energy didn't go unnoticed.

"My mother and I want to know," Maria asked one day, "does Mel *ever* run out of energy?"

Mel was a godsend for Xela AID, and me, as it turned out. Stoic and reserved, he'd been mostly all business in the time I'd known him. But I'd gotten to see through his disguise on that, his first volunteer trip to Guatemala.

That happened the day a group of us had been climbing a steep, muddy path to the village of Santa Cruz perched above Lake Atitlán. A village woman was also climbing that daunting hill. She was half Mel's size, and maybe half-again his 51 years, barefoot, and carrying on her back a bundle of wood about half her size. To her surprise, mine, and the rest of the people in our group, Mel caught up to the woman and, using full-on gringo body language (the kind people use when they're not even *trying* to speak Spanish), he offered to carry the heavy bundle for her. She looked confused at first, but then smiled faintly when she realized he was there to help and not rob her of her wood!

The old woman led, Mel followed, and the rest of us from the Xela AID group followed them both up the path for perhaps half a mile. The woman then took a left turn up a steep, narrow and thickly mudded footpath. In about a quarter mile, it ended at her home, a tiny hut. The hut was fashioned of dangerously sharp-edged, rusting sheets of tattered tin lashed together by nylon rope where there were holes rusted through the tin. Her "roof" was a tattered tarp.

The whole structure couldn't have been larger than five by five feet. She motioned for Mel to set the firewood in front of the shack, then managed a full smile, which was toothless, save two top front teeth. She moved toward Mel ever so gently, put her arm around his waist and on his far hip, closed her aged eyes, bowed her head and gave a squeeze as if a blessing. We all snapped photos. A tear rolled down Mel's cheek. He was a softie after all—the cat was out of the bag.

Mel quickly became devoted to the village. Like service work in Guatemala had "transformed" Pat McElroy's life and mine, I watched Mel's joy grow. He soon began co-leading trips and became the de facto lead construction guy. He and his crews took on everything from repairs and maintenance on our headquarters to computer installations, building chicken coops, retrofitting to create smokeless stoves, installing solar devices, and everything else that faintly resembled construction.

In true leaders' fashion, Mel took the blame for any goofs and deferred all credit to the members of his construction teams. He next volunteered to take on Xela AID's challenging financials (the

Federal government and State of California don't make it easy to run a non-profit organization). On volunteer trips, his preparedness with cash for every occasion became legendary, and he soon became known as, "The Bank of Mel."

Then, some years later, he took on another challenge — me. We were married in 2009. He continues to impress and amaze me.

The home for Lucia and Maria was planned to be built over a span of just twelve days from start to finish. The work was spread over three volunteer trips each a month apart, working four days on each trip.

During the first trip, Mel's construction crew, our Leaders youth group, and Maria and Lucia themselves worked together to clear the land where the house would go. The process of deciding its exact location had been revealing. When through a translator Mel asked Doña Lucia where exactly she wanted the house, she could not come up with an answer. Not because she didn't have an opinion, but because, "No one has ever asked for her opinion," her daughter Maria informed us.

We guessed Lucia was in her late fifties. It was hard to imagine a person so marginalized that she had never before been asked for her opinion. Maria stated this as a fact, assured us it was true, and smiled broadly, seemingly amused that we didn't see that as obvious. A life where my opinion would never be asked, nor would it matter? No right, or opportunity to choose? What would *that* feel like? It would be tempting, under those circumstances, to believe that like my opinion, my life didn't matter either. It is still hard to fathom, and painful when I imagine living like that. Yet it is the reality of many Mayan women, especially of Lucia's generation.

With our gentle encouragement, Lucia found the courage to tell us where she'd like her new home. She created the outline, including which way it should face, with her footsteps. At seeing her daring, I was encouraged and elated! Her victory in finding her voice stunning, as real as bricks and mortar. When she'd finished, a round of applause burst out spontaneously from all of us on site.

With Luis' help, Mel hired a local *albañil* to tutor us in block construction. As we'd seen in earlier construction projects, all the digging out and leveling was done by hand. Concrete was made by mixing ingredients in water in a shallow hole and stirring with a shovel. The rebar was put together as needed by hand-bending iron rods. Although devoid of modern-day technology, the process works. By day four, the first rows of bricks had been laid.

The second group arrived a month later to pick up where the first had left off. Mel moved the project into even higher gear, aiming to have the walls up, a pitched roof on, a stove built, a patio poured and roofed, and water and a *pila* (sink) installed—all in four days. In the meantime, we continued to ask Maria what she wanted. Emboldened by her earlier experience, she became even more forthcoming. We brought her paint swatches, and she went hog wild. She picked a bright, happy, orange for her new home.

"And red for the floor—she'd like a red floor!" Maria translated for her mother. If the lady wanted a red floor, Mel was determined to make it happen.

Lucia then selected the location for her brick stove, and then the outhouse, which she wanted smack dab in the middle of her cornfield. Mel had fun ascertaining which way Lucia wanted to look out of her outhouse. He entertained the volunteer workers by feigning sitting on the pot in various directions. Which way won out with Maria? Looking at her new house, of course.

Mel's team poured the porch, and in the pouring rain, he and his team installed the support beams and the roof. We'd purchased bright orange rain pull-overs for 10 cents each which flapped wildly in the wind and the crew's faces, making it tough to hit the nails.

The *pila* was last to go in before this group had to leave, requiring Mel and team to move the water line. This three-compartment sink is used for everything from washing dishes to holding drinking water. The traditional *pila* is made of concrete. This one would be hard plastic, and indestructible. The only problem was, instead of weighing 500 pounds, it weighted just 50 and could be easily stolen. I guess some of Mel's ingenuity rubbed off on me, because I devised a system of giant rebar hooks for each corner anchored by cement to make the *pila* virtually thief proof. The *albañil* was amused that a woman had come up with the hook design, and when I caught him smiling, he told me so.

"No, it's *not* normal for women to get involved in construction around here," he said. *Maybe someday it will be.*

The third and last group of volunteers to work on the house was the perfect mix to pick up where the other volunteers had left off. It was led by our long-time friend an Advisor to Xela AID Cliff Hague. His group was made up of mothers and their 14-year-old daughters who were thrilled to get the assignment to paint and furnish the new building. Standing 6 feet 6 inches tall, Cliff would be in charge of painting the highest places.

We all painted our hearts out, and when the inside was all white and the outside the bright orange Lucia had picked out, we then hit the market for curtain materials and furniture. We had intended to get two single beds, but it occurred to me to ask Lucia what she wanted. Maria translated the question to Lucia, then the two women giggled, and giggled some more.

"What are you laughing about?" I finally asked.

Maria explained, "We are laughing because we can't imagine it… having a bed *each*. Having two beds for just *two* people. Neither of us has ever slept alone!"

In the end, Lucia asked for one standard bed for the two of them. "It would be wasteful, otherwise," she told us.

On the final day of painting and outfitting, we had several Xela AID staff members whisk the two ladies away for a bit of recreation. Our staff took them to buy food for a month, and dog food—oh, please give that dog something to eat! (I admit it, I sponsored the dog. I sent money faithfully every month for dog food. Maria changed his name from "Toby," to "Toby-Leslie.")

When the staff members returned with the two women, the volunteers were inside the new home, waiting silently. The curtains were drawn so the ladies couldn't see in. I was outside to greet them, and when Lucia opened the door, the group yelled "Surprise!" When they saw inside, the astonishment on their faces was priceless. We'd made the curtains out of local, woven fabric. We'd purchased dressers, and placed flowers upon them. A lovely painting of flowers by a local artist hung on the wall. The bed was queen sized. And finally, there was the custom floor—Lucia's chosen deep-crimson red. They were stunned, speechless. At first, Lucia covered her mouth with her hand. Her eyes at first smiled, and then, she was overcome with joy and cried. Maria cried. We all cried.

It was Lucia's House, a house that Love built—sacred ground.

Now you maybe wondering where Mel was on this last, all-important day. Due to work commitments, he couldn't be on that final trip to finish the house, but knew it would be done right when Cliff stepped in enthusiastically to lead the charge. But it wasn't long before Mel, too, had his moment of delight.

Mel and I returned about three months later with another group and visited Lucia and Maria. I was elated to see "Toby-Leslie." He'd morphed from a bag of bones to become a muscled, beefy dog. I posted photos on Facebook. All the volunteers who'd met Toby-Leslie in his skeletal phase were relieved. With a roof over their heads, Lucia and Maria could weave again. They could earn more money for food, and both of them had gained weight, and strength, too. It's amazing what a little more food can mean for a person's life.

On that trip, Mel got to see the completed home for the first time. Seeing him approaching, Lucia and Maria ran towards him, burst into tears, sprung to his side, and hugged tight in their gratitude. For many minutes they cried and held on to Mel for dear life, "the kindest man ever" to enter their lives, they said—their brightly burning star, their sacred ground.

I know how they feel.

36 – Lessons in Perspective

MY FAVORITE-EVER PICTURE of my nephew, Jordan, was taken in 2007. In it he is 12 years old. He is frozen high in the air in the middle of a running jump. He is having the time of his life with other youngsters, all Mayan children from the village of San Martín. The look on his face is one of pure joy. It belongs naturally to children, and the rest of us hope to reclaim it in later life.

Handsome, clever, and with an improprietous sense of humor like his dad (my brother Justin), at 12 years of age Jordan was already a deep thinker. His pre-teen years were marked by a furrowed brow, and long periods of silence. Something important was going on in that little head, and I hoped it wasn't something too heavy. I'd taken those carefree years for granted, and wished more of them for him.

While Jordan was always courteous and affectionate to his Auntie Leslie, his intensity made him prone to dark spells and apparent despair. I remembered all too well the turbulent youth I'd passed through, and didn't wish on anyone. When it appeared he was navigating low points like I'd had, my heart went out to him. I was also well aware of the abundance I'd grown up with, and how it had created in me a kind of museum-blur when it came to seeing all I had to be grateful for. As a result, as a kid I often felt I was being deprived of something in life, although I wasn't sure what. Jordan was growing up similarly privileged. I wondered if he had some of the same challenges with perspective that I'd had.

By this time I'd done my share of world travel. Nothing in the world had brought me more perspective, more of a sense of gratitude, or more contentment than serving in Guatemala had. And besides, I couldn't think of anything I'd like to do more than share the Guatemalan experience with my brother and nephew. So, I proffered the idea to Justin, and that summer, he, Jordan, Mel and I and a gaggle of other volunteers were off to the highlands. In Jordan's case, new perspective came to him in the person of Diego.

Jordan and Diego

Diego was just five years old when Mel first sponsored him to go to school. He lived next door to Xela AID headquarters in San Martín, and made a habit of coming over to hang out with our volunteer groups. Mel's heart quickly melted for this little guy who, having no sober father in his life (so no father figure at all), was glued to his side as Mel's assistant on each of our visits. Diego would watch what Mel was doing intently, then hand him a nail, hammer, screwdriver or other tool before Mel asked. He became skilled at anticipating what Mel would need.

On this trip, Diego showed up to join the construction team that included Mel and Jordan. By this time, Diego was about Jordan's age. He wore a pair of tattered pants with a broken zipper that didn't zip up completely. His tennis shoes were similarly tattered and had no laces, and his right shoe had a hole at the right big toe. Diego wore a long-sleeved sweater against the wet chill of daytime during the rainy season in San Martín at 8,500 feet. It was smudgy-white and maroon-striped with a tear at the bottom of the right sleeve. This was Diego's daily uniform.

Diego showed up each morning, faithfully. On the last day of our projects in the village for that trip, he joined us for lunch. Although Jordan spoke little Spanish, and Diego, even less English, the two seemed to communicate just fine with punches and pokes and pointing at things amidst smiles and giggling. I loved seeing both Jordan and Diego smile.

That day, women of the village we employed to cook lunch had prepared a delicious chicken-and-rice dish featuring *jocón*, a green sauce that is traditional in the region. But eating chicken is a luxury here since meat is so much more expensive than rice, beans and tortillas. Even though protein is needed for nourishing growing children, eggs are more often sold than they are eaten as families try to make ends meet. Diego downed the chicken like he hadn't eaten in a week. As Jordan poked at his food, I noticed him looking Diego over.

When Diego finished eating before we did, I encouraged him to go get seconds and he leapt up, leaving us at the table. After about 10 seconds had passed, Jordan leaned over and whispered softly, "Auntie Leslie, why does Diego wear the same clothes every day?"

The thinking that had gone into Jordan's question, and the risk associated with asking questions in general for a near-teenage boy was not lost on me. *How observant and brave of him.* I did not answer hastily, but let the silence punctuate.

"That's a good question," I encouraged, speaking softly. "The last time Mel and I were here a few months ago, Diego was wearing the same clothes and shoes. I'm pretty sure they're the only ones he has."

At this, Jordan continued looking in Diego's direction and said nothing for a time. He then nodded his head slightly as in the affirmative, never looking away from Diego. If I had X-ray vision into his thoughts, I believe I would have seen a light flicker on, a new perspective being born.

When Diego returned to the table with another bowl of chicken and rice, the two didn't miss a beat yukking it up with one another, continuing to have great fun.

About a year later, I heard Jordan recalling the trip to a friend. He mentioned that a boy he'd met, Diego, had just one set of clothes he wore each day. This suggested to me that there had been an impact.

We have a lot to be grateful for.

I was especially grateful for that time I spent with Jordan, and that I'd gotten to see him interacting with Diego. I witnessed two young men who couldn't be more different bridging the divides of language, culture, education, and resources and reveling in one another's company. They had become fast friends despite their many differences.

There is hope for the world.

Myth of The Other

I'm sometimes asked to speak about Xela AID's work. This evening, I'd joined several hundred government service workers for their annual awards dinner. It was a festive environment and the crowd was warm and welcoming.

I shared a little about my journey to Guatemala and what had inspired me to start the project—the tamer version, that is. (No strafing from helicopters at an awards dinner.) I talked about the people I'd seen living with curable, untreated illnesses, and how I realized that short-dated medicines and other items we throw away could improve quality of life and even *save lives* in Guatemala. I shared stories about individual people I'd met and had come to love.

I emphasized mutualism, the deeply profound benefits that volunteers derive from relationships in the village we work in. I make sure and emphasize this, because it's easy for those of us who live privileged lives in the developed world to fall into the trap of White Knight's syndrome—thinking we're there to *save* others, that we're superior to them, and that the benefit of our presence is one way. I don't make this point out of a false sense of humility or to be politically correct, but because I have for many years been witness to this mutuality, and because I've also seen that it's easy to overlook. I have experienced for myself the profound, personal benefits of our collaboration and the gifts it bears for all of us who are involved.

A number of people approached me after the talk to ask questions or learn about volunteer opportunities. When the line died down, I walked table to table to thank the guests for their attention and answer additional questions. I was surprised at one table by the comment of a woman I'll call Joan. She announced, 'I know exactly who you are talking about, because they are in *my office* day after day with their hands out.'

I was taken aback, but curious about Joan's perspective and asked what kind of work she did. She said she worked at the Welfare office, and without missing a beat, followed up with this question. "There are plenty of people here in the United States who need help. Why don't you help *your own* instead of *those people?*"

Joan blurted this out so forcefully that it jarred her co-workers who looked around awkwardly, and went silent. I thought carefully about what she was asking, but before I could respond, she continued.

"On a daily basis I deal with them—the bottom of the pile. You could say I'm in the deadbeat and loser business. Sounds like you and I are in the same business."

Her words were like fingernails on a chalkboard. I imagined someone down-and-out coming to Joan for help, and how the additional burden of her judgment must add to their suffering. Did she loathe her job, forced every day to interact with the people she seemed to despise—*those people?* I was momentarily speechless. I took a deep breath.

"Everyone is God speaking," Hafiz wrote. "Why not be polite and listen?"

I listened.

Joan's question had been rhetorical, really just a statement of what she felt and believed, belying, I thought, a deep sense of frustration or anger. Her comments didn't require, or even invite a response. She continued to talk while others at the table squirmed. Then, all hell broke loose. When one of her co-workers challenged her, a heated debate ensued. Others tried to mediate and de-escalate the conversation that was heading someplace I had no interest in going. The dust-up between co-workers continued, and when it seemed I could do so politely, I excused myself and slipped away.

I thought about Joan's comments a long while. I hadn't gone silent because I had no answer. The answer just seemed so obvious that I couldn't wrap my mind around where to start. It was as if someone had asked if it's wrong to knock another person to the ground for fun, and if so, why would that be wrong? Where do you start?

I no longer saw people born or living in the United States as *my* people, and others in Guatemala as *those* people. I don't know how or when my worldview changed.

It might have happened that night on the mountain, when as part of some ancient, hardwired instinct I joined with a mother in her inconsolable grief over the death of her young son. It could have been the day I shared in a child's joy when he opened his eyes and his pain was gone after a year-long eye infection. These experiences seemed to peel layers off me, down, beneath the superficial. Clinging to an "us" and "them" would have been an excuse for inaction.

I understand that being afraid of people who are different than us is deeply rooted. I felt empathy for Joan, because it's a reflex that I, too, have to keep "un-practicing." I don't feel with everyone the deep connection I feel with the Guatemalan people—yet. But I'm working on it. Travel is enlightening, and humbling. It reminds me what a tiny corner of the world I occupy, and that there is ample room for the many and varied truths of others.

In my travels, I've also learned to recognize someone who is interested in exploring another point of view, and one who is not. Not only is it disrespectful to force a point of view on another person, but it is also fruitless. Time is too precious to waste. Wherever we call home, whatever our language, customs, or the color of our skin, life is short for all of us.

"Walk around feeling like a leaf.

Know you could tumble any second.

Then decide what to do with your time."

—Naomi Shihab Nye

Local Wisdom

On an early visit to Guatemala, before meeting Luis, I invited Gaby and Marcos out to have a traditional dinner. They suggested a chicken dish with either *pepian*—a brown sauce—or the green sauce, *jocón*. With the chicken, we'd get *paches,* a rice or potato *tamal* steamed in banana leaves and usually reserved for the holidays.

"You haven't really had Guatemalan food until you've tried *pepian, jocón,* and *paches,*" Gaby told me. I couldn't have that. So off we went, and the place didn't disappoint. It was a truly delicious dinner, and for about the equivalent of only $2.

After dinner we began our walk home along a windy road lined with street vendors. Their small stands were illuminated by the glow of their fires as they prepared tamales, corn on a stick (served with mayonnaise and green hot sauce), and other food to sell. There was a line five people deep waiting for the corn. It was tempting, but too big a risk—I'd been sick before on similar street food and vowed *never again.*

We turned down a street that passed through a neighborhood. It was darker than the main street, but illuminated by the moon. I asked Gaby and Marcos questions about everything from their families to how the government in Guatemala was structured. Besides being interesting, the conversation helped to increase my Spanish vocabulary. It had been an enlightening and peaceful walk, until that point.

Suddenly, I heard a woman screaming. I looked around to see where she was. The screaming sounded like it was coming from not too far ahead of us, and I ran toward the sound. Just around the corner I came upon a man who had a woman by the hair and was hitting her. By sheer reflex, I dove into the fray to stop him. I pushed myself between the two and had taken a couple of pelts to the back, when I felt a grip firmly on my left arm. A decided yank pulled me out of the middle. I looked up to see it was Marcos dragging me away. I heard Gaby saying something to the couple that sounded vaguely like an apology.

The two of them physically moved me down the road and away, almost at a run. I wrenched my neck to see if the man was still hitting the woman, but could no longer see either of them. They had vanished from the street.

"We have to call the police!" I blurted out to Marcos who still had me by the arm. But he said only, *"Después,"* (later). His voice transmitted an urgency, but I didn't understand his meaning.

"We need to go," Gaby exclaimed under her breath. We moved quickly away.

Marcos and Gaby didn't speak for several minutes. When we were well out of the neighborhood and back on a main street, Gaby began to explain.

"There is much violence here, and it is not safe to become involved."

I was agitated and wanted to argue. I couldn't imagine seeing something like that at home and *not* getting involved, or at least calling the police, and I told the two of them as much.

Marcos elaborated. "The problem is that the man involved is a well-known person in the community, and he *is* a policeman.

"Your involvement will not stop his violence, but it will put all of us in danger!"

I let that sink in. I asked questions. They explained that the police were among the most violent and most corrupt at this time in Guatemala's history.

"This is what we live with," Gaby told me.

For me, it was a sad revelation. I was also shaken to understand that here, I couldn't trust my eyes and instincts to know what to do. No matter what my reflex, I would have to trust Marcos and Gaby and the local wisdom they brought to the table.

We were headed toward Xela's Central Park, and I invited them to a coffee shop where we could decompress before heading home. I thought I may even have a drink, and if so, a stiff one after the evening's unsettling turn of events.

In the safe haven of Baviera, a European-style café, over three steaming cups of coffee, Marcos explained to me the error of my ways, kindly.

"There are many things that can only be changed with time and can't be forced on a culture," he said, "and especially not by an outsider who has spent little time here…

"Slow down and give yourself time to learn, time to understand." he coached.

He was right, of course. My reactions were based on my reality at home, and not all of them would be appropriate for here. I'd not only have to learn, but also, *unlearn*—and most importantly, learn to ask those who know.

Marcos added, "Guatemala needs your help, but first, it needs your respect."

The Father's Decision

The waters of Lake Atitlán could have been a mirror they were so still and calm. The effect was such that the two giant twin volcanoes morphed into another two volcanoes reaching downward, their profiles rippling with the water's movement. Reflecting the sky, the lake was a shimmering, turquoise blue. It was a stunning sight at which our volunteers marveled as we prepared to open the day's *jornada*.

We had situated ourselves at the bottom of a dirt foot path that stretched up into the mountains to the village of Santa Cruz de Laguna. There, where the road met the lake, we had turned small homes and snack shacks that lined the road into clinic exam rooms. Hundreds of people had gathered to see our doctors, and waited patiently.

There were many of the usual cases—nausea and diarrhea caused by bacteria, parasites or amoebas. There were skin rashes, some caused by swimming in the lake during algae blooms, some apparent allergic reactions, and some cases of just plain sunburn. There were lice infestations, eye infections, and a self-inflicted wound from a machete (while cutting grass) that needed to be stitched up.

Our career nurse, organizer extraordinaire and de facto clinic director, Jim Mramor, had grown accustomed to the kinds of illnesses we would treat at the lake. Several of the doctors, too, were old hands at volunteering in the developing world, and weren't fazed. On the other hand, a doctor from California who was in private practice and a newbie to jungle medicine was shaken by the sheer magnitude of human suffering in this relatively small community.

"One patient told me she had a UTI for about a *year*," the doctor confided in me. She said she'd found the patient's case unsettling, almost unbelievable.

"How could someone just live with that pain for a whole year?" she asked rhetorically, shaking her head.

From several years of running clinics in the area, I knew that this kind of long-term suffering was common. But I also knew that doctors new to jungle medicine had to come to understand these realities in their own time, just as I had. There was a case we saw that day from which no volunteer, old hand or new, escaped unaffected. It was the case of Hector.

After lunch that day we had all returned to our posts, and at about two o'clock, with two hours of clinic left, Jim took me aside to speak privately. Hector had been brought to the clinic by his mother, father and some other relatives, and was extremely ill, Jim told me. His skin and eyes were jaundiced. He had no strength to walk, and he'd been carried to our clinic by his father. All these symptoms had convinced Jim that the boy likely had hepatitis, and was in imminent danger. Hector was only five years old.

"We don't have what's needed to treat him here, so he needs to go to the hospital," Jim informed me, "and soon!"

As I'd learned to do in situations out of the ordinary, I found Luis to fill him in about Hector's case. Luis immediately went to speak with Hector's family. It turned out they lived across the lake in a small village next to the larger lake town of San Pedro de Laguna. They spoke *Tzutujil,* so Luis, a Spanish speaker, struggled to communicate the urgency of the situation. We quickly located a worker at a nearby hotel who could translate Spanish to Tzutujil.

Jim and me and our three volunteer doctors stood near Luis as he spoke to the family across the listless, yellowed body of the boy who lay on a sheet on a make-shift exam table, his eyes only partially opened. Luis spoke. The translator translated. The parents and other family members listened, then the father spoke back and the translation continued in the other direction. During this back-and-forth, Luis became increasingly agitated, and at one point, began pleading.

"We will pay for the boat to get him to the hospital," he said. "If you don't take him *now*, he may die…"

The family listened intently, and when all had been said, all eyes turned to the father. They spoke to one another in low tones in their native language. The father then asked Luis, "If he goes to the hospital, what is the chance he will live?"

Luis turned to Jim, and the two of them quickly discussed the boy's odds. When they agreed, Luis spoke to the translator. "We believe that if he goes to the hospital now, he has at least a 50 percent chance of surviving—but he must go *now!*" Luis urged.

The father nodded his head, and turned to his family. Again, they spoke quietly. I saw that Luis's eyes had become soft with tears. Mine, too, had filled to near brimming over. It was a tense several minutes.

After emerging from the discussion, the father turned to our group and the translator and spoke, the translator then sharing his message with us. "We will not take Hector to the hospital. We will bring him home. You have been very kind."

And with that, the father gathered the boy up off the sheets and into his arms readying to leave.

Luis continued talking to the father through the translator. He spoke softly in a caring, yet compelling tone. I couldn't believe how calm he was. Every molecule of my body screamed for me to jump up, stop the family from leaving and try to convince, cajole and even beg the father to let us take the boy to the hospital. But by now I knew it was not my place, and I trusted that Luis would do all that could be done.

"You've been very kind," the father repeated. "But if it is his time to die, we want him to die in his own home, surrounded by his family—not in the hospital. We cannot risk him dying there."

With Hector in his arms, the father, mother, and the rest of the family took their leave. They never looked back.

Of course we were all stunned. For a few moments, we remained behind in the room, speechless.

It was Jim who broke the silence. "Make sure and use gloves to remove that bedding," he said, his voice cracking. He quickly took his leave. There was nothing left to say for the moment, and we dispersed back to our various posts.

I didn't understand the family's decision. I did know we had another hour of clinic work to get through today, and that we needed to provide caring service with a smile. We'd also need to find a way to recover to avoid the dark cloud of the last hour hanging over the final days of the clinic. I hoped Luis would have some words of wisdom that would help all of us understand, and move on.

As soon as we closed the clinic that day, I sought Luis out. He had some insight, but it offered little comfort. He said the family's decision was in part for fear of the hospital, which wasn't unearned. In Luis' experience, about half of all people admitted to rural hospitals left with an infection. Some died, not from what they'd gone in for, but from infection. But no matter what the family's reasoning, this decision had upset Luis as much as the rest of us. The difference was, he'd seen it before.

I knew I'd done the right thing in leaving it to Luis to handle, but I still had some questions.

"There must be laws protecting children who may have a chance to live with medical treatment," I pressed.

"There are no laws like that here," he told us. "Here, it is strictly the father's decision."

He added that although he wasn't in agreement, respecting the father's decision was the right thing to do.

"If there is one thing that is in shorter supply in Guatemala than medicine, it's respect for the wishes of indigenous people—like that family.

"Respect," he repeated. "Xela AID must set an example."

When the medical team finally talked over what had happened, the team members understood the need to respect the father's decision. Still, the case was a hard pill to swallow. It had broken our hearts to know Hector had zero chance outside the hospital, and would surely die. The incident haunted me for some years after, and Luis, too, he later told me.

In a book of letters between Mahatma Gandhi and his student Madeleine Slade, a British woman living in a Hindu spiritual community in India, Gandhi gives her this advice on cultivating respect for another culture:

"Go as a learner. Where you can help, speak. Where you cannot, be silent."

Sage wisdom.

Throwing Crusts

Pacaya volcano stands 8,373 feet tall and regularly erupts. The first time Mel and I climbed it, it had erupted just two weeks earlier and we roasted marshmallows on hot lava. The volcano is just outside of Antigua where we stop on our way to Xela, and on this occasion, a group of 15 of us had opted to scale it.

Guatemala is rife with entrepreneurs and a cottage industry has grown up at the base of Pacaya. Besides the climbing sticks you can buy for Q10 that they'll buy back from you for Q5 after the climb, there is a cadre of entrepreneurs who follow behind groups with their horses. These folks bet that one or more climbers will tire along the steep two-hour trail. When that happens, you can purchase a ride on one of their "taxis," as several spent people in our group did. Besides the horses and their keepers, on this occasion, we were also accompanied by a trail dog, a female that had recently had puppies.

When we reached the top, tired and sweaty, we quickly found places to sit and rest and eat the sack lunches we'd brought along. The dog (apparently knowing this drill) sat patiently a few feet from a group of us, fixated on our sandwiches. She seemed to know that if she behaved, we would eventually give in and throw her something to eat.

I was enjoying my ham-and-yellow-Kraft-cheese on delicious, locally made five-grain bread, but figured I could spare some crust for this hungry new mother. I began throwing small pieces to her which she caught in mid-air. She appeared so hungry and had such a sweet face and mannerism that soon, several of us were throwing her scraps.

When my sandwich was gone except for a few pieces of crust, I noticed two young boys not far from us, watching. They were gaunt, obviously undernourished, and fixated on the scene. I had one of those "oh shit" moments, accompanied by a sick feeling. Rather than dwell on the goof of throwing human food to a dog in front of hungry children, I immediately called to the boys whose faces lit up as they came running over.

The two stopped in front of me, then reached out their hands— as if expecting crusts. This shocked me.

I stood up and motioned that they follow me to a small snack stand that a family had erected under a tarp near by. I asked them to pick out what they wanted, and got them their very own snacks. Another volunteer who had made the climb gave the boys some chocolate to share, and the two broke into smiles.

It struck me how the two little boys had assumed they would get crusts, like the dog. I felt sad to imagine that they saw themselves on par with a street dog, and even sadder knowing they could only have come to accept this role if it had been reinforced by their daily experiences—well-intended visitors, no doubt, giving them leftover food. It had become the boys' reality.

What also struck me was that even after twenty-five years of work among those with great need, I had a lapse in awareness and had shared human food with a dog in front of hungry children—an inadvertent act of disrespect. The incident reminded me of the many years it takes to cultivate awareness, and how even with the best of intentions, I can still fall short.

Over the years I've had to forgive myself many times, vowing to do better the next time. I was sure that wouldn't be the last lapse, and of course it wasn't.

37 – Scrubbing Our Assumptions

M Y FATHER USED TO SAY, "Assumptions make an ASS out of U and ME." I came to learn he was right. They can be deadly wrong even with people you know well, and that's especially true across cultures. During the years I've worked in Guatemala I've seen many examples of assumptions being made. And more times than I like to admit, I've been on the ASS end.

When Matthew Met Felix

For the first twenty years of Xela AID, besides volunteering, I also worked a paying job. At Harvey Mudd College I got to interact every day with 16- to 19-year-olds who were bright and energetic. I felt fortunate to work among them and the college's exceptional faculty and administration, and there always seemed to be ways to dovetail my day job with Xela AID projects.

Each year, Mudd students took on solving engineering problems for numerous for-profit companies which paid for the expertise. They also selected a lucky non-profit organization for which the work would be done gratis. Clive Dym, the chair of the engineering department, was in charge of these problem-solving teams called "Engineering Clinics." I told him about our work in Guatemala and he invited me to describe three social problems there that could be solved with engineering solutions. If one or more of them were appropriate to students, he'd consider devoting a team to solving them at no charge.

In the village of San Martín where we'd settled, most people cooked on open, dirty-burning stoves. Not surprisingly, respiratory infections topped the list of maladies we treated. (They are currently Guatemala's top killer.[46]) This was Social Problem Number One.

Chickens ran wild in the village, making eggs hard to find. As often as people got to eat free-range chicken eggs, so did wild dogs or vermin, robbing families of sorely needed protein. Many children were lethargic and had trouble studying or even staying awake—one of the telltale signs of protein deficiency. Social Problem Number Two.

And finally, men and women commonly walked long distances carrying wood and other supplies on their backs held by slings across the forehead. The stream of men and women we treated at Xela AID's clinic for chronic back pain was telling. There were no roads, nor could people afford off-the-shelf backpacks. That was Social Problem Number Three and the last of my proposed projects.

Xela AID was fortunate to be selected as the non-profit organization that would get Mudd expertise at no charge that year. Soon, Mudd students were creating designs for fuel-efficient stoves, chicken coops to corral gallivanting fowl, and backpacks that would be ultra-cheap and easy to make. To be appropriate, everything would need to be made out of local materials. For example, the students cleverly designed backpack frames to be made out of used PVC which was commonly available in the Guatemalan highlands.

Clive traveled to Guatemala with Xela AID, a handful of students, and another professor to implement these solutions, with mixed success. A solar-oven design worked like a charm when there was sun, in what we learned was an ultra-foggy region. (I should have caught a clue from the name of one of the local villages, *"Las Nubes"*—The Clouds). The ovens were also a cultural leap for women of the village who had generations of history cooking on wood-burning stoves. They did not catch on.

A chicken coop was built to withstand an earthquake, but didn't fare well in the torrential rains common to the region. The ultra-sturdy coop fashioned with four by fours and using industrial, weatherproof 3-inch screws and a thick tin roof fell over and floated away in the first major storm.

The backpacks made from used PVC and material from worn-out ladies skirts turned out to be the student team's success story. They were a rectangular shape stretching both overhead and below the buttocks to create a comfortable balance point off the upper and lower back. They sat squarely on the hips. Because of the unique design, I knew one—or a copy of one—when I saw it.

(I saw versions in use for many years after the students left. Each time I did, it made me smile.)

Both engineering missteps and successes were important to the students' learning process. And learn they did—not only about engineering, but about assumptions, too.

A student named Matthew had acquired a young helper, Felix, who showed up on site each day. Felix was perhaps 5 years old. A victim of extreme poverty, he lived nearby in a single-room brick house with his mother, sister, and two brothers. His threadbare clothes smelled of the open fire his mother cooked on, and he had only flip-flops for shoes. Matthew didn't speak a word of Spanish, but it didn't matter because neither did Felix, who spoke only Mám. Felix was quiet and watchful.

After a few days of work, Matthew confided in me at dinner that he'd been surprised at how wrong he'd been about Felix. Matthew had assumed that Felix was "slow," and just earlier that day, realized he'd been wrong. He began to notice that Felix was handing him tools even before Matthew realized he needed them. He'd realized Felix was not only extremely clever as he watched, learned, and anticipated what Matthew needed, but also that he was trying wholeheartedly to communicate and be friendly. Matthew had been entirely oblivious to Felix's overtures and now felt bad. "There are still a few days to go…" I pointed out.

During dinner after our last day at the work site, Matthew told me that after our talk he'd reached out to Felix. He began to teach Felix words in English, which Felix used almost immediately. Felix then taught Matthew words in Mám, "But I couldn't pronounce them or remember them," Matthew told me.

He was stunned about how wrong he'd been about Felix. Like all Mudd students, Matthew was brilliant, and not accustomed to being wrong. "He is smart, very smart. I'm not sure why I thought he was slow," Matthew told me. "Maybe it's because he doesn't speak English, or because of the way he looks, or because he is poor…" I shared with Matthew that I'd made assumptions about people—in Guatemala, and elsewhere—many times, and had been wrong, too.

In his post-trip essay, Matthew bravely concluded the following:

"I was cocky when I left for Guatemala—I knew everything. I don't think that way now. I have assumed things all my life and learned on this trip that they weren't all true. I now feel less certain about things, and that I have a lot to learn."

I knew exactly how Matthew felt.

The Autoclave

One year I visited a small rural clinic in Guatemala where the staff members were using alcohol to sterilize medical instruments. Alcohol is not effective against many germs, so we found and lugged a 50-pound autoclave to Guatemala to give to the clinic. I carried it by hand onto the plane, and fought to get it through Customs. In the process, I wrenched my back. But I didn't mind too much, since I was sure it would be worth all the effort.

In a ceremony attended by the local health minister, we handed over the autoclave. Both he and the clinic director thanked us profusely.

About a year later, we stopped in to visit the clinic. During a tour by the director, I noticed that they were still using alcohol to sterilize their instruments. The autoclave was nowhere to be seen.

When I asked the director if there had been a problem in using the autoclave, she was effusive about how grateful she was for the donation, and proudly, took me right to it. I was surprised to see it in their store room sitting on the floor, still wrapped up nicely, just the way we had delivered it. No one had even tried to use it, so that ruled out it being broken as the reason.

"I'm glad you still have it, but is there a reason you're not using it?" I asked, now brimming over with curiosity.

Matter-of-factly, the director replied: "To sterilize, it is our custom to use alcohol."

In the States, an autoclave would be used. I had not thought to ask if the director of this clinic saw a need for one and wanted one, and if not, if she'd like to learn more about how useful one could be.

Given that I'd not asked the right questions or offered additional information, my assumption had led me down a fruitless path. It was a lesson made more poignant over the course of a week by the shooting pain in my lower back!

Shakedown in Mexico

One year, the Xela AID Board decided we would transport to Guatemala a used vehicle—my aging but still useful Toyota Camry. Luis would use it to help carry out his duties for the project.

Luis was always looking to save the organization money. We could save lots, he told us, if rather than shipping the car by boat, or paying someone to transport it, we were to drive it ourselves. That sounded reasonable. In this case, "ourselves" would mean Luis and I and another volunteer, we decided, figuring three people would meet the criteria for "safety in numbers."

Wolfram was now serving on Xela AID's Board, and had helped hatch the idea for the car for Luis. His chivalry during the harrowing overnight with two flat tires near the site of a spate of beheadings was legendary among Board members, so all eyes were upon him for this mission. He agreed without too much arm-twisting.

Luis had heard from friends who transported autos to Guatemala through Mexico that it could get dicey, but that the challenges were manageable and worth the savings. I never asked what challenges his friends were referring to. I should have.

With a bit of research, we learned that you can't drive a car down the Pacific Coast if you intend to pass *through* Mexico. We'd be turned back at the border. To pass through, we'd have to first drive to Hidalgo, way on the other side, the Gulf side, of Texas.

From Los Angeles, that alone would be a three-day drive. But heck, that's what vacation time was for. So off we drove.

It was hot—no, hot as *hell*. Temperatures during the day topped 110 degrees in the Lone Star State. The car's puny, California-calibrated air-conditioning system wheezed out pathetic puffs of air that were only slightly cooler than the outside temperature. I'm not sure what we were thinking when we decided to do this in July, but now, we were committed.

We took turns driving. To get our minds off the heat, Wolfram and I started teaching Luis words in English, and he reciprocated in Spanish. For my turn teaching English, I started by practicing sentences with Luis like, "My name is Leslie, what is your name?" I would praise the response, "Hello Leslie. My name is Luis."

I taught Luis other sentences including "The road is long," and variations such as "The road is dark" and "The road is bumpy." Wolfram, on the other hand, chose to teach Luis words and phrases that where wholly inappropriate to say to a stranger, and tell him they meant something entirely different.

After listening to Wolfram contaminate Luis' vocabulary for a hundred miles or so, I finally put the *kibosh* on it. I let Luis know he'd been taken in and that he should never say any of the things Wolfram had taught him to any stranger he met. We all had a good laugh along those many long, and very hot and sweaty miles.

Before we reached the border town of Hidalgo, we met a convoy of Guatemalan men transporting cars, and Luis quickly bonded with them. They told us the safest route through Mexico, and also warned us to be off the roads by sunset each night to avoid being robbed by roving gangs. They also warned us to make sure our accommodations had a place for our car, or in the morning, we'd find it up on blocks, wheels gone, or the car missing entirely. What they did not tell us about—maybe because they'd become accustomed—were the constant stops by the police. There were lots of them, and it always seemed to happen when I was driving.

Each time was roughly the same. An officer would stop us and ask to see my passport. I'd hand it to him, and he'd thumb through it for a minute or so, turning it to different angles. He'd ask if I had additional identification. I'd hand him my California driver's license.

Then or about then, Luis would suggest, whispering, "Put some money in the passport and hand it back."

"No way!" I'd retort, or give him a dirty look.

The officer would then ask us all to step out of the car, and next, to unload the car. There we'd stand with the car's doors open, trunk up, and all our luggage outside. Sometimes the officer would continue looking through the passport as if reading every single stamp, word and letter before handing it back and dismissing us. It was an irritating waste of time, but I wasn't about to have money extorted from me. Wolfram didn't like the idea of extortion either, and agreed we shouldn't be intimidated into giving money. Luis must have thought we were both ridiculously stubborn.

Five days and at least a dozen shakedowns later, I still hadn't been worn down. But we'd all grown increasingly annoyed and weary of the routine. The next time it happened, Luis didn't say a word but just looked at me as if to say, 'Hey, it's your choice silly *gringa!*'

He's a patient guy.

I grimaced at imagining giving in and stuffing $50 or maybe more into the passport. It was not only the money, but it was the principle of the thing. For the first time, I wondered, how much *would* it cost? I had never thought to ask Luis.

"How much does he want?" I barked in a whisper.

Luis thought for a moment, then replied.

"Oh, just a few dollars."

Of course, I was incredulous. All the police stops had probably added a full day to our journey.

"Why didn't you tell me?" I crowed.

"I did!" he pointed out.

I hadn't heard him because I'd been too busy assuming.

We eventually made it to Guatemala. When Luis suggested we needed to pay someone off at the border, I didn't argue—much. That one did cost us $50, but I was so grateful to get to Guatemala that I didn't care. On the other side of the border, I got out of the car and literally kissed the Guatemalan soil.

Alan Alda said about assumptions that we need to "scrub them off every once in awhile or the light won't come in." Scrubbing, I learned, means listening, asking questions, and being open to changing my mind.

Otherwise, I might still be in Mexico.

38 – Dignity

ON A CRISP, FOGGY morning, our group boarded our bus in Xela to head up into the mountains to San Martín Chiquito. On the way out of town, a volunteer noticed a woman standing on a corner selling fruit, and suggested it might be nice to have some to snack on during the day. I agreed and asked the driver to pull over and let me hop off for a minute to buy some.

Sweet Bananas

The woman was elderly, with long, gray hair neatly parted down the middle and braided on both sides with a red ribbon running through each braid. She had erected a folding table covered with a bright red cloth upon which sat a selection of fruit, most of which would have been messy to eat. Her bananas caught my eye. She had two large bunches, totaling maybe eighty bananas in all. They were the small, sweet variety that can fit in the palm of your hand.

As I approached, she was speaking in a Mayan dialect with a nearby street vendor who was selling tortillas with black beans, and another vendor who was selling candies. She was dressed in Xela's Quetzalteca-style *huipil* and pleated skirt, so I guessed they were speaking in Quiché, the language associated with her dress. The vendors seemed to know one another well, and the old woman was enjoying a deep belly laugh as I walked up.

When I reached the stand, she immediately offered samples of mango, papaya, and ripe banana. The banana was melt-in-your mouth ready to eat and delicious. We negotiated a price—an art form in Guatemala. She gave me a high price, I came in too low, then we settled on a price about in the middle. That was the custom, and *not* negotiating with a vendor was seen as bad form—even a little rude, Luis had instructed me. I had to be careful, too, not to negotiate too far down to the point that I insulted the person's product or their intelligence. It was a dance, to be sure, and I kept in mind we were negotiating over pennies. I liked to let vendors have the last word. If I paid a price that was a bit too high, I never felt bad about it. I was sure the person would put the extra few cents to good use for their family.

"I'll take forty," I said, thinking that there were twenty of us and each team member might want two as a snack during the day. The woman smiled and began counting.

A moment later, I reconsidered. If I bought *all* the bananas, we could share them with the village children who, living in the highlands, didn't get to eat bananas often since they are cultivated several hours away on the warmer coast.

"Wait, I'll buy *all* of your bananas," I told the old woman. Her smile quickly disappeared and she stopped counting. She looked down at her bananas for a second, then looked back up at me.

In broken Spanish, she told me *no*. "You can buy forty, but no more." She began counting again.

I hadn't seen that coming, and couldn't for the life of me understand why. Maybe an explanation of why I wanted them all would help.

"Señora, I would like to buy all of your bananas so my friends and I can eat them and also share them with the children of the village of San Martín Chiquito where we are working.

"You can go home early today," I concluded with a smile, encouraging her.

The woman looked at me and said, matter-of-factly, "If I sold all my bananas to you now, what would I do the rest of the day?" She returned to counting, and I could tell that our conversation was over.

The woman placed the forty sweet bananas in a paper sack. I paid her, and went on my way.

On the bus I contemplated what had occurred and wrote my conclusions in my journal. I realized that selling sweet bananas on this corner each day was much more than this woman's livelihood. It was also the activity by which she shared time with other people, and affirmed her place in life. Her joy in her work was palpable, as was her sense of pride and dignity as she went about it.

Kahlil Gibran wrote, "Work is love made visible."

I understood the meaning of those words that day, and recall the woman's example when I'm having the odd, bad day.

Graduation Day

A worn bath towel with an American flag design was her shawl in cold months, and her hat in warm months. As I watched her exit Xela AID headquarters on this day in July, she neatly folded it and placed it on her head as her protection against the bright, hot sun beating down through the thin air at 8,500 feet.

Magdalena wore a faded *huipil* and *corte* (blouse and skirt) and walked barefoot. Her hair was mostly gray, and I guessed she was near 60. She could have been older, or younger for that matter. Here in the highlands poverty belt, life is so hard that it's almost impossible to guess someone's age within 10 years. At any age, it was tough to watch someone who could be my sister, mother, or grandmother walking barefoot on the stony, litter-strewn paths of the village. It was a miracle she hadn't stepped on glass or a rusty nail and died already.

Magdalena came to our building three days a week to take classes with Alicia, our literacy teacher. The advantage of being able to read, write, and do simple math is easy to take for granted unless you really think about it. Imagine if all the letters and words you saw looked like meaningless symbols. How hard would it be to travel if you had to do it all by landmark—no reading signs or maps to know where to get on or off a bus. No reading recipes for ingredients, or sizes on clothes; no reading stories to your children. And what if you couldn't count out money to pay, or count your change? This was the world Magdalena lived in. Alicia told me her story.

"She doesn't speak often, and when she does, it's only in Mám—and only in a whisper. In class sometimes it's as if she wants to be invisible."

Invisibility was a tactic to survive, especially during the height of the civil war. At that time, government troops had come through San Martín. They had punished anyone who they believed disagreed with the government and might stir up trouble, or had sold food to or otherwise aided the *guerrilla*. Magdalena told this to Alicia, who was too young to remember those times. Magdalena herself had nearly been killed by a soldier.

Magdalena's husband had drunk himself to death. Two of the couple's sons had followed in their father's footsteps. Magdalena had been left with two granddaughters to raise, and earned just enough washing clothes each day to feed them and herself.

Alicia could not explain how Magdalena had mustered the courage and strength to begin to study. Our headquarters was a good 30-minute walk from her home. She'd made the journey without fail, class after class, three days a week for the last *six months*. Tomorrow was graduation day.

I was fortunate to be in town to see the graduation. The fifteen women graduating spent the lion's share of their time doing household chores. They had very little time for themselves, and had sacrificed every spare moment they could squeeze out of a day to study. They'd probably done it without completely understanding how monumental being able to read and write would be. It would change their lives in amazing ways.

Our volunteer group would get to see this too. Alicia had us take our seats at the back of the classroom. The women came in ceremoniously, and walked to the front where Alicia had placed three rows of five chairs. By setting up a formal graduation and inviting an audience, Alicia set a reverent tone. She wanted the women to know that their accomplishment was nothing trivial. It was great preparation on her part.

After the women were seated, Alicia stood and spoke about how much time and effort each had put in. We followed with a round of applause. She then began calling the women up one at a time to receive their diplomas, to say a word or two if they wished, and to receive the individual applause that in each case brought a smile to their faces. Every one of these women's graduations was a personal victory, and also, a wonderful victory for their children. That's because almost 100 percent of all poor, rural women who become educated, in turn, make sure that their children are educated, too.

When Alicia called Magdalena to come up to receive her diploma, it was an especially moving moment. It was obvious by what she wore, her bare feet, and her exceptionally thin frame that Magdalena was among the extraordinarily poor of the village. Despite it all, she walked purposefully, with stunning dignity, and wore that towel on her head like a crown. Every eye in the room was upon her.

When Magdalena had moved in front of the class and us, Alicia went to hand her a well-earned diploma. But before Magdalena took it from Alicia's hands, she turned to directly face our group. She held up a rectangular piece of cardboard about a foot long she'd been holding at her side. She gripped both ends and turned the cardboard around, holding it up just beneath her chin.

Printed there in her own hand for all to see was her full name, "MAGDALENA JAUREZ PEREZ." Her eyes were steely and defiant, her emotion evident by a stray tear that escaped down her cheek. The room was absolutely silent as she spoke in Mám and Alicia translated. You could have heard a pin drop. Then, the room burst out with applause and cheers and she strode back to her seat, smiling and glowing with pride.

Alicia had translated:

"'From this day forward, I will never again face the indignity of signing my name with my thumb print.'"

That's dignity.

39 – A Covenant Between Equals

AN OLD FARMER IN TATTERED CLOTHES had been waiting in line at a *jornada* we were holding after we'd built our headquarters and clinic. I recognized him as a farmer because he carried a wide hoe, the tool of his trade and perhaps his most valued possession. He'd reached the front of the line and as I began to write down his name, what village he was from, and other vital information, he asked me for some water to drink.

A Cup of Ice

To keep things moving, each of us who had a post also had a volunteer runner assigned. I asked mine, John, if he could get the man a cup of drinking water which he gladly went off to do.

When John returned, he handed the water to the man who looked down at it, then turned to me and asked, "May I have some ice?"

That was wonderful. Few people had running water to drink at home, clean or otherwise. And in-home refrigeration was unheard of. We had a small refrigerator-freezer at the clinic that was stocked with ice to treat swelling. I was thrilled that this humble man had courageously asked for the water he needed, and then, for the small pleasure of ice. It was something most people in the village would have only heard of, but never seen. I hoped he was one of them so I'd get to see the look on his face when he had ice-cold water for the first time.

I smiled at the man, took the cup of water from him, and handed it back to John asking if he'd mind going to our small refrigerator and adding some ice. John's reaction was unexpected. He shot me—then the man—a disapproving look before taking the water and storming off into the clinic. The man could not help but notice John's scowl and looked at me, waiting for my reaction.

I smiled. "He'll be back with your ice water in just a minute, *no hay problema.*"

"Muy amable" (very kind) the man replied.

John soon returned. He handed me the water without saying a word and walked away. I handed it to the man who took it gratefully. He put both hands around the cup, looked into the water, then took a very small sip and smiled, telling me, *"¡Primera vez!"* (first time). I was thrilled. I'd gotten to see it. Too bad John had not.

That evening, our group went out to a local restaurant for dinner. I sat with John to see how he was doing in general, and also, to find out what had upset him about the ice situation. He wasn't shy.

"That guy had a lot of nerve asking for ice," John railed. "Beggars shouldn't be choosers!"

It's an old, well-worn adage. And there are so many reasons why it's wrong thinking.

"Would you have liked some ice in your water?" I asked him.

"Well I might have. But I certainly wouldn't have asked for it if I'd been that man. He was lucky just to get a glass of clean water!"

Father Gregory Boyle devoted his life to helping young people escape gangs in the toughest areas of Los Angeles. He wrote, "Compassion is not a relationship between the healer and the wounded. It is a covenant between equals."[47]

We all need to eat and drink, to be loved and accepted, to stay safe. We all feel the heartbreak of loss. It's so easy to lose sight of our inherent humanity and equality. Recognizing this is the essence of the true giving spirit. It's a mindset that has to be practiced. I've nurtured it for years and still, like John, sometimes forget.

Surprising Generosity

I hadn't been back to my old stomping grounds on Skid Row in Los Angeles for more than two decades. It was a shocker. Where once just a few streets were lined with tents where homeless people lived, in the fall of 2017, block after block of sidewalks were filled with encampments housing a mind-blowing *50,000 homeless people,* according to the latest survey. A trip to the wholesale district to find upholstery material with my sister Mara, and daughter-in-law April, had turned into a painful walk down memory lane made exceptionally heartbreaking because things had gotten so much worse.

After an hour or so of ducking into shops to compare offerings and prices, we found a restaurant to grab a quick lunch, ordered and sat down. A short, very thin man came in wearing torn, dirty clothes, appearing to be homeless. He passed by the tables asking in a whisper if anyone could spare some food. He held out a cap with a napkin in it to collect food offerings. I thought about how after five decades of life I'd never really gone hungry. I also thought about how humiliating it would be to have to beg for food.

Some people ignored the man and he quickly and respectfully moved on. Others put food from their plates into his hat—a chicken wing, a leg, a small tub of black beans. While the giving was all well meaning, it reminded me of a day I was throwing scraps to a dog. I couldn't bear it.

I asked the man what I could get him. "A taco," he told me. "Just a taco…"

I suggested a full lunch, three pieces of chicken. He was delighted about that and also, that he'd get side orders. He picked potatoes and black beans. When he thanked me, I was speechless. I couldn't imagine his burden, and it was such a small gift. I felt tears welling in my eyes, and sat back down with Mara and April.

While he waited for his food, he picked trash up off the floor and threw it away. Maybe he was "paying forward" any kindnesses he'd receive, or demonstrating his own humanity. *I am a person who cares.* Maybe it was both of these things. It is gratifying for each of us, in our own way, to make a meaningful contribution to the world. There is dignity in it.

As the man left the restaurant with his bagged lunch and accompanying drink, my eye caught his and he smiled. What happened next caught us all by surprise.

The man walked out of the restaurant, and through a large window behind us we saw him walk directly to a man who had been waiting outside. He showed the contents of the bag to the man, then patted him on the shoulder, tenderly. He then handed the man the drink and put the lunch bag on his lap. The second man—apparently homeless, or living in a very difficult situation—was in a wheel chair. The first man then wheeled him away. I was deeply touched.

So much generosity, even in the most desperate of situations.

Wrote Kahlil Gibran, "In truth it is life that gives unto life while you, who deem yourself a giver, are but a witness."

So it was.

40 – Worlds

"Each mind is a world."

—Cuban Proverb

THOSE WHO COME FROM QUETZALTENANGO in the Guatemalan highlands are endearingly called *chivos*—translated, *goats*. On a number of occasions over the years, we've had *chivos* among us in the States. I thought it would be valuable to bring select rural Guatemalans to immerse in our culture just as Xela AID volunteers were immersing in theirs when we visited. Since Luis was leading Xela AID in Guatemala, it seemed fitting to bring him to the states for some cultural immersion. Why I picked Las Vegas to initiate him is explained as well as possible in four words: I was thirty-something.

A Single Egg

Six of us squeezed into the car to take Luis on this adventure. We asked him to tell us what he thought about everything he saw. Like little kids opening a package on Christmas morning, we watched his face as he saw the desertscapes emerge and change. He had never seen a desert with its dramatic dunes, tumbleweeds and stately cacti. He told us, "It is like something from the movies."

Once we arrived, we dumped our stuff into a boys' room and a girls' room, both equally gaudy with red- and purple-velvet decor. We whisked Luis out and onto the Strip at dusk, anticipating the look on his face as he watched the sky darken and lights come up. He did not disappoint.

Luis was wide-eyed and almost in disbelief as one after another casino lit up so bright as to "make the night look like day," he observed. But the surprise on Luis' face quickly morphed into something else. While the rest of us cooed on about the audacious displays of bright bulbs and neon, his perspective gave us a taste of a different reality.

311

"I can't imagine what it would be like to have that much electricity to waste!" he said, shaking his head.

Imagine. In his world, electricity is a *luxury* often reserved for a single, dimly lit bulb at the center of a family's home to be used only for necessities after dark. Never just for fun.

I gave Luis $20, and told him not to worry about losing it. I encouraged him to have fun trying out the slot machines—like it was the cost of a night out. He played for hours, but of course lost every penny. He couldn't help but make the conversion to *quetzales* in his mind.

"That money could have paid a child's school tuition for a month. *¡Fíjate!*" (think of it) he said shaking his head in wonder.

An incident at an all-you-can-eat lunch buffet at one of the larger casinos brought another revelation. It was one of those mega-buffets four-lines-thick that was moving hundreds of people through lickety-split to get them fed and out gambling again as soon as possible. As we moved through the line, Luis was gobsmacked by the sheer quantity of food.

"Incredible, just incredible," he remarked, wide-eyed.

While he bravely tried dainty helpings of unknown fare, in the end, he opted for the familiar for his main course. He'd have eggs. We would order those from our server.

We sat down and the server soon arrived. After some back and forth in English-Spanish, we figured out that Luis would have his eggs over easy. She presented him with the specter of, "Bagel, muffin, or bread—white, wheat, rye or sourdough? Toasted? Buttered?" He had her repeat his options several times. He wasn't accustomed to so many choices, and it made him laugh. He then opted for white, untoasted, no butter, "What I normally have," he told us.

Minutes later, the waitress returned with Luis' eggs and white bread and put them down in front of him. His face telegraphed that the eggs were not what he had expected. They were sunny-side up, but runny-raw on the top. He looked at me in dismay.

312

"If you want them cooked some more, just ask," I urged him. He was hesitant, so I asked the waitress on his behalf.

Luis was relieved he wouldn't have to eat raw eggs, and thanked me. He then watched as the waitress took his plate away. After she'd passed behind me, I saw Luis' face go white. I had no idea why. When I asked him what was wrong, at first he could not speak. Then, his eyes grew soft and welled with tears. Still, no words.

"What's wrong Luis?" I jumped in, worrying that maybe I'd embarrassed him by returning the eggs. But it wasn't what I'd done. It was what the waitress had done after taking his plate.

Luis had watched the waitress whisk the eggs away, and instead of taking them back to the kitchen, promptly dump them into a trash can outside of my view. He had never seen good food thrown away, and he was truly mortified.

"I have seen a whole family give thanks and share nothing but a spoonful of rice each, and a single egg…"

"*A single egg*," he emphasized, his voice cracking.

I've learned so much from Luis over the years, including how easy it is to lapse into wastefulness. He's also reminded me how empowering it is to find gratitude for the simplest of things—like an egg.

Worlds.

The Weavers, the Stick and the Ball

One year we brought four weavers from the village to participate in a weaving conference Xela AID was putting on in Southern California. While they were here, we wanted to treat them to all kinds of changes of scenery, locally. (I'd learned my lesson about Las Vegas.)

"Why don't you bring them to visit me in Palm Springs?" my Aunt June urged.

This would have been a no-brainer had it been any time but the dead of summer, when temperatures in her neck of the woods would be excessive. But Aunt June had visited the village and met these women and wanted to share her hospitality. So after they'd been in the U.S. just a few days with heads already full of the wonders of freeways, tall buildings, and ice in drinks as the norm, we set off in my car for Palm Springs where that day, it topped 110 degrees Fahrenheit.

Gloria, Esperanza, Alma, and Doña Macaria were ages 30 to 62, (in that order). None had made it past the second grade, and only Alma could read. Alma, Esperanza and Gloria spoke fluent Spanish, and Doña Macaria spoke only a handful of Spanish words along with her native Mám.

During the Guatemalan Civil War, Alma had been beaten and nearly killed by a soldier who suspected her of selling supplies to the *guerrilla*. Esperanza had been nearly beaten to death by her drunken husband. Gloria was a single mother raising two children. All had block houses except Doña Macaria who lived with her husband in a shack of reclaimed tin and wood. None had running water. None had previously traveled more than a few hours away from their village. All were masters at the art of backstrap weaving, where the angular designs and bright colors of cotton threads tell the stories of their rich Mayan heritage. I was in awe to be in their presence and to get to see my world anew through their eyes.

Upon nearing Palm Springs, Alma pointed to a vast stretch of green grass on the passenger's side of the car, where sprinklers were in full force.

"Where is the water coming from?" she asked excitedly. I slowed and pulled to the shoulder to explain.

"Pipes, underground," I said. To her, water spewing skyward here in these wide-open spaces looked like pure magic!

"And what is being grown here to eat?" she inquired. In San Martín, water is a scarce resource that would rarely be invested in something that was not edible, or saleable.

"Well, it's *grama*," (grass) I explained, adding, "We don't eat it."

"Oh," she said, pausing. "Then is it grown to feed animals?"

"No."

"Grown to sell?"

"No."

"Do you burn it as fuel?"

"Well, no…" I could see where this was going.

"It's used to play a game," I answered, sheepishly.

Alma was silent for a moment, then commented, "There must be many, many children for it to be such a large area to play?" She translated to the others who shook their heads in agreement.

"Well, it's not really used for a game for *children*," I explained. "It's a game that *adults* play."

They were all staring at me now. They looked at one another quizzically.

Alma stated, as if she had not heard me correctly, "It is a game that *adults* play."

"Yes," I replied, realizing how silly this must sound considering that hers was a life of almost constant toil, dawn to dusk. In her world, adults simply did not have time to play games.

"It's played with a stick," I continued, now giggling, "and the adults use the stick to try to hit a small ball into a hole—or 18 holes, that is." Alma translated to the others.

I'd lost them. Worlds had collided. This made less-than-no sense to the four weavers and they were now transfixed looking at the length of rolling green, silent, as if they'd landed on Mars and realized they had no hope of ever communicating with the Martians. I felt like a Martian.

I started the car, moved back onto the road, and picked up speed.

315

After a few minutes had passed and we were well beyond the golf course, Alma asked me, gingerly, as if she half-feared the answer, "Do *you* play that game?"

"No I don't!" I declared, wearing it as a badge of honor.

Alma translated, and at that, the ladies all smiled, looked at each other and at me and started to giggle and speak in Mám.

Alma translated, "We are talking about what it would be like to have time to walk around with a stick hitting a ball into a hole!"

I laughed with them and felt relieved that we were all back on the same planet, at least momentarily.

When the five of us got to Aunt June's house and stepped out of the air-conditioned car, these women from the cold, foggy highlands of Guatemala, got their first taste ever of desert heat. It caused them to have the strangest look on their faces, as if to say, "What the f...?" Then, more giggles. It was sweltering.

Aunt June met us at the door and hugs were exchanged all around for this reunion of special women. Aunt June immediately noticed them sweating and whisked them into the house and the air conditioning and got them cold water to drink. But even inside, they continued to overheat. Their thick-weave *huipils* and skirts are meant to keep them warm at 8500 feet, and Aunt June and I realized simultaneously that her pool might be the answer. But these highland village women didn't know how to swim, and didn't own bathing suits.

"Have you ever been in a pool?" I asked the group. They had not. In their entire lives, none of the women had even immersed their bodies in water, not even in a bath. Never. They washed their hair in water, and steamed their bodies clean in small huts called *chüks*. Aunt June and I were both astonished.

Luckily, Aunt June is a woman of many bathing suits. Each of the ladies selected one. I showed them rooms where they could change clothes. Aunt June and I quickly changed and retired to the pool area, looking forward to experiencing the ladies' first time in a pool with them. When they emerged, it was a sight.

Alma and Esperanza who'd selected one-piece suits had managed to get them on right, mostly, but Alma had hers on inside out. Gloria had figured out her two-piece. Macaria had gotten the bottom of her two-piece on correctly, but was fully askew on top. The women of the village in her age group don't use bras, so she had no experience with how something like this might be worn. She was wearing the top piece backwards with the effect of covering her shoulder blades and fully exposing her breasts. Gloria had not helped, she said, because she thought hers might be on backwards.

Aunt June and I nearly fell off our chairs laughing, and soon, we were all laughing together, including Macaria who had no idea why we were all laughing. I quickly got Macaria righted before she caused a spectacle since Aunt June lived next to a golf course and her pool area was visible to passers by. (Before the day was over, the ladies got to see golf being played for themselves. They were not impressed. The swimming pool was much more interesting.)

The women started out just putting their toes in the pool, afraid to enter further than the first step. But with a little urging, they slowly eased in up to their calves. Before they knew it, they were up to their thighs. Soon, they were comfortably up to their waists. Alma let me take her floating on her belly. All four were wide-eyed and laughing. It was wondrous to see the common experience of a swimming pool through the eyes of these lovely women for whom it was something special and uncommon.

The novelist Marcel Proust said, "The real voyage of discovery consists not in seeking new landscapes, but in having new eyes." As with so many of my experiences with people of the village of San Martín, this moment was a reminder of the simple joys within our reach when we cultivate the eyes to see them.

41 - Alma and the Corn

IN THE *POPOL VUH*, the best-known surviving creation story of the Maya, The Creators first try to make people out of mud, but they melt. They try wood, but the resulting beings have no compassion. Finally, The Creators make humans out of corn and are satisfied with the result. The modern-day Maya sometimes refer to themselves as "People of the Corn." The nomenclature is fitting not only because of the creation story. Corn remains for the Maya an important food source, and is also a symbol of abundance and well being.

Corn kernels and husks abound even in Mayan-Christian worship. In the Mayan village of Salcajá, a six-foot-tall cross stands in the courtyard in front of *La Ermita de la Concepción,* Central America's first Catholic Church built in 1524. The cross is commonly adorned with corn husks and corn-kernel offerings. It is an example of how ancient and modern worship have become integrated, or "synchronized." It's a strategy practiced widely by the Catholic Church in Africa, on Indian reservations in the United States, and throughout the world to align local religious beliefs with Catholic beliefs.

In the case of *La Ermita*, corn was used throughout the 16th, 17th, 18th and 19th centuries to attract the Maya to worship at the small church, even though historical documents indicate that they were not allowed inside. To this day, the cross in the outside courtyard where the Maya worshipped is still adorned with corn at Easter and during other celebrations.

One summer when Xela AID brought San Martín master weaver Alma to Southern California to participate in weaving events, she stayed at my house for a few weeks. I loved learning about her beliefs and customs. My neighbors, however, were not amused when Alma—a modern Maya—demonstrated her deep-rooted devotion to corn.

As I got ready for work on the first morning of Alma's stay, I was already questioning the wisdom of leaving her home alone. She assured me she'd be fine. She would weave. She would study Spanish (she was a native Mám speaker who was working to improve her Spanish vocabulary). She may also cook up a surprise for me for dinner, she said.

I told her there was food in the fridge for her lunch and our dinner. I showed her how to use the phone. I wrote down my office phone number and told her to call me if she had a problem. I left convinced that she'd do fine on her own that day, and also vowed to myself to get home early—just in case. I walked out of the house at 7:30 a.m

Mid-morning, I called to check in on Alma. She didn't answer. She was probably fine, I reasoned. I worked through lunch. At 4 p.m. I made a beeline for the door and made the 30-minute drive home. When I pulled into the driveway, I noticed something different about the way the front yard looked, but I couldn't put my finger on it.

Walking up the path to the door I realized what had changed. There were mounds, LOTS of mounds, between the many drought-tolerant plants of my front-yard landscape. *Mounds of what?*

When I entered the house, Alma was as giddy as a teenager with a secret to tell.

"Leslita," she said. "I have a surprise for you!"

I was bracing, wondering if the surprise was something other than the mounds in the front yard. She took my hand and walked me into the backyard. Smiling ear-to-ear she watched to see the expression on my face as I beheld her handiwork.

I looked around the backyard, and in the beds behind the pool, along the back fence and side fences—basically, everywhere I looked—there were *mounds*. Mounds, mounds and more mounds, just like in the front yard.

"Wow!" I said, managing not to look distressed as I saw on the lawn several piles of mature plants she'd plucked from the soil to make way for the mounds. In one case, she had dug out an *entire hedge* and in its place, fashioned a bed full of mounds.

320

"Wow!" I repeated again. "What *are* those mounds?"

She explained: "I walked out to pick food for dinner, and there was nothing to eat growing here!"

Alma described this as if it would be a revelation to me, something I had overlooked. "No food *anywhere!*" she continued.

I had told her there was food in the refrigerator, and assumed she'd understood. She hadn't. But why would she? She didn't have a refrigerator. As it turned out, she'd never seen inside one.

"So I made this surprise for you," Alma said, now whispering, as if sharing a secret. "Earth is for growing food. It is a sin not to grow food on the land, and bad luck.

"Bad luck!" she emphasized.

She walked me deeper into the backyard, and to the large, mound bed she'd created. "You'll have corn, beans, carrots, and potatoes," she declared.

"Wow!" I repeated yet again, wondering where in heck she'd gotten the seeds, which was my next and obvious question.

"Your neighbor was out front. She speaks Spanish. I asked her to drive me."

I found it amazing that this precocious woman in full Mayan dress, who'd never met our neighbor, Juliette, had marched next door and asked for a ride to go buy seeds. That takes gumption.

Alma walked me around the entire property, backyard then front, showing me her many plantings that must have taken her the entire day. She'd planted the corn and beans together in the old Mayan way, she told me—four kernels of corn and three black beans to a mound, then a prayer. This, she said, was sure to produce two, three, or even four healthy stalks in each mound. A variation on this, if there were no black beans available, was planting seven corn seeds. But the seeds had to total seven, she explained.

Why seven?

321

"Seven is the number of the ending of cycles," she told me. She had no idea where this concept came from, but it had been passed along to her.

I was so fascinated by Alma's description that I asked her to plant another mound so I could watch. After ceremoniously placing each seed in a hole made with her finger then covering it, she said a brief prayer in Mám, then in Spanish (the latter for my benefit). The prayer invoked a triad of blessings, first that of her grandparents, then *Maximón* (a Mayan deity), then Jesus. I got chills watching and listening, imagining the unbroken chain of prayers that, while they'd evolved, stretched back generations. "It's the same prayer as in the very old days...minus Jesus." she clarified.

After selling weavings at a number of events, Alma returned home to San Martín. In the weeks to come at my house, the land produced, and produced some more. Many dozens of corn stalks shot up, most soaring past 12-feet tall. I eagerly surveyed my yard each morning, watching the tiny plants grow. Eventually, ears of corn appeared and grew larger. Everything got plenty of water from the sprinkler system, so I didn't have to do much. For a city-slicker like me who as a kid thought that food came from the grocery store, it was truly exciting to see a food crop flourishing in my own front and back yards. The neighbors however, with the exception of Juliette, didn't share my enthusiasm.

It wasn't too long before the ostentatious crop eclipsed the ornamentals. Giant corn stalks dominating the landscape were a spectacle in our upscale urban neighborhood, and some of my neighbors worried this might be the new norm at my house. One neighbor strolled over several times to comment on the corn, specifically, to ask when I'd be harvesting it and pruning (i.e. cutting it all down). "Some of us have been wondering..." she said. Juliette, who'd been an accessory to the crime, confirmed that there was a gaggle of neighbors who were not pleased. Her final comment on the matter was, "Let them eat corn!"

I thoroughly enjoyed this unorthodox garden and the gossip it generated. When months later I finally dug out the last dying corn stalk and cut it up for the compost pile, I'm sure my neighbors were relieved—until I planted corn again the next year.

Mayan Science

I was fascinated watching Alma create a mound and sow seeds. She seemed to have such a deep sense of connection to the earth, something I didn't have. I wanted to understand more about the tradition of what she chose to plant together, and her thinking while she planted. I did some research.

Science bears out the many-thousand-year-old Mesoamerican practice of planting beans with corn. Corn is a nitrogen depleter, and beans fix nitrogen back into the soil. Without the benefit of modern soil science, farmers would have to observe over generations that fields produce better yields when the two are planted together. It's amazing to consider how closely ancient farmers would have had to observe this, and over what span of time, to come to this conclusion.

Alma meticulously planted exactly four corn kernels, and three black beans, totaling seven. The numbers seven, four and three, all have particular significance in ancient and in modern spiritual texts. Both four and three are considered to be especially significant numbers across Native American and other spiritual belief systems. For the Maya, the number four (like the four kernels planted) represents the four directions and their *Bacabs*, "the gods who hold up the sky at the corners of the earth."[48] Some seven thousand miles away from Central America in the Middle East, the number four evolved as important in the Old Testament, including the Four Horsemen and Four Angels of Revelations, and the Four Winds that appears in Ezekiel.

Alma explained that planting exactly three black beans ceremoniously at the base of each of the corn stalks meant "earth, water, and sky" to her parents and grandparents. For her as a convert to Christianity, she planted the three beans in homage to the Holy Trinity of Father, Son, Holy Spirit.

The "ending of cycles" represented by the seven total seeds of each mound bears out in a traditional belief system of the Maya.

The number seven is half way to 13, the number of days (or "energies") in the repeating cycle which creates the recurring "weeks" of the Mayan calendar. Thirteen number sequences that begin with number one will always end with the number seven. In the Mayan creation story of the Popol Vuh, both the "Hero Twins" and the "Underworld Lords" carry the numbers one and seven, representing the Alpha and the Omega. Omega, seven, represents the ending of a cycle.[49]

For ancient Egyptians, seven represented eternal life. For modern Hindus, seven is the number of *chakras* or energy centers in the human body. There are dozens of uses of the number seven in the books of the Bible, including "seven pairs each" of clean animals on the Ark, "seven signs" in the Gospel of John, "seven qualities" the Lord dislikes, Jesus as the "seven-fold I Am," and many others. The first time the number seven appears in the Bible is in the Book of Genesis where God spends six days creating heaven and earth and rests on the seventh day, giving us the seven-day week. Just as it does for the Maya, seven in the Judeo-Christian tradition also represents a completion, the end of a cycle.

I find it extraordinary that people from all corners of the earth have created a parallel language in numbers. Perhaps it evolved in the search to understand ourselves, our universe, a Higher Power and our relationship to it. These common symbols hint at our connection across barriers of land, culture and vast swaths of time to ancient people such as the Maya, who I am so grateful to have the privilege to work among.

"We are like islands in the sea, separate on the surface but connected in the deep."

—William James.

Enjoy this song I wrote for Alma and the weavers:

• The Weaver's Way

www.lesliebaerdinkel.net/HopeDancing/Songs/

42 - Mayan Wisdom

ON THE FIRST OF ALMA'S STATESIDE VISITS, I took her to the Claremont Farmers' Market. It is one of the markets my son, Oscar, manages. As we walked stall to stall taking in the vivid colors and scents of fresh fruits and vegetables, Alma tutored me on the names of these food items in her native language, Mám. She also taught me their Guatemala-Spanish names, since many words change in the various countries of Latin America. For example, in Guatemala, a peanut is called *mania*, while in Mexico, it's a *cacahuate*. Being that California borders with Mexico to the south, the Spanish we learn here in school and the *Spanglish* we acquire tend to favor Mexican Spanish. It was a good education, and I returned the favor by teaching Alma the English equivalents.

During our walk through the market, we bumped into an old friend of mine who'd once volunteered on a trip with Xela AID. Bobbi Hill had met Alma during her trip with us years before, and was quite excited to see her again. Accompanying Bobbi was her daughter, Sydney, who was many months pregnant.

Dar La Luz

"I'm going to be a grandmother!" Bobbi proudly declared.

Besides being a master weaver, Alma is also a midwife. It was a calling "passed down from mother to daughter through the generations in my family," she'd told me. And this was no insignificant post in life. *Comadronas* are revered, since they bear the great responsibility of shepherding in new generations. In fact, *"dar la luz,"* the term for giving birth, translates literally to "give the light." *Comadronas* keeping vigil prior to a birth are called in Mám by a term meaning "light keeper." This was the term Alma's grandmother had used for her mother when she was away tending a birth. While the term is heard "less than when my grandmother was alive," Alma told me, the *comadrona* tradition continues. More than 70 percent of all births in rural Guatemala are still attended by midwives.[50]

While one could be trained as a *comadrona*, it is widely believed among the Mám that one who has not been gifted through *herencia*, heritage, will face an uphill battle to learn, and could be unlucky in their craft. Since a deep-rooted belief in magical cures and curses continues, midwives with *herencia* like Alma are sought after since they are believed to possess healing wisdom. From first consultation through delivery, a *comadrona* will receive up to Q600 (about $90), depending upon the mother's ability to pay.

As we stood before Bobbi and Sydney, on instinct, Alma extended her hand toward Sydney's bulging belly and looked at her with widened eyes to ask, "Is it OK for me to touch?" Sydney nodded in the affirmative and Alma placed her hand firmly on Sydney's belly and did some pressing here and there. Smiles were exchanged. Alma removed her hand, smiling, and nodded her head in an apparent gesture that all was well with the baby.

"We just got back from the doctor and the baby is due in two weeks," Bobbi told me excitedly. I translated to Alma, who said nothing, and just smiled and nodded.

After saying our farewells, Alma and I resumed our walk through the fragrant fruits and vegetables. When Bobbi and Sydney were out of earshot, and between us exchanging Mám, Spanish and English names for plums and peaches, Alma commented casually, "The baby will be born *tonight*."

I thought for a moment, and then concluded, *Alma must be mistaken*. While she had only visual observation and touch to determine such things, Sydney's doctor had all the tools of modern medicine, and must certainly be more accurate about when the birth would occur. I imagined, too, a modern delivery room, versus the basin of warm water, clean cloth, and clothespin for clamping the umbilical cord that Alma would have. There was little doubt in my mind who was more qualified to predict when the baby would come. So, I explained modern tools to Alma—the blood tests for gestational diabetes and birth defects, the ultrasound, the calendar calculations, a doctor's vast knowledge of the subject, etc. She appeared very impressed, and thanked me for having explained.

Satisfied that we were now both on the same page about the superiority of modern medicine, including the superior accuracy of birth calculations based on science, I walked with her to the next booth. Just as Alma picked up a large, purple, eggplant, she said, casually, "But the baby will be born *tonight*..."

That took some audacity. How could this woman with no formal education and no tools but her five senses and her intuition know more than a painstakingly educated doctor from one of the best medical systems in the world? I decided to humor her, shrugged my shoulders and thought, *Why argue?*

The call the next morning was unexpected—at least, by me. Bobbi thought I'd like to know that the baby had come, well, during the night.

"Mother and daughter are doing well," she merrily told my answering machine while I contemplated the many ways to eat crow.

When I told her, Alma was not surprised at all. No semblance of an "I told you so" passed through her lips. It was as she'd known it was, and there hadn't been a doubt in her mind, nor any need to prove herself.

When I asked her how she knew the baby would come the previous night, she could not articulate it fully. In part, it was "the way the baby was sitting." It was also "the activity" she felt, and more she'd intuited as she touched Sydney's belly.

"It is the sense of another human being reaching out, ready to come into the world—a new light eager to shine," she explained, leaving me more baffled than ever, and in awe.

I can't count how many times I've been surprised by what my Mayan friends know. Theirs is a practical wisdom.

"Say not, 'I have found the truth,' but rather,
'I have found a truth.'"

—Kahlil Gibran

A Lesson in Time

One day two years into our project I was lamenting to Esperanza, a weaver and midwife about 50 years old, that I was dealing with doubts and a little burnout. Our young leadership team had a vision for Xela AID, but we hadn't developed the skills or the support system to get there yet. For my part, I could only work on the project part-time, as I had a demanding full-time, paying job. I knew we needed to find more expertise, and to meet with other groups and learn from them to avoid missteps. I also knew I needed to develop my own skills, and finish a related degree. But all that would take time. I was like the five-year-old who wants to be all grown up before their time.

Esperanza listened intently, then smiled and asked, "Leslita, are you doing all you can do?"

I thought for a moment, then answered, "Yes, I believe I am."

"Then *no se preocupe* (don't worry). Just keep planting and your day will come to reap," she said with great confidence and wisdom.

She concluded, "You can't rush the corn."

The Day Keeper

I read a National Geographic article about a 3000-year-old wall of calculations discovered in a small Mayan ruin outside a larger ruin called *Xultún*. It relates to the Mayan calendar and computes the cycles of the moon and sun. The calculations not only chart the past, but accurately predict planetary and solar movements some 7,000 years into the future. I find that *amazing*.

Besides its astronomical purposes, there have been volumes written about the ancient Mayan glyphs appearing in the Mayan *Tzolk'in* and *Haab* calendars. Used in different regions, the two differ slightly, including a few of the glyphs they use to represent what is called the "energies of the days." The scholarly material I found on the subject was dense, and wading through it made me understand why archeologists go to school for *years* to understand it. In 1995 I was fortunate enough to meet a man who *lives it,* and brought the glyphs to life for me.

Eliü' (pronounced Ay-lee-OO) is straight off an ancient stela at a Mayan ruin. His powerful nose, jutting jaw and compact frame could not be more classic Mayan. Nor could his manner be more humble, or his interpretation of the meaning of ancient Mayan glyphs more profound.

Luis first introduced me to Eliü' after he floated the idea of Xela AID volunteers experiencing a Mayan spiritual ceremony. I had stressed to Luis that Los Angeles was rife with New-Agey shaman*esque* experiences, and that such a dog-and-pony show wasn't what I had in mind. If we were to do it, it should be as authentic as possible. He understood, since in Guatemala, too, there are plenty of pretenders. When I said the word "authentic," Eliü' immediately came to Luis' mind.

"¡Él es Shamán, cien por ciento!" he told me—100 percent, the real deal. Over a cup of coffee at Baviera, Quetzaltenango's famed European coffee shop, Luis elaborated on Eliü's credentials. I was fascinated, and agreed we should talk to him about the idea. I didn't have to wait long. Luis used the house phone to call the "true Mayan Shaman" to join us, and in about 45 minutes, Eliü appeared at our table.

With hat in hand, kind eyes and a gentle smile, Eliü introduced himself to me. Because of his features I had to pinch myself to make sure I hadn't traveled back in time. The only thing that gave him away as a modern man was his uniform. Besides the significant time he devoted to the study of Mayan spiritual practices (he founded an organization to preserve them), Eliü' was also a devoted Scout leader. Earlier that day, he'd taken his troop on an outing at a park and still wore the telltale, blue Scout uniform and neckerchief.

Scouting was what Eliü' and Luis had in common, and over the years they had shared a troop—but not just any troop. The two were co-leaders of a troop of more than thirty orphaned children, boys and girls, since in Guatemala, Scouts are combined. Eliü' had been the primary leader on duty for the past several years while Luis had expanded his work with Xela AID, and the two had remained close friends.

After sitting down, Eliü and Luis began to share stories and updates about individual children in their troop, particularly, two who had once lived in an orphanage Luis founded and ran for a decade. Luis was content to hear that the two children were still in Scouts and doing well overall. Then, as if a timer had gone off and the appropriate amount of chit-chat had been completed, the conversation turned on its heels to a world much less tangible.

Calling me by my first name (I was impressed he'd remembered—its not a common name in Guatemala), Eliü' began to explain in simple terms the heart and soul of his spiritual practice. It is not a religion, he said, but a mental discipline to "grow in goodness." Some of his explanation slipped beyond the bounds of my Spanish comprehension, so I asked Luis to clarify concepts as we went, and I took notes.

"To help us grow in goodness, we learn about the energy of days," he said. "Every day has its own attributes, or energy to it, including the day we are born, today, tomorrow…all days that have ever been and all days that will be.

"The day each of us is born is significant because it represents the energies we will work with in this lifetime—the strengths or gifts, and the lessons we most need to learn as we evolve as souls.

"And for the Maya," he added, "there is no distinction between the body and the soul—they are one."

I was charmed at how poetically Eliü' spoke. His words were so subtly complex that at times Luis had trouble clarifying them to me in simple Spanish (we returned to my notes later and looked up some words to be more precise).

"Our ancestors were great mathematicians who left us information to guide us in the form of numbers. The meaning of the days is a puzzle that cannot be completely solved, because the energies exist as part of us. Like us, the answers are ever evolving. To solve this would be to understand all the mysteries and one would have to be a perfect being—and none of us is that!"

Eliü' laughed aloud and smiled, punctuating that point.

"But those whose life's work is solving the puzzle of the days, understand them as a road map of lessons to navigate by. Those of us who are solving the puzzle, and keeping the puzzle pure, and sharing the puzzle with others, are called Day Keepers.

"I am a Day Keeper, and I am at your service," Eliü' concluded.

I had been riveted as he spoke, and especially impressed at his sincerity. Surmising from his long association with Luis who surrounds himself with goodness, I knew Eliü' was no snake-oil salesman hawking his wares. Everything about him screamed authenticity, and the passion he had for his work as a Day Keeper was palpable. If there was any proven validity to the "energy of days," I did not know. But I did believe after meeting Eliü' that he would provide our volunteers with an experience with a Mayan shaman that was as authentic as possible in modern times.

Eliü' joined our group one evening that week. Several days prior, at his request, I collected and forwarded the birth dates and years of all eighteen of us who wanted to participate in the ceremony. Two volunteers hung back, feeling that participation might be antithetical to their religious beliefs.

We gathered in an open field near dusk. The field was five minutes from an eatery where, after the ceremony, all of us would reunite for dinner. Eliü' placed a red woven cloth over his head and secured it with a cord which he tied at the back, a length of braided gray hair visible down his back. He had us gather in a circle, then with a stick he drew a circle in the center of our circle of people. He looked to the horizon and at landmarks, and within that circle drew two lines at right angles. This created four equivalent segments in the circle.

Where the lines touched the circle were the "cardinal points," which he adorned with thin, colored candles of particular colors: red for the east, black for the west, white for the north, and yellow for the south. He added in the center of the circle green candles to represent the earth, and blue for the sky. His selection of colors was not random, Eliü' explained. The red, black, white and yellow coincided exactly with the four colors of corn so central to Mayan culture.

Eliü' then piled at the center of the circle crystalized resins pressed into balls, including copal and pine sap, and added shards of a fragrant wood he called *palo de jiote*. He then placed a carefully counted number of each of the various colored candles at the center, struck a match and lit the offerings which quickly began to burn. He stirred them with a stick into a hot blaze. The aromatic resins and candles doused us with sweet-smelling smoke, and the fire burned brightly against the night around us. Eliü's face luminesced in the fire's glow.

With great reverence, he handed each of us our own baggie of candles, resins, and rock salt. Each had a note pinned on top. On the note was written our name, birthday, and the name of the glyph assigned to the day of our birth on the Mayan calendar. He told us we would place the contents of the baggie into the fire after he spoke about the energies of our particular glyph. The last thing we would add would be the salt, representing "our humble acknowledgement that we are made from Earth and Sky, and it is to the same that all of us shall one day return."

Then, one by one, he called us forward as our days of birth coincided with each of the twenty glyphs, called, *nahuales*, "representing divine qualities," and the thirteen numbers that, together, form a Mayan "Day Sign" with particular energies.

To the Day Sign *T'zi*, which is Mel's sign and sometimes represented by the coyote, Eliü' ascribed in part the qualities of courage, superior problem solving, being just and faithful, protective and loving, and a trusted guide into the unknown. I thought to myself that these sounded like the man I know and love. (All *that* and amazingly good looking too!)

To my Day Sign, *Iq,* sometimes represented by the hummingbird, he ascribed in part the qualities of good communication, creativity, and the ability to inspire as a leader. He ascribed, too, the challenges of "sometimes being stubborn, and often spreading oneself far too thin"—both of which I can confirm with full confidence. And so he continued reciting the strengths and challenges of the other eighteen *naguales*, repeating a blessing for each group of people sharing the same *nagual.*

"To You, our Heavenly Grandfather-Grandmother, by any name, may all of us of [this *nagual*] make the most of our divine qualities, overcome our challenges, and grow in goodness." As each of us stepped forward to hear our attributes and challenges, receive our blessings, and add our offerings to the flames, Eliü' asked that we ascribe to that act and to his prayer whatever meaning was compatible with our individual spiritual beliefs.

After completing all twenty *naguales*, Eliü reverently bowed to each of the four directions. He prayed for our volunteers' safe return home, and that one day each would return to Guatemala. He then used the stick to move all the candles and incense into the inner circle where they would be completely consumed by flames. With the center flames still dancing, he erased the outline of the small circle, bowed to us, and walked person to person shaking our hands and thanking us for having participated.

It had been a touching ceremony, with grandfatherly wisdom kindly delivered. At about two hours long, it was probably about an hour too long for the average fidgety Westerner. But we'd wanted authentic, and I believe we got as close as we could some five hundred years after the integration of Mayan spiritual beliefs with Christian traditions began.[51]

At the end of the ceremony, the volunteers were inspired, but hungry. Dinner was a treat, and so were the conversations volunteers had with Eliü for several hours in the restaurant.

Planetary movements in the ancient Mayan calendar predicting specific strengths and challenges in the lives of us mere mortals sounds far-fetched, I know. Nonetheless, that night at dinner, I couldn't help but notice how Eliü's ceremony had touched everyone in our very diverse group.

One volunteer raised in the Jewish tradition said the ceremony had felt akin to the mysterious and reverent readings of the Torah he'd heard in his youth. A doctor raised a Jain felt it compatible with Jain teachings of "right knowledge, faith and practice." It so touched her that she felt the Maya might somehow share spiritual roots with her own ancient faith. Another volunteer who'd been disillusioned with religion in general due to what he called "over-literal and narrow definitions of truth," found the ceremony refreshingly spiritual. Even the self-identified atheists among us described it as a touching spiritual experience.

For me, the sweet scent of burning incense took me back to my childhood with my mother at St. Anthony's Catholic Church in Anaheim, California, where I grew up. The ceremony made me feel safe and reassured.

I thought about how this ceremony had resonated so positively with people from such different spiritual backgrounds. It struck me that the quest "to grow in goodness" is a common human theme, a timeless quest. Circa 359 BCE, Socrates taught, "Virtue is knowledge...all living things aim for their perceived good." From the Bible, around 62 AD, the Epistle of Paul to the Philippians says, "Whatever is true, whatever is honorable, whatever is right, whatever is pure, whatever is lovely...dwell on these things..." If one believes we emerged from the primordial soup, were fashioned from the rib of the first human being, or were created out of corn, who hasn't tried to grow in goodness and to be a better person? For many of us, it's a lifelong pursuit.

When Luis clarified some of the words Eliü' had used in his concluding prayer, I realized he had made that same point:

"Whatever our spiritual path, we are united in our longing to act as better human beings, to love and be loved, to be peaceful and happy. Through our active seeking and reflection, may we also become wise."

Amen.

43 - Learning to Weave

A T A LECTURE I ATTENDED by the Dalai Lama, one of the interviewers asked him if he had any regrets. He didn't hesitate in saying that he did.

The Dalai Lama told a story of an old monk who came to him wanting to attempt a pilgrimage up a local snow-covered mountain. This he would do to demonstrate and reaffirm his devotion to God.

Fearing that the old monk could perish in the cold, the Dalai Lama dissuaded him, telling him that his devotion was obvious and the pilgrimage was not necessary. Deflated, the old monk thanked the Dalai Lama and took his leave.

A few days later, a note was delivered to the Dalai Lama. It read, 'If I am no longer worthy enough to undertake a pilgrimage to demonstrate my devotion, then I have no reason left to live.' Soon after, the Dalai Lama learned the old monk had taken his own life. Of course the Dalai Lama was full of regret, and he told the interviewer so.

"How did you overcome that regret?" the interviewer asked, on the edge of his chair awaiting the Dalai Lama's profound answer.

"I never did," the Dalai Lama replied. He then paused, leaving the interviewer looking puzzled.

The interviewer was unprepared with a follow-up question, so for a moment, an uncomfortable silence hung in the auditorium. Then, the Dalai Lama added, thoughtfully, "I had to weave this regret into the fabric of my life."

Over the years with Xela AID, I've had to do some weaving, too.

Starfish

During the first several years of Xela AID volunteer trips, I sometimes succumbed to feeling hopeless. We were confronting what seemed like an endless sea of suffering, and I couldn't see the difference we were making. Since on a given *jornada* we'd have only two or three doctors, out of the many hundreds of suffering people who came, we'd have to select just a hundred or so to be seen. Sometimes, we had to choose from as many as a thousand people who had travelled from hours away with hopes of seeing a doctor and getting well. I was deeply saddened to have to turn people away.

Walking through lines and triaging for what appeared to be the worst cases made me feel like I was playing God. I'd get physically ill. I tried to avoid having to do it, but more often than not, I was needed to assist. We'd seek out accident victims with bleeding wounds, babies who weren't eating or had persistent high fevers or diarrhea, and other cases that were obvious emergencies. If I hadn't found a mental framework to be able to accept that we couldn't help *everyone*, and to be grateful for those we *could* help, I might have quit the project. There were a few stories I held onto like lifelines.

One day my friend Abdi Sami told me this story he'd heard as a child in Iran. I've now heard it repeated many times in slightly different versions.

A woman is walking down a beach and comes to a place that is thick with many thousands of starfish. There had been a storm, and she realizes they've all become stranded and will soon perish in the hot sun. The woman immediately begins picking them up and placing them back in the sea, one, two, three, four, as carefully and as quickly as she can.

Another person, upon seeing the immensity of the task before the woman, comments to her that what she is doing is obviously futile.

"You'll never be able to get all of them back in the water, so what you are doing will not matter!" the person exclaims.

Wholeheartedly dedicated to the task at hand, the woman holds up the single starfish and just before returning it to the sea answers, "It will matter to this one."

Another story I've clung to came from Mother Teresa, who, as a young nun, picked up a single man dying in a gutter and gave him shelter. Shortly thereafter, she formed her own Order, and founded The Home of the Pure Heart in Calcutta. There, some of the city's poorest and most destitute people had been taken in and nursed back to health, while others died in loving hands and with dignity. Shortly before the end of Mother Teresa's life, the Home she founded beginning with one person, had cared for more than 40,000 people.

It mattered to them.

Kimberly

There are at least 15,000 young people in Xela AID's coverage area. No matter how much we advertise and coerce, some people in the region are afraid of doctors or won't go see one until they are on their deathbed (which of course happens in the U.S. too). Some mothers will bring their children in for health screening, and others will not. And even if every single person came in for screening and treatment, not everyone could be cured.

Kimberly still stands out in my memory. She was a pixy of a little girl, as cute as could be, sweet and demure and with a sparkle of mischief in her eyes. If not for her shortness of breath at the slightest exertion, you would have thought she was a normal five year old. But Kimberly was born with a heart defect that by the time we saw her, was beyond repair. Dr. Steve Kent who was volunteering at our clinic in San Martín had to break the bad news to Kimberly's mother.

"Kimberly may live another few years," Dr. Steve had to tell her. "We can make her more comfortable, but there is no hope for recovery."

I will always regret that we couldn't save Kimberly. Her short life and those of other children suffering with diseases that could have been prevented or cured inspires me to continue working to improve medical care in Guatemala.

Our village and region is a start.

Ana

Haunted by Kimberly's case, Dr. Steve acquired an EKG for our clinic. We began a screening program to detect life-threatening heart defects like Kimberly's so that they could be corrected before it was too late for other children. Just a month after we started the screening program, we detected a heart defect similar to Kimberly's in a little girl named Ana. Ana was less than two years old, and the damage to her heart was not yet beyond repair. Time was of the essence, and we were able to advocate within the Guatemalan healthcare system and get her the surgery she needed in weeks rather than the months or up to a year we'd been told she would have to wait.

Post-surgery, little Ana is thriving. The screening program mattered for Ana.

The Greater Good

At a certain point I became concerned that Marcos may have connections to the *guerrilla*. Not that I didn't believe their cause was a just one. But our organization's work depended on access to Guatemala, and on volunteers whose safety was our top concern. Staying safe meant staying out of politics as much as was humanly possible.

Upon occasion, Marcos would ask for medicines for a "community clinic" he was helping. I'd given him boxes of medicines with full faith that it was going to good use—this was Marcos, after all. The same one who'd been on that mountaintop with me the night of the attack. The same one who had presented the conference at the Spanish school years before which had opened my eyes to a new reality, and in doing so, had helped me find a deeply rewarding purpose. I was grateful. At the same time, bringing volunteers to a foreign country was a big responsibility, and one I took seriously. Our collective safety was my ultimate guide. It led me to have to make a terrible decision.

Under Luis' leadership in Guatemala, Xela AID was flourishing and growing. I'd not seen Marcos since we parted ways years earlier over my refusal to spill to the press details of our large donation of medicines to the First Lady. Gaby had come around only occasionally. I'd missed them, and had thought about trying to reconnect, but had stopped short. No matter how I felt, I knew it was best to leave the situation alone. But this night, some years later, Gaby came to find me. She came to the Hotel Modelo in Xela where our group was staying and knocked on my door. It was not good news.

"He's been taken by the police!" Gaby blurted out in a panic when I opened the door.

"They've beaten him. They're holding him somewhere..."

I welcomed her in to sit down, and after she took a few deep breaths she was able to tell me the story. "Slowly," I said to her, so I could understand every word.

Gaby explained that Marcos had become increasingly involved in an organization called *"Derechos Humanos"* (Human Rights) with a branch in Quetzaltenango. The organization was well known for challenging government abuses. As such, it had been targeted by the local police who were, at that time, an extension of the central government and the military, she explained.

"He confronted the police about illegally detaining some men, then they took him away," she continued.

He'd called her from an unknown location, telling Gaby not to notify the authorities and not to try to find him. If she did either of those things, the men holding him would kill him. She was convinced that his abduction had been directed, or at a minimum approved, at the highest levels. She came to see me.

"You've met our President and First Lady. They value the aid that Xela AID is providing. You must send them a FAX saying that

Marcos is the legal representative of Xela AID so that they will personally have him released," Gaby pleaded.

Xela AID had delivered millions of dollars in medicines and invested tens of thousands of dollars in the local highlands economy. In our earliest days, we'd done it all very publicly. Some in power had likely benefited personally. And while we'd gone low-key, we were still on people's radar, Gaby suggested.

"You've got *cuello*," pull, she said. "If you don't do this, and do it quickly, I may never see Marcos again," she told me, now weeping.

I was shaken, and torn. Revolutionary soldiers had, on many occasions, shown up at our mobile clinics in remote villages, sunburned, starved, wounded and debilitated. The *guerrilleros* who came to our clinic the day after three of us were kidnapped, had learned about that *jornada* from me. I'd invited them to come. But on other occasions, Marcos was the common thread. I'd figured out that these fighters appeared at our clinics every year we had contact with him. If he was a *guerrillero,* any links to Xela AID could be devastating for us. We'd be an organization *non grata* in Guatemala, basically, toast.

The policy had been made clear by the Guatemalan military[52] and allies: Help the revolutionary fighters, and you'll be shut out of the country, or murdered.[53] Such terror had rained down on international citizens suspected of supporting local dissenters, from innkeepers to nuns.[54] I had no illusions that Xela AID volunteers would be spared.

I thought for a few minutes. I asked Gaby to wait for me there in my room. I grabbed my leather notebook containing our organization's official stationary, and stepped into the lobby to use the hotel's lone computer. Writing the letter was agony.

To whom it may concern:

Marcos Fernandez volunteered with Xela AID for several years. He assisted us with the distribution of medicine to remote rural clinics. As a volunteer, he always showed great enthusiasm working with our group, which is strictly humanitarian in nature. We are truly appreciative for the service he rendered, and we wish Mr. Fernandez well in his endeavors to assist those in need.

I signed my name and added my title. I gave the hotel receptionist two pieces of stationary and asked that she print out two copies of the letter on the hotel's printer behind her desk. I signed one copy, and went back to my room.

I handed the signed letter to Gaby, and told her it was the best and the *only* thing I felt I could do to help. I encouraged her to FAX it to the published number for the Presidential Palace, and apologized for not being able to do more.

Gaby read the brief document, then again, began to cry. Her crying turned to a wail of grief, as if Marcos were already dead. Between sobs, she said, "This is not enough!"

I was out of words and could only look at her. I could not speak. My eyes were full of tears and my shoulders heavy with the weight of responsibility I felt for the safety of our volunteers, and our future in mission Guatemala.

Then, Gaby stared at me coldly. I suppose there seemed to be a coldness in me, too, as I looked back with firm resolve. Without uttering another word, she left. I felt sick, and traitorous.

The next morning, I told Luis what had happened and showed him a copy of the letter. He told me I had done the right thing in keeping it brief and not embellishing Marcos' roll with Xela AID, even though Gaby had asked for more.

"It is wise, *very wise* to keep a distance," he said.

I believed that was true. But it didn't make me feel any better.

Six months later, Luis filled me in on what had happened to Marcos. As Gaby had told me, when he intervened during an arrest of two suspected *guerrilla* collaborators, he, too, was handcuffed and taken away. The rest of the story was that instead of being placed in the back of the car with the others, he was thrown into a trunk. When he was removed from the trunk, he was hooded, then placed in a filthy cell in some kind of prison facility. There, in a chair, with his hands bound behind him, he was beaten by thugs who said they would stop once he admitted he was collaborating with the insurgent forces. He maintained that he was nothing more than a social worker, even as they beat him, finally, fracturing one of his legs. But Marcos had survived.

I broke out in a cold sweat as I heard the story, and felt slightly faint. By the look of concern on Luis' face, I must have looked as pale and distressed as I felt.

"I am sorry about this news, Leslita, but I always want to tell you the truth," he offered.

My mind boomeranged back to Gaby's visit and raced with other options I might have had. After a pause, my voice cracking and feelings of guilt wracking my stomach, I blurted out to Luis, "I might have been able to save him from that."

Luis reassured me that I was right to stop at the letter. "Any further association could have destroyed everything we have worked for!"

For several months after this incident, I was guilt-ridden and feeling sorry for myself. *How many more people I care for will I have to sacrifice for this cause?* I succumbed to self-pity for a time. I had some weaving to do…

> "A thousand deaths my heart has died,
> and thanks be to love, it lives yet."
>
> —Hazrat Inayat Khan

PART VI ✚ FINDING OUR WINGS

44 - The Lesson of the M.C. Sisters

Spiders, snakes and heights are at the top of the list of what people are most afraid of. Asking people for money is not far behind. Asking for support for one's good cause goes with the territory of running and growing a non-profit organization. What I witnessed one afternoon in 1991 in an emergency room with two Missionary of Charity Sisters still gives me the courage to ask for help for those in need—and chills...

A S THE NEWLY MINTED COORDINATOR for the volunteers of the Co-Workers of Charity in the Los Angeles area, arranging to make and distribute food to the homeless was at the top of my list. That meant coordinating volunteers during the week to pick up donated foods and supplies from grocery stores, churches, and hotels. Canned foods that a store was discarding because of a dent or ripped label were a staple of the drive, as were fruits and vegetables that had been bruised or were on the verge of becoming overripe. A typical food bag might contain a canned ham, or a half-dozen cans of tuna or chicken; peanut butter, ripe fruits and vegetables, soap, shampoo, moist towelettes, toothpaste and a tooth brush, and anything else the volunteers found that week that might be useful to a person scraping by on the streets.

The active Co-Workers in the area numbered near a hundred, and a dozen more in a pinch. A group of about twenty of us would gather with several Brothers at the crack of dawn each Saturday at the Brothers' main house in the Pico-Union District of Los Angeles. One of the Brothers would put coffee on, and we'd bring in many dozens of boxes of donated items. We'd stack the boxes in the kitchen, then open them and categorize the contents into meats, fruits, vegetables, hygiene supplies, and miscellaneous which we'd lay out in piles on tables in the living room. Some of us would form an assembly line and fill the bags while others restocked the piles from boxes in the kitchen. We'd chat as we worked.

On a day we were well-organized and awake, we'd get about a hundred bags done each hour and be finished by 8 a.m. Sisters (nuns of the Missionaries of Charity Order) would arrive about the time we finished, to lead the distribution. The Brother in charge that day would designate teams that included two Missionaries of Charity Brothers, Sisters or a combination, with one or more volunteers. We'd load up cars, then deliver the bags the balance of the morning and early afternoon. I, for one, felt a little anxiety each time we started out. To deliver the bags, we'd be going to places off the beaten path—*way* off. I had to set my common sense aside to visit these places, and call on my faith.

In keeping with their mission to serve "the poorest of the poor," the Brothers and Sisters of Charity had sussed out the bottom-of-the-barrel nooks and crannies of Los Angeles where homeless people were managing to survive, if barely, in the worst conditions imaginable. This included entire tent colonies located in back alleys, under freeway overpasses, and in abandoned, dilapidated old buildings, with no running water. These were the kinds of places parents tell their children in no uncertain terms to stay away from. They are places adults know, intuitively, not to go because of the dangers that abound. But there are suffering human beings in these places.

If it was compassion for others cultivated over decades of vocation, an unwavering trust in God, or both that the M.C. Brothers and Sisters drew strength from, the end result was a stunning fearlessness. This never ceased to amaze me. I certainly wasn't there yet, but aimed to be, one day. In the meantime, I sometimes trembled as we walked.

The Brothers or Sisters in the group always led. We Co-Workers walked behind them into these dark places, intent upon following their example—and hopeful that we shared their apparent guardian angels.

Even if I closed my eyes I would have known we were close to a tent encampment. The smell of these make-shift, ill-equipped living places is unmistakable as you draw near. That's because like millions of people in underdeveloped countries, people living in these encampments have no restroom facilities. So they are forced to go outdoors, behind a rock or tree or in a corner. Such a predicament was hard to imagine before I encountered it, and sad and maddening after. No human being should have to live like that.

We watched out for each other as we walked, aiming not to step in something undesirable. Sometimes when we arrived with food bags, we found that the people there had no interest in talking to us. In that case, we just dropped off the bag or bags, depending on how many people appeared to be living in a tent. Other times, we had lengthy conversations during which recipients would thank us profusely, or share a bit of the story of how they ended up becoming homeless.

All too often, prison time, drugs, and alcohol were involved in their stories. But not always. As I had while working on Skid Row, we'd come across *entire homeless families*—a father, mother and their child, or children. They'd often describe losing a long-standing job or livelihood, being unemployed for some months, and having no financial safety net. I was reminded that I had once been unemployed for six months. The difference was that I had my father to turn to for a loan. They had no one. Hearing these stories was eye-opening. It was a "There but for the grace of God go I," experience.

On this particular day, Brother Simon was in charge of the bag distribution. He assigned me to do rounds with two Sisters. I would drive them, taking a station wagon. Except for my fraudulently successful Thanksgiving assignment with Sister Thomas Moore, I'd spent very little time with Sisters of Charity, and was looking forward to it. I imagined we'd have a calm walkabout. As we passed out the bags, I'd have a chance to ask questions and learn more about their spiritual practice and thinking. But what actually happened this morning was not anything I could have imagined.

Brother Simon provided me with a hand-scrawled map showing cross streets and a walkway to homeless encampments nearby. He marked them with Xs. He handed me the keys to the station wagon, and told me there was a red wagon in the back that could tote about twenty bags at a time. Co-Workers helped us pack the vehicle, and off the three of us went.

I drove us to the location Brother Simon had indicated, and parked. We took the red wagon out of the back and stocked it with bags. We followed the path Brother Simon's map prescribed, and soon found ourselves in a filthy back alley—a place that didn't feel safe to me. *Faith, faith.* I took a deep breath. The Sisters, on the other hand, were fully in their element. Unconcerned, confident—fearless. I so admired their courage.

As we approached an encampment of about a dozen tents, we were met with the unmistakable smells. It's strange how such a small thing could be such a big distraction, but it was. I had to concentrate to keep myself from gagging, and from feeling disgusted. Now was the time to remember the advice Brother Simon had often shared with our volunteer groups: "Everyone is worthy and lovable in the eyes of God."

When we walked up to the first tent, I could see from a shadow that there was a single person inside. One of the Sisters announced us, "Missionaries of Charity with food and groceries for you." The person did not show themself, but pushed a stained hand through the tent's front opening, palm up, and long, slender fingers outstretched. The hand appeared to be that of a woman.

The Sister gently handed the woman a bag. The woman never showed herself, but uttered a "thank you" as she pulled the bag inside the tent. I had been surprised by this hand, as it appeared to be that of a *young* woman who was alone—something we didn't see too much of in these places. As we walked I thought of how frightening it must be to be a young woman living in this place with only a millimeter of cloth between her and the night. I wondered about what had brought her here, and felt heartbroken trying to imagine what her story might be. I knew the food wasn't going to get her off the streets, but I felt grateful to be able to help in a small way—and humbled.

We handed out the balance of the bags to others in that alley. All wore tattered garb. Many were shiny with sweat, their skin rife with back-alley grit. Many averted their eyes when we approached—perhaps feeling shame about their condition. One gray-haired elderly man had a profile that reminded me of my own grandfather. My heart broke a second time.

At the far end of the alley, we came upon a man sitting on the ground. He was just outside a small tent made of black plastic trash bags. His legs were outstretched, and the bottom half of both of legs was visible through torn trousers. His right leg was purple and black and swollen, and was dominated by crusty lesions. When one of the Sisters spoke to the man, he looked up and answered, groggily. The Sister persisted, but the man lost eye contact with her, and right in front of our eyes, fell over.

The sister moved quickly to have a closer look at him, then whispered in my direction, forcefully, "Get the car!"

I did as I was told.

I sprinted back toward the station wagon making mental notes of exactly where the alley was. It took me maybe ten minutes to find the car. I immediately drove the vehicle back toward the alley, and it took every bit of my concentration to find it since we'd been on foot and had taken short cuts to avoid the streets I was now driving on. (Besides that, sense of direction is not one of my gifts.) I was surprised when I navigated almost directly to the alley and got about a hundred yards from the Sisters—as close as I could without knocking tents down.

I jumped out of the car and ran to the Sisters. It would take all of us to move the man. As we lifted him, I gagged without wanting to. Due to the dampness and lack of a way to wash, he smelled of mildew and sickness. It was a state that no human being deserved to be in. His condition didn't seem to faze the Sisters, and again, I was in awe of their fortitude and focus.

He was a large man, and we sat him in the red wagon to get him to the vehicle. While a Sister held him up, I pulled the wagon and the other, smaller Sister, ran ahead and popped open the back of the station wagon. We took the remaining few food bags out to make space for the man, and sat them on the street knowing they'd be retrieved and be put to good use. We strained and hoisted the poor man into the back where he could lie flat, using every bit of strength we had to do so.

As for the delivery wagon, "We'll leave it," one of the Sisters declared, and off we drove.

Our destination was a hospital not far away. One of the Sisters knew the way. During the ride, the man began to moan. We knew he was still alive, at least, but I was afraid he might be dying where he lay and I drove faster than I should have.

When we arrived at the emergency room, I alerted hospital staff who brought a wheel chair. Two nurses transferred the man onto it and took him inside. One Sister stayed with him.

After I parked, the Sister who'd stayed with me and I entered the emergency room to find the other Sister and the man in the waiting area. A receptionist at the window motioned us over. She asked if we could fill out some paperwork, including the man's name, address and other details. But when the receptionist realized that we didn't know him, that we'd picked him up from a back alley, and that we could produce no identification for him or proof of insurance, she told us that he could not be admitted. I questioned her, hoping to hear a different answer if I persisted, but to no avail. Then, in her soft, gentle voice, the Sister by my side asked for the receptionist's help.

"I beg you madam for mercy for this man, this child of God," the Sister said.

But the receptionist knew the rules, and apparently had her orders—no exceptions. She wouldn't budge, even for this M.C. Sister dressed in the flowing white sari with sky-blue piping so widely recognized as the garb of Mother Teresa's Order of nuns.

This was ridiculous! We had a man barely conscious in a wheel chair who likely would die without treatment. How could a hospital turn him away? I began to get angry. I felt my heart race. Picking up where the Sister had left off, I pleaded with the receptionist, and when that didn't work, I argued.

After a few minutes of our circular conversation, the Sister backed away from the window. I turned my head slightly to see her slip behind me and join the other Sister alongside the man who sat slumped over and motionless. I didn't let up with the receptionist, trying every avenue.

"Is there any way you could make an exception to your policy, any way at all, *please?*" I pressed. "This man could die…"

As I continued trying to convince the receptionist, I began to hear the oddest thing behind me—two soft voices that seemed to be chanting. I then recognized the chants as muffled praying. The soft prayers grew louder, and I pivoted around. To my astonishment, the two Sisters were laying on the cold tile floor of the waiting room, faces down. Their arms were stretched above their heads, and their foreheads were pressed on the floor. Their prayers were unintelligible, but pleading in tone.

It was a shocking scene. I looked back at the receptionist and her mouth was hanging open. There were roughly thirty-five people in the waiting room, and every eye was glued on the Sisters. Their humility was awe-inspiring.

As I watched the Sisters, the anger and indignation I'd felt just a moment earlier drained out of my body. I began to feel peaceful. I'd unconsciously clenched my hands into fists, and now they loosened and dropped to my side. My heart stopped racing. In the span of a few minutes, my desperation was replaced by a calm. If anything could be done to get this poor man admitted to the hospital, I believed it was being done by the Sisters in this humble, selfless act.

Her hand now over her mouth in disbelief, the receptionist seemed to levitate away from the window. Soon, a man appeared who I surmised was her manager. He leaned out to assess what was happening in his waiting room. Besides the prayers of the Sisters, you could have heard a pin drop in the large, sterile enclave. There, each person sat motionless transfixed on the Sisters, the homeless man, and now, moved their gaze to the manager. They were on the edge of their seats and I stood motionless, wondering what would happen next.

At first, the manager tried to get the Sisters up off the floor. "If you can just come back to my office we can talk," he called to them from the window. Soon, he was begging.

The Sisters continued their prayers, drowning him out.

When the manager realized his pleas were of no use, he came out into the waiting room. He got down on one knee and spoke to the Sisters, explaining that he understood their concern, but that the hospital simply could not accept someone who did not have insurance. This line of reasoning, of course, fell on deaf ears. From flat on their bellies the Sisters continued to pray and to plead for mercy for a human being who surely would die a slow, painful death if not treated.

The empathy in the room for this broken, homeless man in the wheelchair, and for the Sister's compassion, too, was palpable. At least a dozen people had begun to sob—me among them.

When after several minutes the Sisters showed no sign of ceasing their prayers, the manager left the waiting room. Then, something amazing happened.

In a situation that most people would normally avoid getting involved in, an old woman in the waiting room stood up. She closed her eyes, crossed herself, and joined the Sisters in praying out loud. Soon, another person stood up, and another... Some said the Hail Mary prayer, others, the Our Father. Some spoke stream-of-consciousness prayers for mercy for the man. Some just stood in solidarity.

Soon, *nearly everyone* in the room was standing! I was stunned at the scene and closed my eyes to think about what was happening. Perfect strangers were uniting behind an unwashed, homeless man, like ones they'd passed dozens of times on the street or a freeway off-ramp—like ones they'd averted their eyes from, as I had, on many occasions. Something that only happens in movies was happening right here, in real life. I breathed in this scene, and etched it into my memory. I never wanted to forget it.

The manager retreated.

A few minutes later, the manager reappeared. He peered sheepishly around the edge of the reception window, his eyes full of surprise. He then disappeared again, and what would happen next was anyone's call.

Another few minutes passed, and unexpectedly, the high white doors leading to the admitting area flung open. The manager strode out into the waiting room followed by a young orderly who went over to the homeless man in the wheelchair and took his place behind it. The manager himself then informed the Sisters, loud enough so that everyone in the waiting room could hear, that the man would be admitted and treated.

One of the Sisters looked up. "Sir, do you give me your word?"

"I give you my word Sister," the manager assured. I believed him.

At that, someone clapped. Then another person. Then everyone began to clap, as if the manager had made the promise to them, personally. Each Sister now worked to stand up, stiff from having been on their bellies on the cold floor. The manager and I and several other people helped them up. They brushed themselves off and adjusted their saris. They bowed to the manager, hands cupped together, and blessed him, again transforming the atmosphere of the waiting room. This time, there was a feeling of reverence.

The Sisters and I and most everyone in the waiting room watched the orderly wheel the homeless man back behind the white doors. The manager followed, backing away and saying goodbye to the Sisters numerous times. He sported an expression that was somewhere between relieved and ashamed. I wondered if after that experience he would work to change the hospital policy. I hoped so.

The three of us walked back to the car in silence. I wanted to understand more about what had possessed the Sisters to do what they'd done, how they'd thought of it, how they'd known it would work...if they had known. But there was a magic to that moment—an intense sense of peace, and great power. Speaking, it seemed, would break the spell.

I said nothing.

When we returned to the Brothers' house, I told Brother Simon what had happened. He took it in as if this kind of extraordinary event was an everyday occurrence in his world. By his reaction, I knew that it was.

"There is so much goodness in the world just waiting to be liberated," he told me, his eyes smiling.

I knew he was right. I never forgot those words.

That day I promised myself I would never again let self-consciousness or pride get in the way of asking for help for those who truly need it, from those who are in a position to help. Mostly, I have kept my promise. When I waver, I remember that extraordinary day with the Missionaries of Charity Sisters, and Brother Simon's observation about "so much goodness…just waiting to be liberated."

I was, and continue to be, deeply humbled and inspired by this lesson of the M.C. Sisters.

_____

Enjoy this related song I wrote when I was working on Skid Row with the Brothers and Sisters of Charity:

• There Go I

www.lesliebaerdinkel.net/HopeDancing/Songs/

45 – Foibles and Fixes

OUR FIRST THREE YEARS working in Guatemala underscored the desperation that was shaping this part of the country's history. In rural areas, the unemployment rate hovered around a whopping *80 percent.* To put that in perspective, in the U.S., unemployment soared during The Great Depression from 3 percent to nearly 25 percent.[55] Thirty million Americans were out of work and turned to breadlines and bartering to feed their families. The hardships predicted by a joblessness rate in Guatemala more than *three times worse* than in the United States during the Great Depression was mindboggling. Yet the Mám Maya of the Guatemalan highlands had lived with unemployment rates close to this for decades.

The hope-crushing conditions we became familiar with in rural villages made those of us who were forming and growing the Xela AID project feel even more determined to help. It was also becoming clear that what we were doing with our roving clinics, though relevant in this time of war, would become less relevant after the war ended. Peace talks were already in process, and it looked like some kind of an accord would be signed in a year or so. We needed to focus on the future and find a model for meaningful change for the long term. Analyzing our missteps to date was the perfect place to start.

Best Intentions

Early on I'd scoffed at hearing about aid groups that brought in canned foods which the rural Maya don't use, slacks that women didn't wear (at that time), and Western clothing for men which destroys the local market for hand-woven traditional clothing. Traditional wear is central to Mayan culture both as a source of identity, and as the principal source of income for many local women weavers. How was it, I wondered, that help groups hadn't done their homework before diving in?

But by the end of our third trip to Guatemala, our own blind spots had become obvious. I was surprised by how easy it was to end up with a completely different outcome than we wanted.

On our third trip, when we returned to locations we'd visited on our first and second trips, there were numerous cases where people in great need were waiting for us to come back instead of seeking local help. In one example, one of our doctors examined a woman who had a high fever, could barely breathe and was listless. She was suffering from pneumonia and was on the verge of death. Weeks before we arrived, family and friends had recognized her grave condition and told her they'd chip in for bus fare or a car ride so she could get to the public hospital an hour away. She turned down their help, telling us, "I was waiting for you." The wait nearly cost her life. By failing to identify local low- or no-cost options for health care and encouraging people to use those options, we'd inadvertently encouraged them to wait for our return. We'd created dependence, the opposite of what we were trying to do.

The first family we'd helped by building a small home brought another family from *El Area Mám* to find us in Xela. This family, like the first, had been homeless for many months and had also been sleeping in a corn field under tarps. The homeless family had relatives willing to help, but instead, they waited for us. It turns out that the first family told them that if they waited, we would build them a free house. Habitat for Humanity, whose specialty is building houses, was working in the area. We could have connected local homeless families to them before we left, but hadn't thought it through.

Another misstep occurred in collaboration with a help group that had begun operating in Guatemala about five years before we arrived. They asked us to help them build outhouses, and we agreed. On a trip back a year later, a few of us returned to the community where we'd built the outhouses to see how they were holding up. To our great surprise, we found that every single one of the dozen outhouses was out of service! All of them were being used to keep chickens, or store corn or firewood. When we asked the head of community why the outhouses were not in use, he thanked us wholeheartedly for having built them. He then informed us, respectfully, "We knew it was important to you to

build them, but we don't use toilets here. We have our fields..."
Whoops.

This misstep happened because we and our partner help group had misinterpreted needs and desires, and hadn't spent any time on education. We could have introduced a theme, like the many health benefits of using toilets rather than fields, to see if we could cultivate interest.

In another example, one year, we insisted on implementing computer record keeping. Computers are hard to come by and maintain in rural Guatemala, and at this writing in 2019, good internet service is still a challenge. After spending a full year developing the system and getting completely frustrated by the technology, we retreated to the paper file system our staff in Guatemala had suggested in the first place. Cheap, easy, and now in use, the filing system gaffe and solution demonstrated once again the wisdom of the phrase that in time became Xela AID's mantra, "Local solutions are lasting solutions."

My take-away from these and other foibles was this. To be effective in empowering positive, lasting change, one needs not only the heart for the work, but also, the eyes to see. In the future, we would need to ask lots more questions, listen humbly and with an open mind, plan carefully with local experts, *then* act. Luckily, there were others who had come before us and had learned lots about what not to do. Between what we'd already learned and additional guidance from the old-hand organizations, we quickly got back on track.

We licked our wounds, and sought advice from organizations that had worked for a decade or more in the region, such as the Spanish Red Cross, the local Rotary Club and the Peace Corps. Their collective wisdom pointed to a "sustainable community development" model. This translates to picking one geographic area to fully develop, focusing on education, health, and building job skills to empower people to rely on themselves for the long run.

In the process of implementing this approach, we nearly completely eliminated giveaways. This was based on the old adage that, "If you give a person a fish they'll eat for a day, but if you teach a person to fish they'll eat for a lifetime." Luis later added, cleverly, "If you teach a person to *sell* fish, they'll bring jobs to a community." (This foreshadowed a Leadership Training Program Luis would champion in later years that would include a focus on small business development.) We soon saw it played out that while giveaways create dependence, sweat-equity fosters dignity and self-determination.

The Ladies Who Wooed Us

To develop the potential of a community, we'd have to find one that wanted a partner, and put down roots there. *El Area Mám* was the logical place to consider since it was rife with exceptional need. We'd built a single-room school there in Loblatzán and knew some of the locals. But we were not connected to the community leaders, and not sure who to go to. Alma showed up as if on cue. This was Alma the weaver, the midwife, the one who would one day besiege my flowerbeds with corn. This is how I first met her.

Alma appeared with an entourage of *compañeras* at a clinic we were holding in the Loblatzán school room and asked—or rather, insisted—to see "the man in charge." She got me instead, and appeared delighted.

Alma and the other Mám women were dressed meticulously in beautiful, hand-woven garments. Many had their hair up and neatly wrapped. Alma spoke to me in Spanish as she explained, confidently, that she and her group were hard-working midwives and weavers and were all widows or single mothers. Their village was right next door to Loblatzán where we had built a school.

Alma's village turned out to be San Martín Chiquito, where we'd built the small wooden house in a cornfield as our very first construction project. The town was nearly devoid of adult men, Alma told us, explaining that there were a number of causes. Death from alcoholism was high on the list, trumped only by having "disappeared" (been kidnapped and likely murdered) during the war. Among other causes, young men had left the

358

village to avoid being drafted into the war, or had gone to the United States to work and had never come back.

"We are taking our children's well-being into our own hands now," Alma continued. "We don't want charity. But our community lacks resources, so no matter how hard we work, we can't get ahead.

"If you come to help our community, we promise to work hard alongside you," she implored, then stopped talking and looked directly at me with piercing, dark eyes. She was determined.

This bold woman made a compelling case. John Diehl, a Rotarian ex-pat from the States and long-time resident of Quetzaltenango had warned me about falling into paternalism. He suggested that we'd know the right community for our project to settle in when we found one that was already organized and helping itself. As a second criteria, we should be *invited* by the community to work with them for positive change. Alma's organized force of women and her invitation for us to come work in their community fit the bill.

Our Board of Directors, Bob Rook, Jim Mramor, Karen Edwards, Colleen Dodds, Bob Rhein, Wolfram Alderson and I, discussed the idea of settling in San Martín Chiquito. It was only about 40 minutes outside of Xela and located along a road that was at least partially paved. We agreed it would make a good location for a headquarters. We all got quite excited as we imagined trading in tents, mud and buggy nights for a brick-and-mortar location to operate out of.

A home base as we imagined it would operate as a clinic to start, with an office or two, and some room to grow. Having a clinic would not preclude us having to carry hundreds of pounds of boxed supplies with us from the United States each trip, but we'd have real exam rooms, running water, and an actual bathroom to use rather than a bush. It would be heaven. Karen not only encouraged us to purchase land to build on, but put up the money. It was her $7,000 contribution that secured Xela AID's future in San Martín Chiquito.

Not for Sale

We immediately began to look for land in that community. Our criteria was that it would have good road access, was large enough so we could expand in the future, and that it wouldn't flood. From the times we'd been there and it had rained, we'd seen that the plentiful rainfall quickly pooled in flat areas and turned cobblestone roads into rivers. There had to be good natural drainage.

Finding a piece of land that met these criteria and was big enough for our headquarters and had room to spare for $7,000 was not a problem. For that amount, in and around San Martín Chiquito, we could get two *cuerdas*—just under two acres. The problem, we learned, was getting someone to sell land to us.

Given their centuries of suffering under the reign of the pale elite (think brutal *conquistadores*, crooked light-skinned politicians and murderous generals), local people were understandably resistant to the idea of white people moving in. So when we began looking in the village for land to buy, there was not an inch for sale—to us—anywhere. This included parcels being advertised, or known by word-of-mouth to be for sale. No one in the village wanted to be known as the scoundrel who'd sold land to the *gringos.*

But the bakers dozen of ladies who'd recruited us to the town were not to be thwarted, and Alma told us not to worry. She herself was a land owner and had some standing in the community as a leader. Still, she couldn't ask on our behalf outright. She instead began to make inquiries for her "long-lost cousin" who was moving back from the United States. As quickly as properties had gone off the market for us, they were back on the market for Alma's "cousin." I didn't like proceeding this way, but Alma convinced us there was no other way for us to buy land in that community. The ladies had faith in our plan for a headquarters and clinic, and so did I. I knew that in time, we'd provide real value to the community and change hearts and minds about us. My conscience was clear, and we moved ahead.

We were a bit shocked to learn that in rural Guatemala, land ownership is not always legally registered, but may be an agreement between neighbors. Wolfram agreed to take on acquiring enough documentation to convince ourselves that the land really did belong to the person selling it. He located a legal document that referred to this particular plot, then collected the required signatures from neighbors verifying its owner. Finally, we were convinced, and more importantly, so was a local judge who signed off.

Alma then did the bidding for that absent cousin of hers to buy the property, and at a good price. It had been listed a bit higher, but we purchased it for exactly the $7,000 we had. Imagine Alma's surprise, she told neighbors, when her cousin was suddenly indisposed, could not return, and sold the property to none other than *gringos*.

Once the word got out that we were coming to town, rumors spread like wild fire that the land would be subdivided and sold to build an expensive housing subdivision, or worse, a factory that would pollute the local water supply. Our local ladies helped squelch the rumors and spread the word that it would be a clinic and education center focused on helping the community. Luckily, it didn't take us too long to prove the ladies right.

The Round House

Alma and her entire group of women had in common the art of backstrap weaving. It is ancient and intricate and based on counting threads to make patterns in shapes and colors that recall the sky, the mountains, the corn, the animals of the earth, volcanoes, roses and thorns and more elements of local life. These are often set against a backdrop of red that, in this particular village, represents hope.

"Red is hope because blood is red," Alma explained. "As long as blood runs through our veins, there is hope."

The weavers were in need of a place to gather to weave so they could share their designs and preserve their ancient craft. Xela AID bought a small plot of land behind Alma's home to build such a place. Wolfram, who among his various talents was an artist and a builder, was excited to design the building and lead the construction effort. In honor of the circle with four cardinal points used by Mayan shamans in sacred ceremonies, he created a spacious round house for the weavers. Against the backdrop of small, traditional adobe and block houses with rectangular footprints that dotted the village, the rather large round structure drew curiosity from far and wide. It was beloved by Alma and the dozens of weavers who initially used it.

The women used the Round House on and off for a solid decade, but spent less time there than we, and they, had imagined. That's because despite their vision of weaving together, in real life, they did not weave in large blocks of time. Instead, they squeezed in minutes of weaving here and there throughout the day in between their vast agenda of "wifely" duties. These included plowing the family field, planting, harvesting, grinding the corn, preparing meals for the family (starting at 4:30 a.m.), washing clothes (by hand), bathing kids and self (the latter, in a spare moment, if any). Weaving with a group outside the home was simply not practical as a standard practice.

When the idea for a preschool arose, the Round House was the perfect location for re-purposing. We were fortunate to have volunteers on early trips who were researchers who provided us with baseline data about San Martín's educational outcomes. We saw the alarming data played out, that nine out of ten native Mám-speaking children who began first grade before they knew Spanish dropped out of school before the sixth grade. Add to that the malnutrition that plagues toddlers in epidemic proportion, and it became eminently clear that we *needed* a preschool where we could teach Spanish and serve nutritious meals. But it wouldn't be cheap. We needed a partner.

Luis worked with local parents to complete paperwork requesting the collaboration of SOSEP (*La Secretaría de Obras Sociales de la Esposa del Presidente*), the humanitarian program of The First Lady of Guatemala. As fate would have it, SOSEP was seeking locations for preschools in poor communities. Luis met with SOSEP representatives and negotiated an agreement stating that we'd provide the building and maintenance, and they'd cover operating expenses. We formalized our agreement and the San Martín Tots Preschool was set into motion, with one small additional requirement—the school would need a kitchen to prepare two hot, nutritious meals each day so we could nurse malnourished children back to health. Mel offered to take on the kitchen construction project. He generously footed the bill for this not-insignificant freestanding addition to the preschool complex in honor of his mother and father.

When the Milton and Helen Dinkel Nutrition Kitchen was completed in just over a month, we opened the preschool and welcomed the thirty children we were approved to have, ages one to five. Within a year, the facility was serving fifty-eight children (twenty-eight over the official limit) and bursting at the seams.

"Let's get this done!"

We had begun the campaign to build Xela AID's clinic and headquarters in 1999. Joyce Fournier and her husband Gene Stone were both serving on our Board, and had led the fundraising charge. Wolfram led the building design process. Gene agreed that when it came time to build, he'd stay in Guatemala for a number of months to shepherd the project along and see that the building met U.S. standards for safety. All we needed was the money.

We all asked family, friends and strangers to help. For my part, there wasn't a week that went by when I didn't call on the memory of the selfless and determined Sisters, prostrate on the hospital waiting room floor, to keep me motivated.

Working together, our small Board raised $60,000 for the building. We raised that over several years with only a few gifts over a thousand dollars, and a gaggle of hundred-dollar bricks. We put on fundraising events and auctions, and between us, it seemed we'd asked everyone we knew to contribute. Still, we'd come up short. There was one person I hadn't asked. I'd saved her for last.

Everyone needs an Aunt June. All my life she's been my hero and had been there every step of the way to help me grow up. When I told her we were $10,000 from being able to build a clinic and headquarters for the project, she surprised me with a request. "Let's go to Guatemala and have a look at that land!"

About a month, a five-hour flight and a few rousing rides on chicken buses later, we arrived at the turnoff for the piece of land we'd purchased thanks to Karen's contribution and Wolfram's legwork. My sister Mara and several friends and a family member of Aunt June's accompanied us. We didn't know at the time what an historic moment this would be for our project.

News of our arrival brought dozens of locals out to greet us, several of whom we'd seen during our *jornadas* in the area. Aunt June got to meet 8-year-old Pedro Elias and his father who couldn't stop thanking us. Starting at age six, Pedro Elias hadn't been able to straighten his legs because of a rare form of arthritis. Working out of tents two years earlier, our volunteer doctors had gotten him on the medication that cured him. Aunt June cried when we later showed her pictures of Pedro Elias' scaly and swollen knees and legs before we'd helped. She could hardly believe it was the same healthy, happy young boy she'd met hours earlier.

Aunt June also met Edgar, age 10, who came wheeling up the road with his father behind his chair, helping. He'd had to crawl around his home for years before we brought him his first wheel chair, 12-year-old-sized and a perfect fit. We brought it from the States where it had been discarded...the ever-satisfying magic of turning trash into treasure.

The bunch of us walked and rolled up the dirt road, and soon came to the land which had been a productive corn field and was now fallow and in the waiting. We all took in the vista—a few houses dotting the corn and potato fields that blanketed the hills as far as we could see, in all directions. It was breathtaking.

I stood behind Aunt June and saw that she'd taken both Pedro Elias' and Edgar's small hands in her large, well-worn ones—hands that had taken mine a thousand times over the years. I then saw that she was fighting back tears.

Aunt June turned to me unexpectedly and broke the silence, declaring, "I've got $10,000 with your building's name on it. Let's get this done!"

Those of us who could, including Aunt June, moved off the road and trudged up through the muddy soil to the highest point of our land where one of the local people took a picture of us for posterity. When she made her first and only trip to Guatemala in 1995 and gave the capstone gift that cemented Xela AID's future in the San Martín Chile Verde region, Aunt June was in her prime—a mere 70 years young.

Open for Good

The June Russel-Glennon Clinic and Community Center opened its doors to some fanfare in 2004. It was a two-story, 13-room building including five bathrooms in a community where, at that time, many homes were still made of reclaimed wood and tin. The opening was attended by a volunteer group from the States, Luis and our other local partners including Alma and her weavers, the mayor of the town, more than a hundred citizens, and lots of school children. This included a dozen darling little girls in traditional wear with their hair up, who performed a Mám dance and threw rose petals upon their exit. Every face was smiling.

A Catholic priest and an Evangelical minister also attended. The religious divide is deep and wide in Guatemala, and it gets personal between rival churches. As amazing as the opening of this hard-won building was, the miracle of the day might have been getting these two spatting spiritual leaders within speaking distance of one another.

The area is also divided by language and social class. As such, it was important to make it understood that this new building would serve everyone. I ended the inauguration with this statement, which we had printed and posted at the front door of our headquarters:

"Like the sun that rises and sets each day, Xela AID is for everyone. May all who serve within these walls as ambassadors of

365

its promise, work with diligence and a loving heart for the well-being of the one Guatemalan community."

With that opening, we began the serious, long-term work of partnering for meaningful change with Mám people living in some of the worst conditions in the world. Luis officially retired from his decades of service as a nurse at the local hospital to work full-time for the project.

We soon added other staff members in Guatemala, including a full-time doctor and teachers. In coming years, the project grew and expanded as a direct consequence of the time, energy, and resources of new volunteers, and particularly those who joined the organization's Board of Directors. In many cases, it was a Board member who spearheaded the expansion of a program, or founded a new one. (There's more about this in "Milestones and Key Historic Dates.")

Although we'd make minor course corrections in the years to come, by that time, we'd made our most serious missteps, found a model, and finally, found a home.

46 – WINGS

BRAD FARROW TRAVELED WITH XELA AID on numerous trips over the years, fitting many dozens of prosthetic arms and legs for both adults and young people. Among them was a 17-year-old girl named Jenifer.

Jenifer was a smart, beautiful young girl. She had excellent grades and a sweet disposition and a fortitude that drew me to her. For one so young, she had a very specific vision for her life. She told me she wanted to get married to "a kind and loving man," have two children as her parents had, then become a teacher so she could help other children who weren't as gifted in their studies as she was. (Jenifer's younger sister struggled in school). She told me, "I will one day do these things. *This is my purpose.*"

I marveled at Jenifer, considering that at age 17 I had little idea of what my purpose might be and was struggling to envision my future. She had so enthusiastically and articulately stated her purpose. There was just one snag, and the reason Jenifer and her mother had come to see Brad and me. Jenifer had lost a leg to an aggressive cancer. Her parents' painful decision to have it removed had saved her life.

Considering both the infrastructure challenges in Xela—high curbs, crumbling cobblestone streets, and virtually no wheelchair access—and local attitudes that both feared and scorned the differently abled, Jenifer's path had been difficult.

"How will she ever be able to work and take care of herself when she is wedded to crutches?" her mother confided to Brad and me, worried and tearful. "And what young man would be able to see past her missing leg and love her?"

Jenifer's mother was broken-hearted. For her part, Jenifer recognized the missing leg as an impediment, but believed it was one she could overcome with a prosthetic.

"I would work hard to make use of it," she offered. "Will you help me?"

Both mother and daughter were, as you might imagine, incredibly grateful when Brad committed to manufacturing a prosthetic leg for Jenifer. They were elated when a few months later he delivered and fitted the finely crafted, life-like limb.

Jenifer cried with joy upon taking her first steps with her new leg. These were her first steps on her way to a new life full of hope and possibility. She knew it, and so did we.

This was just the kind of moment that makes all the hard work worth it—the moment you realize that your efforts have made a positive, meaningful impact in someone else's life. It's love full circle.

On a trip I made to Guatemala about a decade after our last visit with Jenifer, a young woman came to the hotel where I was staying. She was accompanied by her mother and a young girl I believed to be her little sister. To my surprise, the young woman was in fact Jenifer, who was now 27 years old. She told me proudly that she was still using the prosthetic leg, and hiked up her skirt the tiniest bit to show me. Next, she and her mother unfurled an enormous, beautifully made quilt. The two had artfully designed it using hand-woven cloth typical of Xela. The quilt also featured an embroidered, very touching message of thanks to Brad and to Xela AID.

My next surprise was when Jenifer told me that the little girl accompanying them was not her sister, but her very own daughter. Through tears of joy she credited the prosthetic leg she'd received with making it possible for her to find work, to find a "true love," to marry and eventually start the family she'd always dreamt of. And in just months, she would complete her schooling and become a teacher.

"It took a bit longer than I thought, but it's happening," she said, beaming through tears. "I am fulfilling my purpose!"

We all had a good cry.

When the three readied to leave, Jenifer approached me with open arms and stood on her tippy toes to give me a long, warm hug.

Choked up and still sobbing, as we held each other she whispered in my ear.

"It's not just a leg you gave me. You gave me *wings*."

At hearing this, I was overcome with emotion and cried. It was true for Jenifer, as it is for each of us…

Purpose gives us wings.

PART VII ✚ EPILOGUE

In Conclusion

Since I began sharing the full story of how I ended up starting a development project in Guatemala, I have been asked many times how I got over the strafing from a U.S. helicopter and other extraordinary events that occurred in the refugee camp just before Christmas so many years ago. I re-lived that night many times over the years, feeling sad, enraged, betrayed, and many emotions in between.

I finally took a page from the Dalai Lama's book. I stopped struggling against what had happened, and accepted that this experience would always be with me, and that I must "weave it into the fabric" of my life. I accepted that I might always shudder and feel sick at loud sounds that trigger a flight response etched into me that night. And as my friend Dorothy Satten once suggested with regard to painful experiences or changes, I decided I would not let what had happened shrink me—make me fearful, or feel less than my whole self.

These changes in thinking opened the door for me to observe the experience from a new perspective. From that new vantage point, I no longer felt bitter or a victim. I've been able to see that night as just one in a world full of examples where goodness is held hostage by fear, greed and the other most unbecoming traits of people and nations alike. I also realized that if it weren't for that night, I might not have ended up on my own path to purpose. I learned to bless that experience.

I still tear up at the Pledge of Allegiance. But now, not because I have an idealized view of my country of origin. The raw emotion I feel comes from hope—an abiding sense that we will one day live up to the vision of our founding fathers as a nation that embraces "liberty, and justice for all" people on this magnificent earth we share.

I still believe.

I subscribe to Brother Simon's sense of our world brimming over with "goodness just waiting to be liberated." Xela AID is one of many thousands of human development efforts in the world by which goodness is liberated. It brings caring people together to help one another. And when that happens, the possibilities are endless. Each of us, too, can choose daily to exercise that goodness in small ways that make a positive difference in the lives of others, and in our own.

I did see a living quetzal, as Brother Simon suggested I might one day. While on a trail in the Ecuadorian rainforest with a professional birder, Mel and I and our friend Cliff Hague saw not only one, but a pair of quetzals building a nest high up in the canopy. Our guide had ticked thousands of birds off his sighting list, but had never in his thirty years seen a quetzal in the wild. He likened the chances of seeing a nesting pair to the odds of being struck by lighting. It was our utterly fantastic luck—maybe. Or maybe, it was a message… "Some things are just a mystery."

As a young adult, my nephew Jordan mentioned his fond recollection of his volunteer experience at age 12, and meeting Diego.

"I think that kind of experience is one that everyone should have to get a perspective," he observed.

I agree with him, and have often wished I'd first volunteered at age 13 instead of 30. I believe I would have gained perspective and insight that would have made my young adult life less challenging and more peaceful and productive. If I were Queen for a Day, volunteer service would be grade school, junior high and high school requirements.

While math, reading and science can get you a career, compassion, generosity and gratitude will get you a happy life. There's no better way to nurture those virtues than serving alongside those less fortunate.

"The best way to find yourself is to lose yourself
in the service of others."

—Mahatma Gandhi

I am grateful to Xela AID for the practice it gives me at loving service, and for the abiding purpose it has brought to my life. I am grateful to be in the presence of so many kind, generous, and dedicated people. There is much to be done, and it is a joy to do it together. We welcome you to share our journey of purpose— our hope, dancing.

With gratitude,

Leslie

xelaaid.org & localhope.org • leslie@xelaaid.org

———

Enjoy this song I wrote for Karen Edwards—one of Xela AID's life-long and most dedicated supporters—and for all who work to make the world a little bit better.

• 'Cause We Were Here

www.lesliebaerdinkel.net/HopeDancing/Songs/

PART VIII ✚ ADDENDUM

Where They Are Now

AUNT JUNE out-lived three husbands, all service men, from the Navy, Army, and Marines in that order. Offering Mel and Leslie advice, she said, "I married first for love, then for money, and then for fun. The last marriage was by far the best." The secret of a good marriage, she told them, is to "Laugh a lot!" At this writing Aunt June is alive and well and, at a spry 93, might yet find herself an Air Force man.

DR. DIEP NGUYEN, originally from Vietnam, and DR. JUAN RIUZ who met on Xela AID's first service trip, married and had five children. In 2014, the couple returned to Guatemala with three of their five children to volunteer on a Xela AID trip—love, full circle.

DR. JOHN PADILLA – A highly skilled and devoted plastic surgeon who made several trips with our project, John performed hundreds of life-saving cleft palette surgeries on children in Guatemala and China. Sadly, he died in a plane crash in 2004. Were it not for his generosity and dedication to serving others in need, it is likely that Leslie never would have met her son, Oscar. She will be forever grateful for what Dr. John made possible for Oscar, and for her.

JESSICA BUBOLO (GALBO), who introduced Leslie to Luis Enrique de León, married and moved to Telluride, Colorado, where she and her husband founded and continue to run the Rock-and-Roll Academy.

BROTHER SIMON, M.C. – During his short life, his loving example brought hope to the hopeless, and inspired countless individuals to serve others in need. His respectful partnering with those less fortunate to bring about positive, lasting change, was the ideal upon which Xela AID was founded.

FATHER PETER HICKMAN founded and led St. Matthew's Church of Orange, then founded the Ecumenical Catholic Communion, a Catholic movement he grew into a confederation of independent Catholic churches. The Communion now flourishes across the United States and in Europe. He stepped down from his role as Bishop in 2015, leaving six Bishops in place to continue his inclusive ministry. He most certainly found and realized his purpose, and inspired Leslie and many others to do the same.

BOB ROOK retired from Panasonic and moved with his wife, Carol, to Austin, Texas, where he later authored *White Sands Missile Range: Missile Park Museum*, a book about that museum in Alamogordo, New Mexico. He was a driving force in launching Xela AID.

BOB RHEIN and Leslie worked together in publishing, public relations, and marketing for various firms and in non-profit organizations for some thirty years, after which Bob retired and began lending his valuable services to charities. He co-authored with Leslie, *Earth Keepers: A Source Book for Issues and Action* (Mercury House 1995), and later, co-authored the book *Catalina A to Z: A Glossary Guide to California's Island Jewel.*

SAM went on to earn a Master's Degree and became a successful therapist specializing in marriage and family counseling. Upon retiring, he traveled the world, then returned to Texas to live near family. Sam and Leslie remained friends, and even played a few songs together at Sam's retirement party.

GABY and MARCOS – Gaby worked for two more decades teaching Spanish to international students. She and Marcos influenced hundreds of people, including Leslie, to become involved in efforts to combat poverty and champion social justice in Guatemala. After his release from incarceration, Marcos continued working for *Derechos Humanos*. When the revolutionary party—the URNG—was officially recognized in 1998, Marcos became Secretary. He never admitted having direct ties to the party during the war years. Gaby and Marcos have two children who are enjoying the fruits of their parents' sacrifices as they are freer than in the past to speak their minds and to work openly for a just society.

JAN JOHNSON, a combat survivor who the author grew up with as a cousin, was the first person she spoke with about her experience in the refugee camp, and the depression and anxiety she felt in its wake. Never able to heal from the trauma of his experiences on the front lines in Vietnam, he died of a drug overdose in 2015.

TAYLOR BLADH, the first person to sign on for a Xela AID trip, set a high standard of care and compassion for future volunteers. His enthusiasm helped to fuel that first trip, and a second. At this writing, he maintains an optometry practice in Diamond Bar, California.

RUDY VARGAS, a beloved documentary filmmaker and passionate advocate for social justice over many decades, with colleague Rick Cass, created the first promotional film for the organization. He stayed involved with Xela AID as an advisor for more than a decade until his untimely death from cancer in 2009. *¡Que viva la lucha!*

RICK CASS continued his career making educational films in Cal Poly Pomona's media division. He retired in 2016. In a personal note delivered to the author with footage he'd shot in Guatemala, he counted his journey with Xela AID as "one of the most influential experiences in my life."

MURPHY TAMMARO died in September of 2012 of complications related to diabetes. His obituary stated, "He is predeceased in death by the two great influences in his life, his father, Fred, and best friend, [Brother] Simon."

LUIS ENRIQUE DE LEÓN, who became Xela AID's first Director in Guatemala, continues in that position nearly three decades later. The author is exceedingly grateful for the trail he's helping to blaze for the project's long-term success. His will be an exceptional legacy.

While leading a water catchment construction project in a remote mountain village, WOLFRAM ALDERSON shared a cold, wet night and a few hundred mosquito bites with a dozen Xela AID volunteers, among them DAGMAR BEYERLEIN—who he later married. The two live comfortably in San Francisco where he uses his art and advocacy skills to enact social change.

KAREN EDWARDS helped guide the organization for two decades. In 2011 she died of breast cancer at age 61. At a ceremony in Toronto she was remembered by scores of women whose lives she helped turn around through Cinnamon Toast, the dignified housing project she founded and ran for women recovering from substance abuse.

COLLEEN DODDS continues as a close friend, advocate and supporter of Xela AID and with Karen Edwards, is recognized as an Emeritus Board Member. She continues to volunteer in Guatemala and bring family along, and has introduced two of her daughters to the child she and Karen sponsored, Rosa—now grown with a family of her own.

ROSA and ADALBERTO HERNANDEZ — Rosa earned a teaching credential, and went on to become a teacher. She was the first woman ever to teach at the school she attended, and at this writing, is still teaching there. Her father died of lung disease suspected to be tuberculosis, or perhaps Bird Fancier's Lung (BFL). Rosa, too, was struck ill. Thankfully, she recovered, married, and had two children. Adalberto became principal of the same school he and his sister attended as children. They were the first two children to receive educational scholarships through Xela AID, but not the last. Rosa now acts as the organization's coordinator for educational scholarships in her village of Santa Cruz de Laguna.

ESTRELLA VASQUEZ, LUIS MIGUEL LOPEZ VASQUEZ and JUANA GOMEZ all realized their dreams. Through Xela AID's educational scholarship program, the trio became three of the first Mám speakers in the village to complete higher education. Estrella became a nurse, Luis Miguel became an architect, and Juana became a teacher. As of this writing, Estrella and Juana are giving back to their community as members of the project's staff, and Luis Miguel, by tutoring children in Xela AID's Study Center.

NATHANIAL DAVIS, former U.S. Ambassador to Guatemala, ended his career as a Professor of Humanities at Harvey Mudd College in Claremont, California, where he taught political science from 1983 until his retirement in 2002. During an event in Claremont in 2010, the author recognized Mr. Davis and sat down to talk with him about his visit to her office many years before. Mr. Davis unfortunately did not appear to remember her, or who he was. He died in Claremont in 2011.

BAXTER was never heard from again—so far.

OSCAR married APRIL on a March 3rd—the anniversary of his coming to the United States, and Grandpa Hank's birthday. They were surrounded by friends and family, including Oscar's birth parents, Rafaela and Marco Sr., who beamed with pride. Leslie was ecstatic to participate in the ceremony alongside of Doña Rafaela as Oscar's second, doting mom.

MEL DINKEL and LESLIE BAER married in 2009, and continue to build a life together they both love (with gratitude to Dorothy Satten for her wisdom). At this writing, Mel serves on Xela AID's Board of Directors and as its Treasurer and Chief Operating Officer. Leslie serves as Executive Director. Together they co-lead volunteer trips each year and relish their time in Guatemala. They keep in mind Aunt June's secret to a good marriage and make sure to "Laugh a lot!" It's working.

Milestones and Key Historic Dates

1992

• **Founding** - Xela AID is founded during the Guatemalan Civil War in December by Leslie Baer. She is accompanied in the project launch effort by Fr. Peter Hickman, Bob Rook and Bob Rhein of St. Matthew Ecumenical Catholic Church under which Xela AID begins operating as a non-denominational project.

1993

• **First Volunteer Trips** - In July and December, Xela AID undertakes its first two volunteer trips. Organized with the help of a local language school, the group holds medical and optometry clinics and builds a small home for a family living in extreme poverty. (Yearly volunteer trips continue through the present.)

• **First Coordinator, Guatemala** - Luis Enrique de León joins Xela AID as the organization's first Coordinator in Guatemala and works as a volunteer.

1994

• **First Building** - Xela AID builds a single-room school at Loblatzán, the organization's initial block structure. It welcomes thirty children. Heartened by the success of the single classroom, the community soon adds additional rooms.

• **First Educational Scholarships** - Karen Edwards, Colleen Dodds, and James Mramor soon after, sponsor children from Santa Cruz de Laguna to go to school. This launches the Work-Study Scholarship program which is run and expanded by volunteer Ana-Maria Flores. It becomes the first pillar of Xela AID's education program.

1996

• **Weavers Gathering Place** - Xela AID constructs a round building designed by then-Board Member Wolfram Alderson. The unique "Round House" is a place for weavers to gather and share designs to preserve their ancient craft. It becomes home to Xela AID's first sponsored weaving cooperative.

• *In Guatemalan History* - **Signing of the Peace Accords** – The Peace Accords are signed by the Guatemalan government and the revolutionary forces after a civil war that lasted more than three decades and during which at least 200,000 people were killed or "disappeared"—more than 80 percent rural Maya such as those served by Xela AID. The conditions of poverty and unequal opportunity that fueled the war remain largely unchanged.

1998

• *In Guatemalan History* - **"Never More," and Murder** - Roman Catholic Archbishop and human rights defender Juan José Gerardi Conedera releases the report *"Nunca Más"* (Never More) which includes interviews with more than a thousand survivors and witnesses to atrocities committed almost exclusively by the Guatemalan military. It is the first investigation to include the names of the implicated individuals, totaling more than a thousand people. Two days after presenting the report, the Archbishop is murdered in his home in Guatemala City.

1999

• **Land Purchased** - Xela AID purchases approximately two acres of land in San Martín Chiquito with funds donated by Board Member Karen Edwards. Fundraising begins for a headquarters and clinic.

• *In Guatemalan History* - **Truth Commission Report** - After interviewing eleven thousand people and pouring through declassified information from the U.S. government, the Guatemalan Truth Commission completes its final report, "Guatemala: Memory of Silence." The report states, "agents of the state committed acts of genocide against groups of Mayan people. State forces and related paramilitary groups were responsible for 93 percent of the violations documented. Insurgent actions produced 3 percent of the human rights violations and acts of violence." People killed are estimated at more than 200,000—83 percent Mayan, and 17 percent Ladino. Subsequent to the Commission's work, a *diario militar* (military logbook) was found of the names of people unlawfully arrested, tortured, and put to death by a government security unit. The Forensic Anthropological Foundation of Guatemala (FAFG) continues to exhume mass graves contributing valuable information for further investigations.

2000

• **International Weaving Conference** – "**World Weaving 2000**" hosted by Xela AID at the San Juan Capistrano Mission in Southern California brings together eighty weavers from twelve countries and welcomes more than ten thousand people over two days. Xela AID then-Board President Joyce Fournier and volunteer Alana Jolly coordinate the event.

2003

• **Capstone Gift** - A $10,000 gift from June Russel-Glennon completes fundraising for Xela AID's headquarters and clinic and construction begins with then-Board Member Gene Stone supervising in Guatemala.

2004

• **Xela AID Headquarters Inaugurated** – The Xela AID June Russel-Glennon Clinic and Community Center is completed. An inauguration is held including local political and religious officials, a volunteer group, and many local citizens. Mám children are featured dancing during the ceremony.

• **First Full-Time Staff, Guatemala** - Luis Enrique de León becomes Xela AID's first full-time paid staff member in Guatemala. He is followed by medical and educational staff.

• **First Sponsored Children Enter Workforce** – The first children sponsored through Xela AID's Work Study Scholarship Program in 1994 graduate and take leadership roles. Rosa

Hernandez becomes a teacher and her brother Adalberto, a school principal. Third sponsored child Gregorio Simaj becomes his village's first literate mayor. (At this writing in 2019 more than six hundred children have received scholarships through the program whereby sponsored children pay their good fortune forward by tutoring other children in need.)

• **Preschool Launched** – The organization enters into a partnership with SOSEP, the project of the First Lady of Guatemala, and converts its Round House weaving cooperative into Xela AID San Martín Tots Preschool. This is made possible by a donation from Mel Dinkel honoring Milton and Helen Dinkel that funds the addition of a required kitchen. The preschool initially serves thirty children, but quickly grows to nearly sixty.

2005

• **First Emergency Response** - In response to Hurricane Stan, Xela AID sends funds and local teams who provide emergency shelter and deliver clean water and blankets to victims.

• **Loblatzán School Expanded** - Xela AID adds a second floor to the School at Loblatzán made possible by a donation from then-Board Member Dr. Flora Johnson. The new classroom increases the schools capacity from seventy children in two shifts to one hundred and forty.

2007

• **Loblatzán Additionally Expanded** - The local community continues adding on, and the School at Loblatzán which began as a single classroom built by Xela AID serving thirty children grows to five classrooms serving two hundred children daily over two school shifts.

• **Study Center Established** - Xela AID then-Board Member Sheryl Fontaine spearheads *Centro de Estudios*, a study center where children struggling in school can be tutored in their native language. Juana Gomez Perez, a graduate of Xela AID's Work Study Scholarship Program (WSS) program, becomes the Study Center's first teacher.

- **First Formal Advisors** – Dr. Karen Yoshino, assessment specialist, and Clifford Hague, strategic planner, become Xela AID's first two formal Advisors. Karen creates the organization's first professional tools for measuring progress. Cliff leads visioning sessions which result in an organizational goal to become a model for sustainable community development that can be scaled and replicated in rural settings worldwide.

2011

- **Weaving Cooperative Built** - The *Tesoros del Corazón* Weaving Cooperative is formalized when a storefront is built and dedicated at Xela AID headquarters. The Weaving Cooperative is made possible by a generous gift from Board Member Kathy Burt and Don Logan in honor of their daughter Amy.

2013

- **Incorporated as a Legal Entity** - Xela AID Partnerships for Self Reliance becomes a freestanding 501(c)(3) not-for-profit organization through the efforts of Mel Dinkel, the organization's first Chief Operating Officer, Treasurer, and full-time volunteer. Leslie Baer Dinkel becomes the organization's first Executive Director under its official non-profit status.

- **First Board Chair** - Entrepreneur Susan Rikalo becomes first Chair of the Board of the newly minted legal entity, Xela AID, a 501(c)(3) not-for-profit charitable corporation.

- **First Free-standing Office** – At the encouragement of its new Board Chair, Xela AID opens its first freestanding office in Long Beach, California, creating a comfortable gathering place for Xela AID's growing work force.

- **First Director, Guatemala** - Luis Enrique de León is the newly incorporated Xela AID's first Director and Legal Representative in Guatemala, expanding the responsibilities of the position he's held informally since 1993.

- **First Paid Employee, U.S.** - Amy Logan becomes Xela AID's first paid employee in the United States as office manager. She later becomes stateside Director of the Work-Study Scholarship Program and joins the Xela AID Board as its youngest member.

389

• **Leadership Training Program Launched** - Xela AID formally launches the leadership training program developed by Director Luis Enrique de León with an initial twenty students. Board Chair Sue Rikalo becomes Coach and Benefactor and grows the program into a two-year, certified course. Elmer Mazariegos leads the program to success as its first full-time Coordinator. Graduates have taken leadership roles in local government, and as regional representatives of both youth and women.

• **Women's Literacy Program Formalized** - Board Members Sherry Robin and Bailey Smith become Coaches and shore up Xela AID's fledgling Women's Literacy Program, positioning it for expansion. It is led locally by Alicia De León, who goes on to become one of the village's first college graduates. Colleen Dodds establishes the Karen E. Edwards Women's Empowerment Program Fund to further strengthen and grow the program.

• **First Foundation Grant** – The SG Foundation (named for philanthropist Stuart C. Gildred) awards Xela AID its first foundation grant (special thanks to CFO Dee Reed and Executive Director Pamela Gratten). Numerous grants follow. Foundation grants augment personal gifts to enable the organization to professionalize and expand services, and this year, serve nearly 6,000 people through all programs which now include, Education, Health, Leadership Training, Small Business Development and Clean Environment Initiatives.

• *In Guatemalan History*: **Guilty of Genocide** - A Guatemalan court finds former military leader Efrain Rios Montt guilty of crimes against humanity, including genocide. From a BBC report: "The three-judge tribunal sentenced the 86-year-old to eighty years in prison. Montt was convicted of ordering the deaths of 1,771 people of the Ixil Maya ethnic group... Survivors described horrific abuses committed by the army against those suspected of aiding left-wing rebels. In blisteringly critical language, Judge Jazmin Barrios said that as de facto president it was logical that Montt knew what was happening, but did nothing to stop it. Hunger, systematic rape, and forced displacements were all used as tools of war against the Ixil people..." It is the first time a former head of state is found guilty of genocide by a court in their own country.

2014

• **Evolving Brand** – After struggling with its name Stateside ("Xela AID" is hard to pronounce and has to be explained), "Local Hope" is adopted for use in the U.S. The new name aims to communicate the organization's commitment to local, lasting solutions, and its evidence-based belief in the power of hope.

2015

• **Montessori Preschool in the Making** - Xela AID Board Member Sherry Robin designs and supports a Montessori teacher training program and test preschool in preparation for the launch of an official Xela AID Montessori preschool that will be constructed on Xela AID land behind the existing headquarters and clinic. (A small school was opened in rented space as a test, at this writing in 2019, serving sixteen students.)

• **Third Floor and Welcome Center Added** – Needing a kitchen large enough to prepare meals for hungry volunteers, a third floor is added to Xela AID headquarters. It is inaugurated as The Betty Rikalo Welcome Center. Its namesake was known by her family as a hostess extraordinaire, and the Center was made possible by a capstone gift from her older sister, Dolores Tukich, on behalf of the Tukich and Rikalo family estates.

2016

• **Campaign for the Center for Learning Innovation** - Xela AID launches a campaign for the Center for Learning Innovation. The 16,000-square-foot three-story building will double the organization's capacity to serve. Building design is led by Mel Dinkel. Rony Escalante is selected as the project architect. The new facility will include Montessori and public preschool classrooms serving up to one-hundred-and-twenty children, additional classrooms, a state-of-the-art computer laboratory, and an eleven-room inn. Interior design is led by Kathy Burt.

2017

• **Partnership with Rotary for Clean Water** - An eighteen-month-long effort led by the Rotary Club of Avalon on Catalina Island, the Rotary Club of Quetzaltenango, Guatemala, and Xela AID results in a $119,000 Rotary Foundation Global Grant to provide clean water and sanitation. The effort, dubbed "San Martín Thrive," will serve nearly fifteen thousand people in the San Martín Chile Verde region. Additional support comes from Rotary District 5320 and the Rotary Clubs of Signal Hill, Las Alamitos/Seal Beach, Huntington Beach, and Placentia.

• **Commitment to Sustainability** - Xela AID's Board ratifies a resolution to use only cutting-edge, sustainable energy technologies and to become a model for sustainable community development that can be replicated and scaled.

• **First Six-Figure Grant to Xela AID** - The SG Foundation contributes a $100,000 matching gift for the Center for Learning Innovation.

• **Partnership with Art Ambassador For A Colorful World** — An open-air art studio to welcome visiting artists will be incorporated into the Center for Learning Innovation.

2018

• *In Guatemalan History:* **Montt Dead** – Rios Montt, Guatemalan dictator convicted of genocide, dies at 91.

• **Breaking Ground** - On March 23, a ceremony is held to mark the beginning of construction on the three-story Center for Learning Innovation to be located on Xela AID land behind its current headquarters. It will model leading-edge practices for the efficient use of resources, will bring two dozen additional jobs into the community, and will provide a sustainable source of income for Xela AID to continue to serve in perpetuity under local supervision—the best outcome we could hope for. Writes Board Chair Sue Rikalo to the balance of the Board members, "We are the little train that could."

And the journey continues...

About the Author

Leslie's career has spanned reporting, editing magazines and books, hosting radio programs and writing and producing documentary films, among other creative adventures. She is also an accomplished singer-songwriter who has recorded three solo albums and a compilation. Her joy is serving with her husband Mel in the  Guatemalan highland headquarters of Local Hope / Xela AID Guatemala, the community development organization she founded in 1992. The two share a passion for exploring new places and cultures, and their travels have spanned the canals of Britain's lowlands to the top of Mt. Kilimanjaro. They share their Southern California home with their cat Tasha, and a menagerie of squirrels, ducks, tame stingrays and a wobbly-legged great blue heron they call Clive, all of which grace their backyard lagoon.

If you have enjoyed this book, please don't hesitate to post a review on Amazon.com and other venues where you find it, and tell others about it!

100% Proceeds to Charity

What's Next?

According to UNICEF, more than 80 percent of rural Guatemala's population still lives in poverty without consistent access to clean water, medical care, quality education and jobs. Xela AID Partnerships for Self Reliance continues to flourish and to partner with families to break the cycle of poverty and to support them in becoming healthy, educated and self-reliant. Find more information about how to volunteer or support its work at www.xelaaid.org (also www.localhope.org).

Other Published Works
Giving 100% of Proceeds to Charity

MUSIC BY LESLIE CAROL BAER DINKEL

The Weaver's Way

One Step at a Time

I Could Have Never Come This Far

Carpe Diem

BOOKS
Real is Better than Perfect: Stories and sayings for self healing
Dorothy B. Satten

Coming Soon - *Bite the Peach: Stories from a juicy life*
Leslie Baer Dinkel

Find them at lesliebaerdinkel.net

End Notes

Related documents for this section may be accessed at
www.lesliebaerdinkel.net/HopeDancing/EndNotes

---

[1] Inter-American Commission on Human Rights Report, 1992.

[2] Lowell, Bud, "Mary Ramerman Ordained A Priest," *WXXI AM News,*
November 2001.

[3] Tribune News Services, "Woman Ordained to Priesthood in Breakaway
Catholic Church," *Chicago Tribune,* November 11, 2001.
http://articles.chicagotribune.com/2001-11-18/news/0111180292_1_rev-
mary-ramerman-bishop-peter-hickman-catholic-churchmunion

[4] Overview of the Ecumenical Catholic Communion.
http://www.catholiccommunion.org

[5] Cabales, Victoria, "Homeless in California — what the data reveals," Cal
Matters report based on Department of Housing and Urban Development
data, June 18, 2018. https://calmatters.org/articles/homeless-in-california-
what-the-data-reveals/

[6] "Skid Row includes 50 blocks in Los Angeles and 47,000 people are now
counted as homeless." Los Angeles Homeless Services Authority Report, 2016.

[7] There are differing ideas about what the diety *Maximón* symbolizes. Over
time, his meaning has evolved and diverged by community where in some, he
is revered, and others, feared.

[8] Knoema World Data Atlas-
https://knoema.com/atlas/Guatemala/topics/Demographics/Mortality/Infant-
mortality-rate

[9] Doyle, Kate; Kornbluh, Peter. National Security Archive, "CIA and
Assassinations: The Guatemala 1954 Documents."
http://nsarchive.gwu.edu/NSAEBB/NSAEBB4/

[10] Xela AID's maiden voyage participants included 43 in all. Bob Rook and I
were the group's neophyte trip leaders. The adventurous balance of our team
included: Daniel Barclay, Paul Black, Taylor Bladh, Henrik Bothe, Jessica
Bubolo, Rick Cass, Mirella Morra, Dave Dickson, Joyce Downing, John and
Ann Finneran, Steve Frutos, Rev. Louis Graves, Fr. Peter Hickman, Nathan
Hickman, Vicki Hoskins, Karen King, Louise King, Danette Le Bron, Bro.
Joseph McLachlan, Dr. Diep Nguyen, Chris MacDonald, Thea Makow,
Joseph Masestas, Patricia McElroy, Ralph McGee, Carla Nagel, Trina Nettles,
Kim Pappas, Joy Parker, Bob Rook, Dr. Juan Ruiz, Laura Saari, Jeff Sherman,
Dr. Jan Singh, Murphy Tammaro, Janamia Thompson, Rudy Vargas, Mike
Valles, Jacqueline Warner and Lisa Wines. Kathryn Tuma manned her post at

accounting stateside with Bob Rhein, our dedicated communications officer who also worked from home base but joined us on the second trip.

Valles, Jacqueline Warner and Lisa Wines. (Kathryn Tuma manned her post at accounting stateside with Bob Rhein, our dedicated communications officer.) also worked from home base but joined us on the second trip).

[11] N.G.O. - A "Non-Governmental Organization," most often providing health or humanitarian services or pursuing community development work.

[12] Rudy Vargas and Rick Cass captured Ann's gifting of her shoes on video, and included it when they created Xela AID's first introductory film. The mother's "May God give you many more shoes" nearly always gets a laugh from Spanish speakers because it is derived from the oft-used saying, "May God multiply your blessings."

[13] The Guatemalan Truth Commission, also called the "Comission for Historic Clarification," was established in 1994 as part of the peace process between the government of Guatemala and the party known as URNG (Revolutionary National Unity of Guatemala). Its charter was to "clarify past human rights violations and acts of violence that caused the Guatemalan population to suffer." Guatemala's Peace Accords were signed in 1996. The Truth Commission operated until 1999.

[14] Kristof, Nocholas, "So What's So Scary About Girls?" *New York Times*, May 10, 2014. https://www.nytimes.com/2014/05/11/opinion/sunday/kristof-whats-so-scary-about-smart-girls.html?_r=0

[15] Perry, Robert, "U.S. Sponsored Dictators," Global Research Centre, 2013. http://www.globalresearch.ca/us-sponsored-dictators-tales-of-reagans-guatemala-genocide/5331929

[16] Paul Baker relocated to Nicaragua and married human rights activist Fatima Hernandez. http://www.telesurtv.net/english/blog/Paul-Baker-Hernandez-A-Lifetime-of-Solidarity-and-Music-20151217-0042.html

[17] Baker-Hernandez, Paul. *Song in High Summer*. Paul Baker, 1989

[18] Hauser, Thomas, *The Execution of Charles Horman: An American Sacrifice*. Harcourt, Brace, Jovanovich, 1979

[19] Lambert, Bruce, "Edmund C. Horman, 87, Is Dead; Insipiration for the Film 'Missing." *New York Times* Obituary, April 18, 1993. http://www.nytimes.com/1993/04/18/obituaries/edmund-c-horman-87-is-dead-inspiration-for-the-film-missing.html

[20] Doyle, Kate; Kornbluh, Peter. "CIA and Assassinations: The Guatemala 1954 Documents," National Security Archive, May 23, 1997. http://nsarchive.gwu.edu/NSAEBB/NSAEBB4/

[21] Barrett, David. M., "Sterilizing the 'Red' Infection: Congress, the CIA, Guatemala 1954." Central Intelligence Agency, Vol. 144, No. 5.

https://www.cia.gov/library/center-for-the-study-of-intelligence/kent-csi/vol44no5/html/v44i5a03p.htm

[22] Kornbluh, Peter, "Chile Declassified." *The Nation*, July 22, 1999. https://www.thenation.com/article/chile-declassified/

[23] Central Intelligence Agency Report, "CIA Activities in Chile." September, 18, 2000. https://www.cia.gov/library/reports/general-reports-1/chile/

[24] Taylor, Stuart, "Libel Suit is Filed Against 'Missing.'" *New York Times*, January 11, 1983. http://www.nytimes.com/1983/01/11/movies/libel-suit-is-filed-against-missing.html

[25] Davis vs. Costa-Gavras Decision: http://www.leagle.com/decision/19851991619FSupp1372_11857/DAVIS%20v.%20COSTA-GAVRAS

[26] Special to the Times, "Point Four 'Hoe Army' Sought by McMahon." *New York Times*, January 26, 1952. http://www.nytimes.com/1952/01/26/archives/point-four-hoe-army-sought-by-mmahon.html

[27] Blum, William, 2004. "Killing Hope: U.S. Military Interventions Since World War II," ZED Books Ltd, 2003

[28] Blum, William, 2005. "Rogue State: A Guide to the World's Only Superpower," ZED Books Ltd, 2006

[29] Peace Corps online archives, "US. History, The Peace Corps." http://peacecorpsonline.org/messages/messages/2629/4074.html

[30] Wise, David, "The Spy Who Got Away," regarding former Peace Corps volunteer Edward Howard. *New York Times*, November 2, 1986. http://www.nytimes.com/1986/11/02/magazine/the-spy-who-got-away.html?pagewanted=all

[31] Staff Writer, "American Official Asked Fulbright Scholar to Spy on Cubans, Venezuelans in Bolivia," *The Chronicle of Higher Education*, February 8, 2008. https://www.chronicle.com/article/American-Official-Asked/40417

[32] Friedman-Rudovsky, Jean, "Recruiting Spies in the Peace Corps." *In These Times*. March 12, 2008. http://inthesetimes.com/article/3562/recruiting_spies_in_the_peace_corps

[33] Peace Corps Online, "Volunteer Detained for Questioning in Gambia." March 30, 2010.

[34] Staff, "Amid Spying Accusations Moscow Bans Peace Corps." *Chicago Tribune*, December 28, 2002. 1http://articles.chicagotribune.com/keyword/peace-corps/featured/3

[35] Cole, Matthew, "The Pentagon's Missionary Spies," *The Intercept,* October 26, 2015. https://theintercept.com/2015/10/26/pentagon-missionary-spies-

christian-ngo-front-for-north-korea-espionage/
[36] Tribune News Service, "Peace Corps Worker Slain," *Chicago Tribute*, October 18, 2001. http://articles.chicagotribune.com/keyword/peace-corps/featured/3
[37] Peace Corp Website, Eligibility. April 2019. https://www.peacecorps.gov/about/agency-jobs/eligibility/
[38] Silberman, Zach, "The Military Understands Smart Power," USGLC, March 8, 2013. https://www.usglc.org/blog/the-military-understands-smart-power/
[39] Government Online Archives. "Foreign Assistance Act of 1961." https://legcounsel.house.gov/Comps/Foreign%20Assistance%20Act%20Of%201961.pdf
[40] Nikandrov, Nil, "USAID Spying in Latin America." Global Research, October 1, 2012. http://www.globalresearch.ca/usaid-spying-in-latin-america/5306679
[41] "Is USAID the new CIA?: Agency Secretly Built Twitter Program to Fuel Anti-Castro Protests." *Democracy Now*, April 4, 2014. https://www.democracynow.org/2014/4/4/is_usaid_the_new_cia_agency
[42] Nelson, Steve, "Another USAID Cuba Spy Program Exposed." *U.S. News*, August 4, 2014. http://www.usnews.com/news/articles/2014/08/04/another-usaid-cuba-spy-program-exposed
[43] Wadi, Ramona, "USAID: A Wolf in Humanitarian Clothing." MintPress, November 17, 2015. http://www.globalresearch.ca/usaid-spying-in-latin-america/5306679
[44] Victoria Sanford, "Buried Secrets: Truth and Human Rights in Guatemala." Palgrave Macmillan, 2003
[45] Victoria Sanford, "Buried Secrets: Truth and Human Rights in Guatemala." Palgrave Macmillan, 2003
[46] Center for Disease Control, April 2019. https://www.cdc.gov/globalhealth/countries/guatemala/default.htm
[47] Boyle, Gregory, "Tatoos on the Heart," Simon & Schuster, 2010
[48] Visser, Margaret. "Much Depends on Dinner: The Extraordinary History and Mythology, Allure and Obsessions, Perils and Taboos of an Ordinary Meal." McClelland and Stewart Limited, Canada, 1986. Page 34.
[49] Shele, Linda; Freidel, David. Parker, Joy. "Maya Cosmos," HarperCollins, 1993.

[50] Midwives for Midwives, 2019. "Reproductive and Maternal Health in Guatemala," http://midwivesformidwives.org/guatemala/

[51] Montejo, Victor D.; *Cultural Survival Quarterly Magazine*, June 1997. https://www.culturalsurvival.org/publications/cultural-survival-quarterly/pan-mayan-movement-mayans-doorway-new-millennium. Various scholarly works propose that the Ancient Maya long-count calendar has been in use since 3114 BC. With the Spanish conquest of Guatemala in 1525, elements of Catholicism began to be incorporated into Mayan spirituality which later saw additional Christian influence. Daykeeping saw a resurgence in the 1980's due in large part to Guatemala's civil war. The war inspired a "Pan-Maya" movement to unite the speakers of the country's many Mayan languages around a shared ethnic identity.

[52] Holocaust Museum, "Genocide in Guatemala," Installation. https://www.hmh.org/la_genocide_guatemala.shtml

[53] Miller, Phil, "How the British Army Cooperated." *Vice,* May 2016. https://www.vice.com/en_us/article/murder-in-the-jungle-guatemala-british-army-civil-war

[54] Cushman, John, "Nun Tortured in Guatemala Seeks U.S. Files." *New York Times*, April 1, 1996. http://www.nytimes.com/1996/04/01/world/nun-tortured-in-guatemala-seeks-us-files.html

[55] The Balance. Unemployment Rate Since 1929. https://www.thebalance.com/unemployment-rate-by-year-3305506

Made in the USA
Columbia, SC
07 September 2019